THE FIRE LINE

THE FIRE LINE

THE STORY OF
THE GRANITE
MOUNTAIN HOTSHOTS
AND ONE OF THE
DEADLIEST DAYS IN
AMERICAN
FIREFIGHTING

FERNANDA SANTOS

FLATIRON
BOOKS
NEW YORK

www.flatironbooks.com

Design by Meryl Sussman Levavi

PHOTO CREDITS FOR INSERT:

Images of the Hotshots before the Juniper tree, Chrisopher MacKenzie self-portrait, and the photographs of the men just before the fire overtook them are all courtesy of the photographer and his estate, Christopher MacKenzie.

Image of Anthony Rose with his wife Tiffany. (Courtesy Tiffany Rose)

Image of Bill and Roxanne Warneke. (Courtesy Roxanne Warneke)

Image of the Ashcraft family. (Courtesy Juliann Ashcraft)

Image of the Steed family. (Courtesy Desiree Steed)

Image of the Turbyfill family. (Courtesy Stephanie Turbyfill)

Image of Sean and Amanda Misener. (Courtesy Amanda Misener)

Image of Eric and Amanda. (Courtesy Amanda Marsh)

Image of Kevin and Joe Woyjeck. (Courtesy of the Woyjeck family)

Image of Eric Marsh. (Courtesy of Wade Ward)

Image of the devastation of the fire. (Courtesy Getty Images/Laura Segall/Stringer)

Image of Christopher MacKenzie coming home. (Courtesy Getty Images David McNew/Stringer)

Image of memorial. (Courtesy Getty Images)

Image of Yarnell tribute at Station 7. (Courtesy Getty Images/Christian Petersen)

The Library of Congress Cataloging-in-Publication Data is available upon request.

ISBN 978-1-250-05402-9 (hardcover)
ISBN 978-1-250-05403-6 (e-book)

Our books may be purchased in bulk for promotional, educational, or business use. Please contact your local bookseller or the Macmillan Corporate and Premium Sales Department at 1-800-221-7945, extension 5442, or by e-mail at MacmillanSpecial Markets@macmillan.com.

First Edition: May 2016

10 9 8 7 6 5 4 3 2 1

To Mike and Flora,
for the love, laughter, and support.

To the Granite Mountain Hotshots,
who strived to be better, always.

CONTENTS

Prologue   1

PART I

The Guys   11

Saving a Tree   36

A Bolt of Lightning   58

Calculating Risk   69

A Sleeping Fire Awakens   75

Promises and Goodbyes   93

PART II

A Treacherous Combination   111

Trouble in the Sky   118

Change in the Winds   138

CONTENTS

No Answer 144

Gone 158

Two Thousand Degrees 174

Coming Home 179

"We Take Care of Our Own" 189

An End, and New Beginnings 201

Author's Note 219

Acknowledgments 223

Chronology 227

Notes 231

Index 265

He had decided to live forever or die in the attempt.

—JOSEPH HELLER, *Catch-22*

Greater love has no one than this, than to lay down one's life for his friends.

—JOHN 15:13

Dulce et decorum est
Pro patria mori.
For generations
we've sold these goods
to young boys
who burn for glory.

Dulce et decorum est
Pro patria mori.
Indeed, how sweet,
Pray tell
Poppy covered warrior.

Dulce et decorum est
Pro patria mori.
How sweet was the Somme?
Such little ground
was gained with
half a generation gone.

Dulce et decorum est
Pro patria mori.
When weapons
far outpace the men
what an empty word
is glory.

—JOHN F. McCULLAGH, "Pro Patria Mori"

THE FIRE LINE

PROLOGUE

PAGE 88 OF THE *YARNELL HILL FIRE SERIOUS ACCIDENT INVESTI-gation Report,* the official account of the deadliest wildfire in the United States since 1933, offers a distanced, emotionless diagram of a fatal last stand against flames and heat. Coffinlike shapes represent nineteen firefighters killed in the Arizona wildfire on June 30, 2013, all members of the Granite Mountain Hotshots. It's an arresting chart—loyalty, death, and immeasurable grief, graphed in numbered geometric figures arranged in precise disarray:

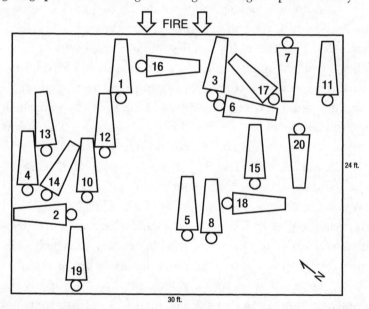

The chart depicts the firefighters' bodies in the hollow where the wildfire trapped them—a steep mountain to their backs, a high wall of flames ahead. A list of names below it keys to the individuals who lost their lives:

1. Eric Marsh; 2. Jesse Steed; 3. Clayton Whitted; 4. Robert Caldwell;
5. Travis Carter; 6. Christopher MacKenzie; 7. Travis Turbyfill;
8. Andrew Ashcraft; 10. Joe Thurston; 11. Wade Parker;
12. Anthony Rose; 13. Garret Zuppiger; 14. Scott Norris;
15. Dustin DeFord; 16. William Warneke; 17. Kevin Woyjeck;
18. John Percin Jr.; 19. Grant McKee; 20. Sean Misner.

Number 9, Brendan McDonough, is missing. He'd been assigned lookout duty a half mile away.

On that hot and dry June day, the Granite Mountain Hotshots had risen with the sun, as usual. They'd taken their assigned seats in the crew's four personnel carriers and traveled through forty-three winding miles, from their home base in Prescott, Arizona, to a speck of town—649 residents, barely 9 square miles—called Yarnell, a hideaway for hippies, artists, retirees, and others looking to forget and be forgotten. The men had parked near the end of a dirt road, on the edge of the wild, and sized up a fire that was chewing at a ridge west of town. They'd trudged uphill in single file for what should have been a usual day's work—sawing off brush, tossing it aside, and scraping the ground down to mineral soil, to starve the approaching fire of the vegetation that would keep it burning. The task is called cutting fire line, and it's how wildfires are fought.

The sun pounded down upon the Hotshots. They marched upslope, bowed under the weight of fifty pounds of gear, their eyes on the rocky ground underfoot. Parched chaparral coated the majestic Weaver Mountains, highlands that rise from the Sonoran Desert's leafy flatlands. It hadn't rained in Yarnell since April. For the fourth consecutive day, temperatures had soared above one hundred degrees and lingered there, disrupting the usual easy summer in that cool mountainside retreat. In flame-resistant pants and long-sleeved shirts that some had folded up, others had closed by fastening a strap of Velcro around their wrists, the men lumbered past massive granite boulders that blasted waves of heat at them. In their gloved hands, they each lugged one of the tools of their trade: picks, axes, shovels, Stihl 440 chain saws.

The fire hadn't looked like much to them when they had

rolled into town that morning—a swirl of saffron smoke against a boundless blue sky. Sparked two days earlier by lightning, the fire had crept north of its point of origin, a gnarled cluster of chaparral plants—catclaw acacia, scrub oak, and manzanita—near the tip of Yarnell Hill, seventy miles northwest of Phoenix.

The Hotshots took positions on the fire's slowest-spreading edge, its heel, an area close to its point of origin. Yarnell stood to their right, ringed by thick, tall brush, land that hadn't burned in forty-seven years. To their left lay a charred patch of about two hundred acres—an area firefighters call the black, because the vegetation there had already burned. They marked it as a safe retreat if the fire turned on them.

Their first task was to find a strategic starting point for the fire line they aimed to build as a barrier to the flame's spread, and as an anchor to a hand-carved buffer zone clear of everything flammable. They settled on a gap on the fire's southwest corner, along the dense wall of a steep, rocky slope facing toward the town of Congress, away from Yarnell. They swung their tools, pounding, digging, slicing, and clearing the ground around the fire's southern perimeter—a line about a yard wide around a bent elbow—and onward along the fire's eastern fringe, its right flank. The task is a sort of savage science, strategic in its planning, primitive in its execution, punishing bodies and minds. Stooped, the men attacked the hardened soil with furious precision, determined to take away the fuel that would otherwise feed the fire if it ran toward Yarnell.

Then, everything changed. As forecasters had twice warned, a powerful thunderstorm blew in from the north. It crashed head-to-head with the fire, which was rolling toward Yarnell's small neighbor Peeples Valley, a community of ranches and middling homes with about half of Yarnell's population and twice the acreage. The collision was at once fearsome and spectacular. Winds gusted to forty, then fifty miles per hour, bending the northbound flames eastward and shoving them southward at a speed of a mile in four minutes, a hundred yards in fifteen seconds—faster than any gear-laden firefighter can sprint. Smoke cleaved a horseshoe in the air, stamping the fire's changing orientation in gunmetal gray against the darkened sky.

From her home in Yarnell, Adria Shayne gasped at the apocalyptic sight. She grabbed her pets and, stunned, drove away in her battered pickup truck, leaving her house and everything in it heating up behind her. Propane tanks hissed and exploded as she escaped. Glass windows shattered. Ammunition fired spontaneously. Flames rolled through the west side of town, then barged inside a neighborhood at its southern tip, Glen Ilah, burning homes at random, skipping some, as if in a drunken game of hopscotch. Pipes cracked and water gushed underfoot. Ash shrouded the sun, turning the day dark.

From a knoll northeast of the rest of his crew, McDonough, the assigned lookout, swung a pocket-size psychrometer, an L-shaped instrument that measured temperature and humidity on the fire line. Lookout is a physically easy task that requires intimate knowledge of fire, weather, and their wicked tricks. The easy part suited McDonough that day as it was his first back at work after two days at home nursing a cold, and a night out with friends.

Facing north, McDonough felt the wind that had caressed his neck shift and slap his face. He saw the fire suddenly rolling toward him, no longer away from him. Over the radio, he warned the crew's captain, Jesse Steed, that the flames had charged close to the knoll. Steed agreed when McDonough said he'd pull back to safety: "I've got eyes on you and the fire, and it's making a good push," Steed had said. McDonough had looked back over his shoulder as he left and saw flames devouring the perch where he had just stood.

The nineteen Granite Mountain Hotshots stayed in the burning wilderness.

•••

Eric Tarr, a police officer–paramedic with the Arizona Department of Public Safety, was part of a three-men team assigned by the state to drop water on the fire from a collapsible bucket suspended from the belly of their Bell 407 helicopter, *Ranger 58*.

The Hotshots had vanished and it had fallen upon Tarr to go looking.

The helicopter circled the smoldering Weaver Mountains. Smoke nearly smothered its jet engine. Swirling winds kept shoving its nose down. The fuel gauge dropped perilously toward empty. With two minutes of flying time left, Tarr glimpsed a fleeting apparition through an opening in the haze—a cluster of scorched fire shelters.

Fire shelters are portable cocoons, mandatory since 1977 for those on the fire line, a last-resort protection against heat and smoke. They're made of layered fiberglass cloth, silica, and aluminum foil and are stuffed inside a hard-plastic case strapped at the base of each firefighter's backpack. Firefighters grasp handles marked LEFT HAND and RIGHT HAND and shake the shelters, which unfurl like rounded pup tents. They then step into the shelters, drop to the ground, and roll on their bellies, wedging the shelters' openings underneath. They keep their faces turned to the ground, their legs spread, and their feet to the fire, protecting their airways and torsos. Within, they slip their arms through straps on each side, lessening the chance of the shelters' blowing away. The shelters are not supposed to hug the bodies inside like blankets, but to wrap them loosely, like sacks. Deployed, they look like giant silver bullets.

The shelters Tarr saw at the bottom of the canyon that day looked like burned ash logs, tightly arranged on ground the Hotshots had half-cleared and brush they'd half-sawed.

The aircraft looped twice, counterclockwise, over them. Tarr clung to the hope that someone might have survived, even though none of the shelters had stirred during the helicopter's transits. The firefighters' radios had gone silent since their superintendent, Eric Marsh, had tautly announced, "Our escape route has been cut off. We are preparing a deployment site and we are burning out around ourselves in the brush, and I'll give you a call when we are under the sh—the shelters."

The pilot, Clifford Bursting, circled the helicopter closer to the ground, worried whether the carbon-composite rotor blades would withstand the heat radiating from the land.

Tarr spotted an opening. Trees burned on one side. A picnic bench burned on the other. It would have to do.

Bursting lowered the helo farther. Tarr stepped out and inhaled. The roof of his mouth throbbed. Scorching air seared his nostrils and then his windpipe. His throat burned. His eyes stung. He grabbed his medical kit. It had a pulse oximeter, which measured the level of oxygen in the blood, a stethoscope, and some basic bandages, moist and sterile, for wrapping burned skin.

Tarr began a lonely hike uphill, toward the shelters.

The fire had scorched the dusty ground black and turned the high desert's golden soil to charcoal. The sand crackled under the soles of his insulated boots, as though he were treading on eggshells. Ahead, thick smoke caressed the granite boulders the fire had seared. To his left, flames still danced against the pale-gray sky. Tarr saw planes above, but couldn't hear them. The air didn't stir.

As usual on the job, he carried a pistol in his holster. His vest held handcuffs and a canister of pepper spray. A rectangular case latched to his backpack contained his own fire shelter, in case the flames menaced him. He knew they could.

From upslope, past a ranch spared by the blaze, a muffled voice pierced the desolate stillness, startling him.

"Hey! Hey!" Tarr bellowed. "Can anybody hear me?"

He picked up his pace. His heart pounded. He heard that voice again.

"Is anybody out there?"

At the crest of the rise, he halted.

His search ended.

The Hotshots had collapsed in the jagged circle. Eleven of them had their feet to the fire, as they'd practiced. Billy Warneke lay between Marsh and Clayton Whitted, the crossbar of an *H* linking lines of bodies—one at right angles to his feet, the other to his head, where the flames must have first touched the men.

Tarr looked at his wristwatch, noting the time—six thirty-five in the evening. He moved deliberately from east to west, stopping at each shelter, tallying the magnitude of the disaster.

The bodies lay in a lonely hollow. Together, they represented the greatest single loss of firefighters since the 9/11 attacks, and the largest death toll of professional wildland firefighters in more than a century.

"We have nineteen fatalities," Tarr said, and heard that muffled voice again. This time he recognized it as his own, echoing from a firefighter's scorched radio.

PART I

...

THE GUYS

T HE MAN FLASHED A BROAD, GAP-TOOTHED GRIN and introduced himself: "I'm Darrell Willis," chief of the Prescott Fire Department Wildland Division. Willis felt at ease and proud as he looked upon the select group of young men facing him on the inaugural day of the 2013 fire season. The Granite Mountain Hotshots, the only municipal Hotshot crew in the country, stood at attention in front of their chief. "Your life has changed today," Willis told them. "You're in a fishbowl, and people are going to judge you by your actions." A lot of people, other skilled crews, a lot of fire brass, would watch and wait for them to falter, he said. They had to set an example, work hard and work right, prove the doubters wrong, on and off the fire line.

Willis had broomstick posture and a trim physique for someone old enough to be their father. At fifty-eight, he still ran four or five miles a day, and still had what it took to fill in when injury or illness left a hole in the crew. He wore a snug, dark-blue shirt, tucked in khaki cargo pants. He kept his cell phone clipped to a black leather belt. His thick head of hair was parted crisply to the right, and when he spoke, he sounded firm and deliberate, locking eyes in turn with each of the men before him, as if individually addressing each. He oozed discipline.

The men trained their eyes on Willis in obedient attention, a cast of wildland firefighters looking to impress. They'd settled on assorted chairs and behind rows of Formica desks in the ready room at Station 7, the Granite Mountain Hotshots' base in Prescott, Arizona, a mountain city of thirty-nine thousand ringed by parched forestland that lightning often sparked. Seven of them were veterans, returning for another season of duty, seven months of stifling fires in the wild. Seven were newly hired. One of the rookies, Kevin Woyjeck, sat in the front row, a studious recruit drinking it all in on the crew's first day at work, April 9, 2013. He had a faint dimple on his chin, freckles on his nose, and a trace of facial hair. He was twenty-one, a firefighter's son, like Willis. And like Willis, he'd fulfilled a childhood dream when he'd joined the fire service.

Willis glanced at Woyjeck and stifled a smile, smitten by the sight of a kid so purely happy to be accepted. Willis admired the kid's earnest conviction that this was indeed the right place for him. Woyjeck's innocence was refreshing in the macho world of Hotshots. In the opening of his résumé, he'd typed, "Objective: To be part of a hard working, professional, and well respected crew, while continuing to gain experience in my chosen career."

Woyjeck wanted to work for the Los Angeles County Fire Department, where his father, Joe, was a captain. Kevin had strategized, filling out his résumé with the most suitable experiences, ones that would make him maximally attractive before he applied. He'd got his EMT license right after high school and worked for a year for a private ambulance company. Then, he was hired by the Bear Mountain Hand Crew, a wildland team in South Dakota, after passing a drug test and answering a handful of questions over the phone. In 2013, he'd thought about going to Alaska, where wildfires burn across gorgeous landscape—and where he could also do a lot of fishing; Woyjeck loved fishing. But his father reasoned with him, saying that Alaska was too far and too difficult for his parents to get to. Woyjeck had asked, "Where, then?" Joe had heard good things about this crew from Prescott, Arizona, the Granite Mountain Hotshots. Woyjeck spent hours online, researching it, learning about its history, its mission. He liked what he saw. The location also made sense: his father had relatives in and near Phoenix, and Anna, his mom, had grown up in Tucson, a few hours' drive away.

Woyjeck joined the Granite Mountain Hotshots as a soldier, not a leader, embracing the crew's strict hierarchy, and accepting the shut-up-and-buck-up attitude that went with his newbie post. He was there to learn.

"Woyjeck! Give me the ten and the eighteen," Willis, about to school him, said loudly and firmly. It was a joke, not a test. The returning crew members knew that. In their world, pranks and ribbings equaled affection.

To graduate from the fire academy, Woyjeck had had to memorize the Ten Standard Firefighting Orders and the Eighteen Watchout Situations—basic rules, steps that everyone on the fire line is expected to take to keep himself and one another alive and safe. Fire Order No. 2: "Know what your fire is doing at all times." Watchout Situation No. 12: "Cannot see the main fire, not in contact with anyone who can." The US Forest Service, by far the country's largest employer of Hotshot crews, had developed the guidelines in the 1950s in response to fire-line fatalities. They're lessons learned in the hardest possible ways.

Woyjeck stuttered, too nervous to recollect them on that cool, overcast day in Prescott, before coworkers he hardly knew. His father had taped a card listing them inside the helmet he had worn when fighting wildfires in Southern California. Grant McKee, another rookie, still twenty years old on the season's opening day, kept a similar card in his wallet. He'd picked up the habit from his cousin Robert Caldwell, twenty-three, in his fourth fire season with Granite Mountain and newly promoted to squad boss, one of six official full-time positions on the crew that year.

Caldwell had smarts, but no patience for school. He'd struggled to get through four years of high school in Prescott and graduated out of stubbornness, to prove to his parents that he could do it, even though he saw no need. He had a knack for doing things well his own way, with a big, fun personality. On eighties nights at Coyote Joe's, a bar on Whiskey Row, where residents and visitors go in Prescott to eat and have a good time, he wore neon-pink shorts that glowed on the darkened dance floor, illuminating his gangly legs. On his first job, working for a company that operated wildland firefighting equipment in neighboring Chino Valley, he'd held a flashlight with his teeth and spent a night fixing a truck his boss had struggled to start for days, just to prove himself. Unlike friends who had gone away for college, Robert didn't want to leave Prescott, and he certainly didn't want to spend the rest of his life doing office work. With the Granite Mountain Hotshots, his free spirit and larger-than-life personality could thrive.

He and his girlfriend, Claire, had talked marriage and he'd told her they'd have to go through a fire season together first to see if she could handle it. The last thing he wanted was a woman calling him on the fire line, nagging him about stuff he could do nothing about—a broken sink, a clogged toilet—and berating him for leaving her alone. He felt he had no choice. He had a job to do.

They married after his first fire season with the crew. But still, he told Claire before every fire, "I see you when I see you." It was his gentle reminder of the unpredictability of a profession practiced at the whim of the weather, a warming climate, and the escalating intensity of that cunning natural force—fire. He often said that he'd rather die in his boots than in a suit.

Hotshot crews are cohesive units of twenty firefighters, extensively trained, hugely fit, and routinely courageous—but, as they often said, only as strong as their weakest link. If the burning wilderness is a battlefield, they're the infantry, engaging the enemy on foot. They use the weapons of construction workers and landscapers: rakes, axes, shovels, pounders. They go where few other firefighters go, closer than any of them to a burning wildfire. In bureaucratic terms, they're an interagency resource— they fight fires wherever fires are burning and only engage in fires that fit the official definition of *complex*. The size of the fire matters, but the difficulties it presents—and, increasingly, the number of homes it threatens—determine the risks, challenges, and manpower deployed.

The Granite Mountain Hotshots was one of 107 Hotshot crews in the country in 2013, the only one to have a city as its employer, and only one of two to operate under the auspices of a structural fire department. The arrangement compressed disparate worlds, mushed them together in a city hugged by forest—concrete and wildlands, brick walls and the big sky, bureaucracies and risk-takers in a tug-of-war between the tamed and the wild.

Life on the crew revolved around busy schedules and austere routines: training, fires, meals, sleep, and travel, often in carriers known in the Southwest as buggies. Their Caterpillar diesel engines and stiff suspensions made for loud, brutal rides. Granite Mountain had a retrofitted Ford F-750 for each of its squads, Alpha and Bravo. Most other Hotshot crews rode green buggies, identifying them as part of the Forest Service. Granite Mountain's buggies were white, a deliberate distinction. With heavy-duty steel-ladder frames and axles, they were workhorses on rough roads in to assignments, mile upon mile of cracked asphalt and dirt crisscrossing gorgeous corners of the country few others ever visit.

In 2011, the crew traveled 16,150 miles in those white buggies, ending their season in a million-acre preserve sliced by one thousand miles of water trails in northern Minnesota, where flames were skipping over lakes and burning through duff despite a light snow. In 2012, the buggies covered 19,450 miles in five months, from West Texas to western Idaho, corkscrewing along the counterclockwise pattern that usually defines the summer cycle of fires in the American West. The Hotshots were like migrant farm workers chasing harvest time from state to state.

In Jesse Steed, the crew's captain, a veteran of eleven wildfire seasons, they had found the ideal player-coach. Steed, thirty-six, offered the Hotshots warm guidance and set punishing physical standards they had to follow. On hikes along Trail #33 on Thumb Butte, a steep and circuitous climb to a ridge just below the mountain's rocky crest, whoever reached the top first had to turn around, join the person at the tail end of the line, and hike with him back to the top. When the Hotshots got to a certain cattle guard along the way, they had to carry one another on their backs. They had created and nurtured a culture of loyalty, a system that rewarded teamwork and endurance—group gold, not individual glory. That was the crew's spirit. Willis, Steed, and Granite Mountain's superintendent, Eric Marsh, stressed it to the new recruits on that first day at work.

A firefighter's job requires unquestioning trust and unwavering commitment, Marsh told them. It's an honor profession, like that of a priest or a doctor. There's no room for lapses of integrity. Among his men, Marsh focused the point further. He knew he could get them to be great wildland firefighters, but could he also make them honorable? "Every decision you make from now on affects others," he'd tell the men at the start of every season. "Look around. They are you."

His emphasis on obedience, in its purest form, reflected his needs as a commander, perhaps even his vanity. But it was effective, if flawed. His search for the most susceptible characters—"the perfect people," as Willis described them—wasn't random. Marsh had a sort of sixth sense for plucking them out of a crowded field of pretenders.

It all started with hiring.

Landing a job at the Granite Mountain Hotshots required persistence and patience, rituals of a peculiar courtship. The wholly personal process was entirely different from the dispassionate hiring procedures mandated for federal crews. For those positions, candidates register on a Web site, usajobs.gov, and click on answers to some questions—about citizenship and military service (veterans have hiring priority), the types of jobs they'd accept (permanent, temporary, seasonal), and if they're open to traveling and relocating. Then, they upload a résumé and wait for the phone to ring. Back in the government office, the candidates are ranked in descending order, based on preferential status, experience, and skill. Their names are organized on lists, and the lists are shared across ten regional centers in charge of wildland firefighting operations in the United States. The Southwest Coordination Center, in Albuquerque, handles the final selection of candidates for jobs in Arizona or New Mexico. New hires for federal Hotshot crews might not meet a crew's superintendent until their first day of training.

Marsh, forty-three, liked to size people up before they even turned in a job application. In November, with a fire season ended and with another several months away, young men came knocking at Station 7, looking to introduce themselves to the boss, maybe get a word in with him. Marsh took time to learn about these young men and took particular interest in those who expressed kinship with the outdoors—perhaps they'd grown up shoeing horses on the family ranch, camping, hunting, fishing, exploring the land. He knew that comfort with nature couldn't be taught. Some of these young men returned after that first meeting to work out with the crew's leaders—the Overhead—and observe them. To Marsh, that level of dedication made them promising prospects. Often, he'd move such an applicant onto a short list for interviews. In a single year, the Granite Mountain Hotshots received an average of ninety applications. Of those applicants, about twenty made it to the short list.

During interviews, also in the ready room at Station 7, Marsh leaned back on his chair, crossed his arms, looked into a candidate's eyes, and asked, "When was the last time you lied?" His speech had a memorable rhythm, unhurried, almost musical, a drawl of the North Carolina mountains of his youth that he'd never shed. He looked for signs of honesty—"what's in their soul," he'd told Willis. Everybody lies, but do you have enough character to admit it? That's what he'd taught the crew's leaders to search out. Jesse Steed had mastered the question-and-answer drill. He liked to say that if a man can own up to a stupid lie, he'd be truthful, no matter about what or to whom.

The question disarmed men who'd prepped to discuss fitness regimens, work experiences, and those rules of wildland firefighting they'd memorized. Billy Warneke, twenty-five, had written those Ten Standard Firefighting Orders and Eighteen Watchout Situations on index cards. Roxanne, his wife, had flipped through the cards and quizzed Billy from the passenger seat of his Ford F-150 during drives to the movies and the supermarket. He'd dressed up for the interview, putting on black pants, a black shirt, and a plain red tie; Roxanne had convinced him to wear it instead of the tie that pictured the red-haired cartoon character Yosemite Sam holding a long-barreled pistol in each hand. Though the orders and situations never came up during Billy's interview, the question about his last lie did. Billy came clean. Roxanne had called from work, asking if he'd washed the breakfast dishes. "Yes," he'd replied, although the dishes lay dirty in the sink; he'd played *Call of Duty* on PlayStation 3 instead.

The interviews were the last hurdle, and for the Overhead, a last chance of catching false positives.

Marsh had a soft spot for underdogs—some called them misfits and losers. To these men and women, he spoke plainly about the alcoholism buried in his own past. He used such conversations to straighten errant paths, and to inspire. He liked to say, "We turn boys into men."

He knew how experiences could scar and bruise, and Marsh connected with the recruits about what it takes to overcome the bad hand life can deal you. In their stories, he looked for strength of character, resilience, discipline, respect, compassion, generosity, confidence. He despised arrogance. He searched for leadable firefighters who could also be leaders, men bound by a shared certainty of their greater identity and utility as a team.

Brendan McDonough had laid it all out during his interview in 2011—the drugs he'd used, the trials of a fatherless childhood, his criminal record. He'd been caught on surveillance video driving away from a car break-in at a Walmart parking lot in Prescott and had pleaded guilty to acting as a lookout in the theft of a GPS and radar detector from the vehicle. He'd felt remorseful and ashamed. He had a baby daughter and wanted to do right by her. He yearned for a steady road and a guiding hand. McDonough was soft-spoken and respectful, a yes-sir kind of guy who also knew the dangers lurking behind his idea of a good time. He clearly lacked direction. He told the Overhead that he'd been through Fire Service Exploring, a Boy Scouts' program for kids ages fourteen to twenty-one. It had taught him to get geared up fast, hook up the breathing mask and tank urban firefighters wear to enter burning buildings. He could find his way around a fire truck, he said. Those were unimportant skills for wildland firefighters, but they attested to a desire for a stable path. Marsh gambled and took him in.

Steed had become Granite Mountain's second-in-command in the fall of 2011. Slowly, he and Marsh forged a yin-yang partnership of roles and styles: Steed was the extrovert and Marsh, the introvert; Steed was effusive and Marsh, stern; Steed was expressive and Marsh, reserved. They weren't exactly chummy. Their relationship was best defined as businesslike, a union of utility. But they'd learned to respect their divergent leadership styles. Steed liked to give the guys some room to do things their own way and have a say in how the work got done. Marsh was more of a micromanager. He'd internalized norms and expected no less than loyalty to them—and to him.

The firefighters under his command called him Papa.

If Marsh was a father figure to the men, respected and feared, Steed was their big brother, a handsome guy who gave hugs and said, "I love you, bro." His marriage to Desiree—a no-nonsense blonde he'd met on a blind date his cousin had set up—survived despite the challenges of his absence for long stretches during fire season. Divorce is a common ending for Hotshot love stories. His children adored him. On the fire line, he was a beast. While digging line on a blaze in 2012, he'd shouldered a tree as it fell toward him and shoved it the other way, protecting the crew. They called him Noble Steed.

Andrew Ashcraft, twenty-nine, second-in-charge of the crew's chain-saw operations, had nicknamed him Greek God. His last name was fitting: *steed,* a spirited horse, ready for battle. He was a beardless Paul Bunyan, and a personification of the Hotshots' confidence and strength.

But it hadn't always been so. Steed had come close to dying in 2010, after a dirt-bike accident in the Imperial Sand Dunes in southeastern California landed him in intensive care with aspirated pneumonia, a blood clot in one of his lungs, and a fractured fibula and tibia in his left leg. It took three weeks of hospitalization, two corrective surgeries, several plates to hold together his bones, and three months in crutches for him to get better. Steed had his own idea for getting back in shape: running a marathon in Phoenix. He finished the race in 3:37, eight minutes and thirteen seconds a mile, a black compression band wrapped around his left calf. He'd trained for it by running along the undulating back roads of his hometown of Prescott Valley, Prescott's neighbor to the east, and on a treadmill at Station 7. The gym there was christened Steed's Dojo, honoring his extreme workouts.

Steed carried a set of playing cards in his backpack, and at the end of a workday, or after a long run, the guys got ready to sweat some more. If Steed drew a ten, they had to drop and do ten push-ups. If he pulled out an eight, eight push-ups. A jack cost them eleven. They carried on like that clear through the end of the deck, feeling as if their arms were about to fall off. They finished red in the face, panting and sweating. Steed would just look at them, flash a mischievous smile, and ask, "Having fun yet?"

Travis Turbyfill knew the routine; he'd mastered it in the Marines. Like Steed, Turbyfill, twenty-seven, had a solid marriage—his wife, Stephanie, had learned to appreciate her independence during fire season. They had two girls, Brooklyn and Brynley, born a year apart. He was one of the tallest and broadest guys on the crew, and goofy even as he pushed through a Filthy 50 at Captain CrossFit, the gym across from Station 7: fifty repetitions of ten different exercises, each more punishing than the next—box jumps, pull-ups, kettle ball swings, lunges. His laughter was earnest and loud, like a child's. He had big hands, thickened by the toil of wildland firefighting, yet he could hold a tiny brush and paint his daughters' nails pink.

Turbyfill, Steed, and Marsh had put together a list of items the men needed on that first day of the season: sturdy running shoes, breathable hiking socks, workout clothes, a water bottle, a pen and a pocket-size notepad to write down what they had to remember. A Hotshot crew's fundamental purpose is to starve a fire of the vegetation that's feeding it, physically removing the grass, shrubs, and trees from the fire's path. It is brutal work. The Granite Mountain Hotshots had to be in condition to saw thick brush and timber, hack away stumps and roots, and scrape the ground to mineral soil, opening clear breaks in the wild, ribbons often as wide as a road—"our superhighway," they would say.

The weeks they spent training before their first fire showed who could handle a Hotshot's tough existence on the fire line. The job required sixteen hours of hard toil for fourteen days straight, often without a bed to sleep on or toilets or showers to cleanse the gunk that embeds in ears and under nails and laminates the skin. Smoke infiltrates their lungs, and they were warned they'd be coughing it out long past the end of the season. On the fire line, it can be scorching by day and freezing by night. The Granite Mountain Hotshots knew they had to be ready for all of that, and more. They had to endure poison ivy, ticks, gnats, snakes, and spiders. They learned to shake their boots when they woke up in the wild to expel the scorpions that might have crawled inside. They had to lug at least six quarts of drinking water, their heavy packs, and enough fuel to keep their chain saws going. They had to be comfortable with being uncomfortable. That's what set them apart.

Rookies such as Woyjeck, McKee, and Warneke, the third Marine Corps veteran on the crew, made $12.09 an hour—no health insurance, no paid holidays, no paid sick leave. They were among the fourteen crew members hired for the fire season and dismissed just in time to exempt its employer, the City of Prescott, from covering benefits legally required for full-time employees; roughly three out of five Hotshots in the United States work under similar rules during any given fire season. The Granite Mountain Hotshots each had signed a form accepting their status, a "temporary employment acknowledgment," attesting that they understood the job came with no perks and protections, and that they could be dismissed at any moment, "with or without notice, and with or without cause." That many of them got hired again right after the summer never factored into the benefits equation. Some of the guys didn't know much about the rights and wrongs of labor law. Others did, but kept their mouths shut, rather than risk never being hired again.

Back in 2009, Marsh wrote in his annual self-appraisal, under suggestions for making his and his coworkers' jobs more effective, that his seasonal Hotshots should be able to accrue sick and vacation days, "as the budget allows." This was in the throes of the recession, and the idea stayed on that piece of paper, shelved and forgotten. Year after year, seasonal crew members came aboard holding on to a single promise: making good money working overtime. They trained their focus on the certainty of having the time of their lives toiling together usefully in beautiful country and sleeping under the stars.

There may be glamour in a Hotshot's job, but certainly no riches.

The job is for the young; fourteen of the twenty men in the Granite Mountain Hotshots' final roster for 2013 were still in their twenties. Most had been born and raised in and around Prescott. They were runners, hikers, hunters, bikers, climbers, skateboarders, guitar players and singers in garage bands—just kids.

In high school, one was a wrestler; another, a champion shot-putter. Two were baseball stars, and six were starters on football teams. Four had graduated from four-year colleges, seven had dropped out of college. Eight never enrolled. Anthony Rose, twenty-three, quit high school when he left his mother's house, in Illinois, for his uncle's, near Prescott, at the age of sixteen. He got his GED in 2012, the same year he joined the crew. He didn't know what it meant to be a Hotshot exactly, but he knew he loved beating back flames, staying dirty, and traveling to places he'd never get to see otherwise.

The men were skilled with their hands, able to build or fix pretty much anything. Wade Parker, twenty-two, a talented athlete with a big smile and a huge heart—in middle school, he'd get off the bus early to protect a younger boy from a bully—made hunting bows out of bird's-eye maple and rosewood in his father's workshop. At ten, he'd caught his first game, a white-tailed deer shot with a .270-caliber Winchester near Nogales, Arizona, not far from the US-Mexico border. Clayton Whitted, twenty-eight, squad Alpha's boss and the crew's second-most senior member, was the Granite Mountain Hotshots' spiritual guide and resident jokester, and an able laborer at home. He hung drywall partitions, laid floor tiles, and installed cabinets in the kitchen of the house he shared with his wife, Kristi. He painted the cabinets vibrant turquoise.

Whitted had a nurturing side. He carried a compact version of the New King James Bible in his backpack and kept a bigger copy, held together by duct tape, in the buggy. He'd written the names of every Granite Mountain Hotshot he'd worked with on it, so he wouldn't forget to pray for them, and he did, every day. He met Woyjeck and immediately took him under his wing. Woyjeck was mature beyond his age, careful in having a clear plan for his future, and deliberate in following it. However, he was still a mama's boy, calling and texting home almost every day, with all sorts of news to share, and with practical questions. He and his father followed each other on their iPhones, using the Find My Friends app, so father always knew if son was on a fire, and where. Clayton and Kristi Whitted invited Woyjeck for dinner one evening. Woyjeck phoned his mother, Anna—should he bring anything? Cookies or some other dessert, she'd told him, and maybe beer.

Woyjeck liked to have a beer with the guys on the crew and loved to dance to country music at a honky-tonk called Matt's Saloon on Whiskey Row on Saturday nights, having a good time because he could. Unless they were fighting fires, the Granite Mountain Hotshots took Sundays and Mondays off. Woyjeck had bought a twelve-pack when his younger brother Bobby came to Prescott from their home in Seal Beach, California, to help him get settled. He was in a new town, in a new apartment, a furnished studio on Montezuma Street, just past Prescott's historic Courthouse Square. He was wary of spending that first night alone: "What if the place is haunted?" he'd asked Bobby, only half-jokingly. Bobby had left, though, telling Kevin the time had come, he had to do it on his own.

Andrew Ashcraft had got in trouble in middle school. He and his friends had lit a fire in a trash can for warmth while waiting for the school bus on a cold winter morning. For community service he had to take a fire-safety class and was hooked.

He was handsome and charming—celestial-blue eyes, a broad smile, and a mustache he worked hard to grow and groom. "Excuse me, you dropped your name tag," he'd tell pretty girls he'd met, holding a packet of sugar in his hands. It was a cheesy pickup line, but somehow, it always worked.

With Juliann, it was different. She was the prom queen, smart, serious about her life and her future. Andrew had tried to conform to her idea of what a family man should be, looking for office work, even putting on a tie and the buttoned shirts she'd press for him. It wasn't long until they realized they were fighting a lost fight, so he convinced her to adopt another strategy. She acquiesced, but still set her rules. He'd work outdoors, yes. Sure, he'd fight fires. But he'd be calculating on his approach to the job, work hard to be the best that he could be, and make it a career so they could have stability at home. She wasn't cut out for the uncertainties of the job. He knew that and accepted it, as he accepted the challenges of the path he'd embraced.

Travis Carter, thirty-one, went to the University of Arizona on a football scholarship, but was injured, forced to abandon the sport he loved, and dropped out. He'd grown up on a cattle ranch near Yarnell, on land his ancestors had settled right after the Civil War, a place he planned to run one day. Carter was shy and quiet, but loved the outdoors and the camaraderie of life on the fire line. And most of all, he loved his children—a boy named Brayden and a girl, Brielle. College, in the end, had turned out to be lost time for Carter. In firefighting, he'd found his way.

Scott Norris, twenty-eight, and Dustin DeFord, twenty-four, though each in his first year with the Granite Mountain Hotshots, had fought wildfires for three seasons on other crews. Norris was a gentle workhorse, swinging a tool or wielding a saw with the deliberate discipline of a man who knew that everybody working a fire had to pull their weight. He liked to write, loved to hunt, and laughed at his own jokes, which often involved speaking with a faux Scottish accent. He had moved to work and live closer to his girlfriend, Heather, a Prescott police officer. DeFord, a minister's son with forearms as thick as Popeye's, was studying to be a preacher, but had wanted to serve the community before delivering sermons to it. That had been a lesson from his father, a pastor and firefighter back home.

Joe Thurston, thirty-two, had majored in zoology and minored in chemistry at Southern Utah University, a short walk from his childhood home in Cedar City. He was in his third fire season, a firefighter with truly Western roots. His uncle A. C. Ekker was a quintessential American cowboy and a rodeo champion. He'd graced the cover of *National Geographic* and guided the actor Robert Redford on a horse ride to Robbers Roost, one of Butch Cassidy's favorite hideouts. Thurston didn't grow up the broncobuster type, though. After college, he'd leaned toward a more orderly career, aspiring to become a brewmaster. His wife, Marsena, got a job managing a women's-clothing store in Prescott while he found work at a brewery downtown. There, he met a man who fought fires in the summer and followed his example. He'd heard the work was hard, but the money could be good if there were enough fires to fight in a season, which there always seemed to be. He immediately felt at ease when he joined the Granite Mountain Hotshots. Something about the men, their camaraderie, and the independence he'd maintain even within the crew's strict hierarchy suited him well. His mother, Gayemarie Ekker, remembered how happy he was, how comfortable he was with himself. For the first time in his life, she said, he was in charge of his future.

Christopher MacKenzie, thirty, was single and a bit of a Don Juan, with a huge shoe collection, entering his ninth fire season. He was genuinely caring; when he talked to someone, he made that person feel as if she were the only one around. He'd remained a daredevil on the snowboard circuits long after high school and had often come home tending to some injury—a bruised knee, a dislocated shoulder. One day, his father, Mike, a retired fire captain in Moreno Valley, California, asked if he'd rather be a broken-down snowboarder or a less broken-down fireman. MacKenzie settled on fighting fires.

Sean Misner, twenty-six, was a fourth-generation firefighter.

His grandfather Herbert McElwee had amassed fifty-eight years in the business, rising from wilderness fire lines to chief of the Montecito Fire Protection District, on the coast of Southern California. He'd had an appropriate nickname—Smokey—and a talent for storytelling. As a boy, Misner had sat on the carpet by his grandfather's feet, listening to him describe differences in drifting smoke: "If it's thin and white, it's safe. If it's dark and dense, call Grandpa." Misner's uncle Tim McElwee had been the first superintendent of Crew 7, Granite Mountain's precursor, an early defender against the wildfires that burned at its doorstep.

Misner had moved to Prescott a month after marrying Amanda. They'd had a modest ceremony before thirty-three guests, under a poolside palm-thatch roof at the Hilton Garden Inn in Las Vegas, in September of 2012. He was short—one of the shortest on the crew—and skinny; handsome with his bright-green eyes, olive skin, and a broad, easy smile that adorned his face on every picture that day, unsolicited proof of his happiness. He'd worn a yellow rose in his lapel, matching her bouquet. She had black cowboy boots on under a white princess gown. Sean's first job in his new town was parking, refueling, and detailing airplanes at the municipal airport. Amanda had stayed in California, working with mentally disabled adults, as they couldn't live on Sean's income alone. Prescott quickly grew on him. He'd called Amanda and told her that it seemed right to raise a family there. People were friendly, the mountains were pretty, and he had relatives in the area. Prescott also offered him a better chance of getting into a wildland crew, since it had two—Granite Mountain, in the city, and the Prescott Hotshots, out of the Prescott National Forest.

She joined him. On New Year's Day, 2013, Amanda bought

two pregnancy tests at a dollar store near their rental home in Prescott Valley. The tests read positive. All of a sudden, a lot more rode on their dreams and Sean's career plans.

They weighed the choice. An entry-level seasonal firefighter made about a dollar less on Granite Mountain than on a federal crew, and no one on Granite Mountain earned hazard pay—a 25 percent bump over base pay for every hour spent on the fire line, available only to federal employees, such as the Prescott Hotshots. But the Granite Mountain Hotshots had a solid reputation as an aggressive crew that rarely turned down assignments and always played it safe. Its members were known as good guys—family men—and Amanda liked that. For Sean, the biggest advantage lay in the classes and training available for people who wanted to get better, and the chance for advancement that came with it.

The Hotshots forged meaningful connections through common interests, faith, blood, and hardships. Some worked out at Captain CrossFit. Several attended Sunday service at Heights Church in Prescott, where Whitted had deployed his goofy sense of humor and gentle persuasiveness to bring the youth to whom he ministered closer in.

Some of the bonding was familial, and some enriched by the same jobs they'd had. One of Ashcraft's brothers-in-law, a contractor, had employed Garret Zuppiger in the winter. Zuppiger was a congenial redhead with a business-management degree. Still, he'd returned in 2013 for his second wildfire season because he loved the way the job challenged his body and intellect, how it tested his limits. He'd planned on making it his last, though. He had a girlfriend he cherished, and they'd talked about moving to the Oregon coast and settling down there.

Robert Caldwell's wife had introduced John Percin Jr., twenty-four, to the Granite Mountain Hotshots. Claire Caldwell had been a bartender at El Charro, a mom-and-pop Mexican restaurant off Courthouse Square known for good food and generous drinks. Percin, the middle son of an upper-middle-class couple, bused tables there, a job he'd dreaded and appreciated—he felt good being useful again. He was a recovering methamphetamine addict. He hadn't found it easy working close to the bar. He'd given it his all at El Charro, though, wiping tables so fiercely Claire thought he was going to rip them off the wall someday. His coworkers had a nickname for him—Diesel—because he never seemed to run out of gas.

On both his résumé and the official job application that Percin had filed with the City of Prescott, a proliferation of exclamation points celebrated his newfound enthusiasm, the self-confidence he'd gained back. Date available for work: "2 weeks due to current job!" Special accomplishments, publications, and awards: "Wilderness program in Montana, organ donor, HS diploma, GED, basic wildland class!" Additional comments: "I am honest, hardworking, motivated young man!" He'd even bragged about hiking more than one hundred miles without ever showering.

For Percin, the Granite Mountain Hotshots offered a final shot at salvation.

Prescott has long been a place of healing. With clean, dry air, and cool nights followed by days of sunshine, it drew tuberculosis patients in the late-nineteenth and early-twentieth centuries. Fort Whipple, two miles northeast of Courthouse Square, was a tactical base for the US cavalry during the settlement of the West, then headquarters for the volunteer regiment of cowboys the Rough Riders, who fought under Teddy Roosevelt in the Spanish-American War. The fort itself became a tuberculosis sanatorium during World War I, one of many in Prescott.

These days, the city has scores of sober-living homes, or halfway houses, for recovering addicts: there's no exact count because the state requires no license. Just in Prescott, drug rehabilitation is a $70-million-a-year industry, by one estimate, with about four hundred workers, mostly recovering addicts themselves.

Percin had worked hard to get fit—hiking, running, lifting weights, and struggling through many a deck of cards' worth of push-ups, under Jesse Steed's watchful gaze. The workouts drained him, but he hadn't felt this happy in a long time. Then, he hurt his knee—another failure, he thought. It happened before the crew had fought any fires in 2013, during an intensive eighty-hour training session hiking on Granite Mountain and sawing on Mount Francis, a seventy-one-hundred-foot peak west of Prescott.

Marsh pulled Percin into his office, a spartan room to the right of the door into Station 7, by the *H* the men had inscribed with black linoleum in the white floor. It was one of the initials of Granite Mountain Interagency Hotshot Crew, a stamp of proprietorship in a building they'd reshaped with their handiwork and sweat. Marsh knew Percin's story. Percin had bared his heart during his oral interview, and his frankness had endeared him to Marsh, Steed, and the other supervisors. Percin had clawed himself out of a pit. There he was, smiling, ready to give his all and go on rebuilding his life. Having a guy like that on the crew had value, and Marsh told him just that. Marsh also told Percin to stay focused, nurse that wounded knee. Soon, his time would come to fight fires in the wild.

Marsh knew what it meant. He'd become sober on September 7, 2000, and he'd remained sober.

Marsh grew up an only child, whose driven, successful parents wanted the same for their son. His father, John, had taught high school biology. His mother, Jane, worked at one of North Carolina's biggest banks, climbing the ranks from teller to manager in her twenty-six years on the job. They were a tight-knit family—Marsh had been raised to respect his parents, which he did, and his parents had pledged to stick by him, no matter where he went, what path he followed, which bumps he hit along the way.

Along with the constant guidance he received from his parents, Marsh valued the lessons he learned from Darrell Willis and Duane Steinbrink, Willis's predecessor as Wildland Division chief. They became Marsh's moral compass after he got hired in Prescott. They'd taught him to push his crew to work harder than any other crew, be nicer than everyone else, and go the extra mile, always. It was a masterful solution for command and employment of dysfunctional people, and a helpful tool of self-control.

Marsh told the Hotshots to open doors for others, and they did. He told them to help the elderly cross streets, and they did. He told them to change strangers' flat tires, and they did.

When he spoke, his men stopped and listened.

He'd adopted the motto of his alma mater, Appalachian State University, for the crew—*esse quam videri*, "to be, rather than to seem."

He had bound imperfect men into a wholesome brother-hood, softening his own sharp edges year by year in an ongoing exercise of redemption. Marsh's ambition, grit, and unrelenting sense of justness were the spine of the Granite Mountain Hotshots. These traits also matched the vision of Willis, one of the crew's founding fathers, who'd fought his own youthful battles with alcohol. Marsh and Willis both preached redemption through hard work, not handouts. For Marsh, polishing rough diamonds was an unacknowledged mission, a way of atoning for his own hurtful stumbles. Marsh's noble goals validated Willis's sense of the Granite Mountain Hotshots as a crew of second-chancers.

· · ·

In the ready room on that first day of the 2013 season, as Willis spoke, he took stock of the men before him, measuring their potential not by the certifications they'd acquired or the considerable physical skills they had shown, but by the eagerness they'd demonstrated to learn the job, and do it well and fit right in. Sitting behind those desks, they'd signed the City of Prescott Oath of Office, vowing to discharge, faithfully and impartially, the duties of wildland firefighters. On the walls, posters reminded them of some of the deadliest wildfires in history: Montana's Mann Gulch Fire, which killed thirteen firefighters in 1949, and the South Canyon Fire in Colorado in 1994, which killed fourteen.

The men were all clean shaven that day, their faces youthful. In flannel shirts and hoodies, they looked like local high school seniors taking a final exam.

Formalities concluded, they filed out of Station 7 under a setting sun. Woyjeck retreated to the studio apartment he'd rented, still agonizing over his failure at listing the fire orders and watchout situations when Willis had asked him to. So he stayed awake late into the night, studying them. Next morning, he approached Willis and said, "I'm ready to recite the ten and the eighteen, sir." And he did just that.

The 2013 season started with a promise of rebuilding and reinvention for the Granite Mountain Hotshots. They'd had rough beginnings and grand goals. They'd been created to protect Prescott from devastating fire, an ambitious mission in a city that had pushed development into its surrounding forest, taunting a lion with a stick. During its previous six seasons, the crew had fought fires all over—as far north as British Columbia, as far east as North Carolina, and as far south as the Mexican side of the border with Arizona. But until that first day of the 2013 season, no big fires had burned around Prescott.

That was about to change.

SAVING A TREE

THE GRANITE MOUNTAIN HOTSHOTS THRIVED ON misfortune: the more the wildlands burned, the more they earned. Fire paid the week's groceries, the month's rent and car loans, and the semester's credit-card charges for school supplies. Billy Warneke prayed for fire so he could afford health insurance for the baby he and his wife, Roxanne, were expecting that December—a girl she'd chosen to name Billie Grace. That spring, two other seasonal members of the crew, Anthony Rose and Sean Misner, also had first children on the way. Cumulatively, the guys were raising thirteen kids, including a stepson Robert Caldwell had embraced as his own. They were eager to work. They needed fire to survive.

May dragged on, though. In Prescott, they'd found themselves doing a lot of off-season chores: chopping brush, chipping wood, clearing dead and dying vegetation from around homes and creating "defensible space," areas free of fuel. They were hungry for adventure, too, but they were marking time, groundskeeping—the least lucrative part of their job—eight hours and done.

Travis Turbyfill kept calculating the hours he'd have to work, how much the rest of the guys on the crew would have to give of themselves once the season got going to make up for the sluggish month. He walked around restless, anxious. But his wife, Stephanie, welcomed the slowness of May. An almost leisurely pace had settled in, with Travis home so often, for so many nights of family dinners and horseplay with their girls on the living-room carpet. She told herself to enjoy having Travis home instead of worrying that he was not out making money.

In June, the slog turned into a sprint. The Granite Mountain Hotshots drove to New Mexico and fought the Thompson Ridge Fire, sparked by a downed power line in the vastness of a thirsty national preserve west of Santa Fe. It was their first significant run of 2013, ten days on the line and one hundred hours of overtime. This one, like most of their assignments, began with a phone call. Eric Marsh had programmed his cell phone to play a bit of "It's a Long Way to the Top (If You Wanna Rock 'n' Roll)," by AC/DC, whenever dispatch rang with a job for him and his men. It was his digital-age version of the old firehouse bell, and it blared the sound of money.

On June 18, 2013, after the New Mexico excursion and two mandatory days off, Marsh's phone rang. The Hotshots again rushed out of Station 7, this time just up the street, to a fire that had ignited around eleven o'clock that morning, eight miles northwest of Prescott, near a popular target-shooting pit called Doce (DOUGH-see), for which the fire was quickly named.

Marsh had taken to telling his supervisors, "I'm no spring

chicken." But he constantly pushed his body to its limits—on ice-climbing excursions to Ouray, Colorado, the "Switzerland of America," and all-day endurance mountain-bike races through the desert. In one of these races, before the start of the 2013 season, he'd fallen and broken his collarbone and had had to sit out work for six weeks with light duty. He'd just returned when the Doce Fire sparked, and he felt rewarded—finally, a respectable blaze burning right on the crew's doorstep. Darrell Willis had instructed Marsh to load up the buggies and follow the swirl of dark smoke off Iron Springs Road, west of Skyline Drive, where forest and city join.

The sun blazed up above. The brush, dried and brittle, looked dangerous. Searing weather stoked the flames. Steady winds fanned the fire, and in seven hours it brazenly pushed across four thousand acres of pine, fir, aspen, and piñon-juniper trees. It seemed unstoppable. From their homes in Prescott, people watched the fire, sweeping ashes from their porches and decks. One man placed his Sony NEX-7 on a tripod and filmed flames and smoke for a while, then mixed a somber violin concerto into the video and posted it online.

The fire marched straight toward a cluster of elegant houses in a planned community called American Ranch on the edge of the Granite Mountain Wilderness. The Wilderness spreads upward along a stack of granite boulders to seventy-six hundred feet, forming Granite Mountain. Its footprint covers almost ten thousand acres in the Prescott National Forest. Prolonged drought and recurring fires had weakened its trees, leaving them more vulnerable to ruthless bark-chewing beetles, which are endemic to the forest, but have grown so pervasive they are slowly destroying it. Left dead and dried standing, these trees had become matchsticks for ignition.

American Ranch had risen from private tracts developed in a volatile transition zone demographers call the wildland-urban interface, a dangerous new frontier of real estate entrepreneurship in the West. In this interface many retirees, empty nesters, and second-home owners find serenity and isolation, and cities and states find an expanding tax base. But building there is like building on the edge of an eroding cliff. From 1990 to 2008, 60 percent of all single-family homes built in the United States were built in the interface, many of them in the West, where more than 3 million residences are in areas of moderate to very high wildfire risk. In Northern California, which includes such picturesque tourist destinations as Yosemite and Lake Tahoe, an average of thirteen thousand homes stood under the threat of wildland fire each year between 2000 and 2010—more than twice the number of homes under the same threat in the 1990s. In Prescott, an expanse of fire-prone lots had transformed into some of the city's priciest communities. Hundreds of splendid houses stood in the Doce Fire's path.

The Hotshots piled into their buggies as flames licked backyards at American Ranch, threatening boarding stables, country clubs, miles of trails, and fulfilled dreams. Homes there sell for half a million dollars or more. Incident commanders, or ICs, ordered an ambitious aerial assault to protect the subdivision. By afternoon, fifteen aircraft were dropping water and chemicals on the flames and continued until dusk. One, a converted DC-10 airliner, dumped eight loads of fire retardant—each consisting of twelve thousand gallons of diammonium phosphate, a fertilizer, as well as water, red dye, and several other chemicals—in and around American Ranch. It coated and cooled the vegetation, slowing the flames.

Still, by nightfall, 460 families had evacuated their homes.

On their way out, some stopped at the Texaco gas station on the corner of Outer Loop and Williamson Valley Roads and dropped a few dollars in a collection jar used to buy Gatorade for Hotshots who were hiking in and out of the burning wild.

The Granite Mountain Hotshots were structured like an army platoon, broken into self-sufficient squads. Marsh, their superintendent, served as a link between the fire's commanders and the rest of his crew, tweaking assignments as needed and working out strategies. Jesse Steed, their captain, made sure that plans turned into action and got done right. The squad bosses—Clayton Whitted, of Alpha, and Robert Caldwell, of Bravo—became the leadership's eyes and ears on the line, each supervising seven men.

Whenever the Hotshots hiked, Whitted and Caldwell walked last, making sure no one straggled behind. They each had a right-hand man, lead crew members who marked the fire lines the squads would cut, branding branches with color-coded tape along the way. For Whitted, it was Chris MacKenzie, who wore a big calculator wristwatch and got ribbed for it. For Caldwell, it was Travis Turbyfill, who kept a weathered copy of *Goodnight Moon* in his backpack and read it to his daughters over the phone while out on assignments, lulling them to sleep.

To cut fire line, they mostly worked in single file, spread along as much as a mile of land in a sequence of workers and tools. First came the ones whose job was to saw off trees and brush— the sawyers, trailblazers of the wild. They lopped down the vegetation that blocked the line the crew had set out to clear. Then, the swampers swept the ground, tossing or hauling away whatever the sawyers had cut—thick slabs of timber, spindly tree branches, thorny brush. Sawyers and swampers work in a ballet with precise, practiced choreography; a wrong move and the saw might chop off a human limb. They function in pairs, staying together for the entire season, bound by shared experience and growing trust.

The crew had four teams of sawyers and swampers; how many teams worked at the same time depended on the terrain. Travis Carter—the injured college football player who, the story goes, once sustained himself in plank position for ten minutes—was the crew's saw boss. Saw bosses often work on the fire line as swampers, so they can listen and relay orders, warnings, and instructions broadcast over the radio. Not Carter. He loved running a saw and was good at it. He had a knack for looking at the land ahead and figuring out what needed to be cut and what could be left standing. The key was to remove the big stuff that flying embers could ignite, and to fell it in just the right direction. In the crew, he was one of three Hotshots certified to cut all types of trees—advanced fallers, they're called; the others were Steed and Whitted. To swampers, Carter was the ideal partner, able to slice a tree he'd just felled into pieces small and light enough to be dragged, carried, or tossed away from the line.

Andrew Ashcraft was the saw team's lead crew member. He and Carter rode the saw truck together and took turns driving. On the fire line, Ashcraft was Carter's swamper—on paper. In practice, they took turns running the saw. Ashcraft had hoped to master Carter's job for the 2013 season and convince his wife, Juliann, to let him stay on, despite the pressures and responsibilities she'd had to carry alone during his long absences, which never got easier.

"They say, 'Jump,' I say, 'How high?'" Ashcraft told her.

"You give yourself 110 percent to the crew," Juliann responded. "I'm here trying to juggle day cares, and make dinner, and make sure our kids have their baths, and that I read a book to them, that they're well dressed, go for a walk, play outside."

Ashcraft had joined the crew two years earlier, after giving up on college—he'd lasted six months at Embry-Riddle Aeronautical University, in Prescott—and a job as a mortgage-loan officer that he'd quit after a week. At first, he'd struggled with the physical demands of lugging saw, chaps, and fuel on long, hot hikes, forty more pounds over his shoulders and in a pack that already weighed at least that much. But while others tired and complained, Ashcraft cowboyed up, huffing like a plow horse and moving right along. He ignored the pain and swelling on a leg he'd shattered plummeting thirty feet while rock climbing; doctors had patched the leg back together with plates and screws. He earned a coveted award that first season, Rookie of the Year, a recognition of the firm determination Marsh looked for in all his men. Ashcraft was one of the seasonal employees who worked year-round, side by side with the six full-time members of the crew, all, like him, in supervisory positions. His wife, Juliann, worried; they had four children, and Ashcraft was much invested in a job that offered no benefits, kept him busy all year, and gave them no guarantees. Through Willis, Marsh had pushed city officials as hard as he could to free up money to restore the two full-time positions the crew had lost to budget cuts during the recession, to no avail. On the job, Ashcraft persevered. By Doce, he'd grown confident in his abilities, and so strong that when it came his turn to saw, he played rock, paper, scissors for a chance to cut the toughest ground, just to prove he could. He was competitive through and through.

The grunt work of breaking and clearing the land fell to diggers, most often a job for newbies. It didn't require special skill, but it took perseverance as well as strength to tolerate unforgiving hours hacking at packed dirt with a heavy hand tool. It was brutal. Warneke thought he'd prepared for it: he'd run three miles from his home to the gym every morning, forty pounds of sand stuffed in the backpack he'd previously worn on duty in Iraq as a scout sniper with the Second Battalion, Fourth Marines, the "Magnificent Bastards." But he looked miserable at the end of his firefighting shifts. He'd also fallen sick with a cold that hadn't gone away since he'd returned from the Thompson Ridge Fire in New Mexico. To preserve his energy at the Doce Fire, he'd judiciously avoided raising the tools overhead, a trick he had learned in training that all diggers strived to follow. They bent their arms and drew compact ovals in the air before striking a tool against the soil, as miners do underground. It's the least strenuous and safest way.

Granite Mountain's diggers carried rhinos, combis, and sometimes rakes they called monkey paws, whose long teeth were great for pulling vegetation out from between rocks. A rhino has an eight-inch steel blade at the end of the handle, for digging the ground. A combi is a trenchmaker—a small shovelhead for breaking and scraping the land when folded at ninety degrees. At the Doce Fire in the Prescott National Forest, combis tore away the hard soil after the sawyer-swamper teams opened the way. At the end of the line, the diggers used a tool they'd concocted by attaching a pounder's flat head to the long hickory handle of a Pulaski—a wildland firefighter's most consistent helper.

Pulaskis combine two tools in one head: an ax on one side and an adze on the other. The adze loosens the dirt and rips out brush. The ax cuts brush too short for the sawyers to bother with and snaps roots underfoot—fire carriers that eyes can't see. Pulaskis became standard firefighting tools of the US Forest Service in the 1930s, prior to the retirement of Edward Pulaski, a district ranger credited with their invention. Pulaski, the ranger, remains a colorful hero in wildfire history. Much of the Northern Rockies had gone up in flames in 1910, in a series of fires christened the Big Burn. Amid sudden and unavoidable danger, Pulaski hustled his ragtag crew of fortysome men down a mine shaft in Idaho, ordered them to lie facedown, and threatened to shoot whoever tried to leave; an inferno passed above. All but five survived.

The Big Burn consumed approximately 3 million acres, most of it in a weekend, sweeping across Idaho, Montana, and Washington, in bone-dry forests speckled with small communities built of lumber and lit by oil. The Forest Service, established in 1905, learned from the battle and adjusted its strategies and ambitions. Thirty years later, the agency promulgated a policy that aimed to have every wildfire corralled by ten o'clock the morning after it started, before higher temperatures and lower humidity settled in, aiding the spread of the flames. Other federal land-management agencies adopted the strategy, and in 1943, the Wartime Advertising Council added its own contribution, using cute cartoon characters to enlist the public in the fight. Bambi starred in the council's first campaign. But after Disney balked, it introduced Smokey Bear, the Forest Service's adorable mascot, pointing his finger and intoning, "Only you can prevent forest fires." During World War II, caricatures of Adolf Hitler and Hideki Tojo, Japan's ruthless prime minister, appeared on posters above flaming trees and the legend "Our carelessness, their secret weapon."

Over millennia, the cycles of forestation and fire renew soil, plants, and habitats. Fire acts as the forest's janitor, clearing the vegetation that has clogged the ground beneath trees. But foresters and bureaucrats, backed by much of the science of that time, gradually villainized the fire part. The ten o'clock policy ruled federal protocols for four decades—first as a militaristic strategy that matched the nation's wartime hubris, later as an administrative obsession that endured in spite of well-researched and steady criticism by fire ecologists, who advocated for allowing certain fires to run their course, and an emerging appreciation among average Americans for the beauty of the wildlands. Their arguments were legitimized by the National Park Service's decision to eliminate the ten o'clock policy in 1968; ten years later, the Forest Service followed it. States chose their own courses of action. Arizona was among those that continued to push a strategy of full suppression.

The 10:00 a.m. policy had been misguided, but for a while, Mother Nature masked the problems it caused. Periods of unusually high rains through the mid-1990s warded off fire while underbrush grew lushly. Then, influenced by climate change, an intense drought gripped the West. On forest floors, shaggy rugs of shrubs dried up and became tinder—ladder fuels, in firefighters' parlance, that help fire climb from the ground to the crowns of trees.

Fires began to burn hotter, longer, and more spectacularly; between 2000 and 2010, they consumed an average of 7 million acres of land a year, up 66 percent from the prior decade. In that same period, the Forest Service directed ever more of its budget to fighting fires—40 percent by fiscal year 2012, up from 13 percent in 1991. The agency found itself in a troublesome cycle: the more it spent on fire suppression, the less funding remained for clearing the dying, dead, and overgrown vegetation that fuels fires on wildlands. In 2014, the Forest Service estimated that 65 million to 82 million acres of federal public lands needed work, about 40 percent of the entire national forest system.

The expansion of frontiers of development into areas prone to burning compounded the threat. By 2014 in the West, 17 million homes were situated in these areas. Two million of them were in Arizona, the second-highest tally among eleven states. (California ranked first, with 8 million residences at risk for wildfire damage.) Scott Hunt, the Arizona State forester at the time, spoke of large fires turning into megafires because of drought, warmer temperatures, and many more people living where people shouldn't live. The Forest Service predicts a net loss of up to 37 million acres of forestland to development by 2060—an area larger than Pennsylvania. Politicians and incident commanders don't like images of homes consumed by wildfires on the nightly news. Increasingly, decisions to fight fires aggressively have started with how many homes might burn. And every such decision puts wildland firefighters in danger.

• • •

Within twenty-four hours, 672 firefighters assembled in Prescott to battle the Doce Fire—an army, responding both to the urgent need to contain the blaze, and to the political pressure to stop it before it destroyed expensive properties and comfortable livelihoods.

Fire hadn't threatened Prescott since the Indian Fire had scorched a swath of national forest in another part of town in 2002, under similar conditions: gusty winds, hot temperatures, and extremely dry grounds. The Granite Mountain Hotshots didn't exist then, not even in the minds of Darrell Willis, at the time the chief of the Prescott Fire Department, and Duane

Steinbrink, a former battalion chief whom Willis had lured from retirement to lead the newly formed Wildland Division. The city had a fuels-management crew—a brush crew of men, mostly, and occasionally a woman—who cleared overgrown vegetation around local homes. Steinbrink rounded them up and led them on an offensive against the Indian Fire. Several hadn't fought a big fire before, but they helped tame those flames before the inferno swallowed the southern side of Prescott. That gave Willis the opportunity he'd been looking for to restructure the fuels-management crew and expand its reach.

In the years that followed, Prescott's homegrown band of wildland firefighters matured. The five types of hand crews require successively more training, greater physical abilities, and deeper commitment—Hotshot crews stand at the top and Type 3 crews at the bottom. Willis's Wildland Division climbed its steps tenaciously, its ambitions increasing with each victory it scored. The brush crew became a Type 2 initial-attack crew, trained in aggressive tactics for countering nascent fires. Then, the Type 2 crew became a Hotshot crew.

They progressed along a bumpy road.

In 2003, Eric Marsh took to the job like a bear to honey, but he was hotheaded, aggressive, and prone to shouting. Steinbrink and Willis puzzled over his tangle of competence and testiness, giving him an ultimatum if he wanted to be a superintendent— "Be nice."

Hotshots are esteemed in the insulated world of wildland firefighters. Crews come from all over to fight a large fire, meeting in fire camps, which rise overnight in the light of the blaze. Camps function as bases for fire commanders. For everyone else, they're refueling stations. They have dedicated phone and

Internet lines, individual showers with scented soap inside semitruck trailers, and busy kitchens that serve three balanced meals a day to men and women who may well have burned as many as six thousand calories as they toiled. The money to pay for all that comes from the federal or state agency with jurisdiction over the burning land.

Marsh accepted the responsibility of building Prescott's Hotshot crew. He began carrying a book that listed the standards for such crews. It guided his actions. He worked his firefighters harder than ever, trained them hard, and spoke daily about the significance of the undertaking. Firefighting has a great oral tradition; it's easier to remember a lesson if it comes wrapped inside an anecdote. Marsh enjoyed sharing his battle stories and encouraged the more experienced crew members to do so—How had they got a big tree that was leaning into the fire line to fall away from it as it got cut? How had they spotted a sudden, dangerous change in weather? If they succeeded—and Marsh never voiced doubts—they'd make history. That goal became their common identity.

Infused with newfound purpose, Marsh felt valued, he told Willis—even if his crew still drove to fires in beat-up minivans bought at a state surplus sale.

Marsh nailed down the Hotshots' trainee status with the federal fire bureaucracy in 2007. He renamed the crew and gave it a new logo, the silhouette of Granite Mountain against a setting sun. He got the surplus-sale vans they rode replaced by the white buggies.

The Forest Service called a year later, in 2008. The Granite Mountain Hotshots had qualified. They were in the Klamath National Forest, in Northern California, fighting a fire that leaped along the crowns of Douglas firs and Jeffrey pines, right over lakes and rivers. Up on the fire line, Marsh announced the news proudly to the crew of eighteen men and one woman standing before him.

•••

Whenever they stopped by a camp, all of the Granite Mountain Hotshots changed into clean T-shirts before meals. Some, such as Clay Whitted and Dustin DeFord, bowed their heads in prayer before chowing down.

Yet until the Doce Fire came along, few people in Prescott knew the crew existed, much less what they were about. Some who'd spotted them cutting brush in the off-season mistook them for uniformed landscapers—they wore matching yellow shirts and moss-green pants, fire-resistant garments of their trade. Elected officials, meanwhile, had more than once tried to get rid of them as the recession pinched the city's budget. Mayor Marlin Kuykendall and some City Council members questioned keeping a crew that fought fires far from Prescott; privately, a few city officials referred to the Hotshots as "brush bunnies," a play on "dust bunnies." The Hotshots heard about the nickname and were incensed. They didn't take crap from anyone.

A new fire chief, Dan Fraijo, took over the leadership of the Prescott Fire Department in February 2013, after nine months as interim leader of a department rattled by budget cuts and in-fighting. In a memo to Craig McConnell, the city's manager at the time, Fraijo laid out advantages (eight) and disadvantages (three) of keeping the Hotshots and the Wildland Division. Willis had offered his own list of advantages and disadvantages in a separate document, prepared in the crew's defense. The memo and document spelled out the unusual system of grants and reimbursements that funded the Hotshots and showed that they brought in more money than they spent. In fiscal 2013, they'd generated a net profit of $88,000, after $1 million in expenses. The city got reimbursed $39.50, per hour and per man, whenever the Hotshots worked on federal land. The reimbursement amounted to more than the overtime rate of the crew's highest-paid member because it assumed the inclusion of other costs, such as fuel for saws and vehicles, replacement of tools, and general repairs. Essentially, Willis argued, the crew members subsidized their own jobs.

Marsh typed up his own memo, on a word processor in his office at Station 7:

"Who are the Granite Mountain Hotshots? This is a simple question with a complex answer. We are many things to many different people. 'An oddity' in a workforce ruled by federal crews. 'A bit of a mystery' to other city workers. 'Crazy' to relatives and friends. 'Chameleons' to one another.

"Maybe to answer the question of who we are, it would be helpful to explore who or what we are not. We are not nameless or faceless, we are not expendable, we are not satisfied with mediocrity, we are not willing to accept being average, we are not quitters."

He named the file "towhomthefuckitconcerns." He renamed it before it got to City Hall.

•••

Granite Mountain overlooks to its northeast an enclave of ranches and estates called Williamson Valley. To the southwest, the mountain faces a minuscule community called Skull Valley, so named because the bones of American Indians killed in an intertribal battle lie scattered in its fields. The wind blew in from the direction of Skull Valley as the Doce Fire burned, pushing the fire over Granite Mountain and toward Williamson Valley. Tony Sciacca, a former superintendent of the Prescott Hotshots, was one of sixteen incident commanders in the country certified to manage the most complex wildfires, which threaten communities and are burning on dry, dense forest, under trying weather conditions—hot temperatures, low humidity, strong winds. On the Doce Fire's second day, he had taken control. Sciacca lived in Prescott; from his front door, he could view Granite Mountain. While mowing his lawn, he'd spotted the first whirl of dark smoke near the Doce target-shooting pit and had warned Willis, who'd warned Marsh, who'd sent the Granite Mountain Hotshots on their way.

Workers had set up a fire camp at Prescott High School. With students on summer break, empty classrooms morphed into dormitories and offices for teams assigned to run the operations, planning, logistics, and financial elements of the firefighting. Sciacca presided over morning and afternoon briefings there, offering updates, distilling objectives and doling out assignments to firefighters after they'd grabbed egg-and-sausage burritos in the cafeteria. He'd named Marsh division supervisor, an on-the-ground leader in charge of a section of the blaze and the crews working there. The direction of the wind, the intensity of the fire, and the dryness of the fuels it burned told Sciacca that the easiest and safest place to anchor a fire line was to the west side of the fire. There, crews had the wind to their backs, pushing the fire away from them. Flames were devouring the shrubs— scrub oak, catclaw acacia, manzanita—that thrive in the high desert's dry summers and mild, moist winters.

The Hotshots assembled by the Doce target-shooting pit. Marsh ordered a bulldozer operator to run his blade along the ground for about a hundred yards, starting at the edge of the fire. Some of the Hotshots then picked up drip torches. The torches are like watering cans, but filled with a mix of diesel and gasoline, and equipped with igniters that light at the pull of a trigger. They dripped the oil on the vegetation and burned the line from the end of the dozer scrape to an old road ahead—a retreat if anything went wrong.

Steed directed the crew to dig, and they set to it, carving a line parallel to the fire, out from the anchor point they'd fashioned. They were working west of Granite Mountain. Hand crews on the other side of the fire, to the mountain's east, were digging a parallel fire line. Eventually, they'd corral both ends of the fire, encircling the blaze. Meanwhile, airplanes and helicopter pilots showered water and fire retardant on and ahead of the flames, so the ground crews could pinch the fire's head, box it in, and save the American Ranch subdivision ("a Western lifestyle community").

In saving homes threatened in the Doce Fire the Granite Mountain Hotshots became local heroes, no longer hometown strangers. They found this odd; they were just a small part of a big operation, one crew among many, but they were getting attention from people who'd never cared for them before. Home-baked pastries appeared on their doorsteps and car hoods, banners of praise and thanks adorned porches and car windows. In public meetings, people got up and praised the Hotshots' courage.

"It was, like, nobody knew the guys, then, all of a sudden, they were heroes," Stephanie Turbyfill recalled. The Doce Fire had made them cool.

The men spent their nights during the Doce Fire at Station 7, another oddity for them and for their families. For once, they

had a good fire going and didn't need to travel to it. The Hotshots enjoyed it and savored the visits from wives and children,
who stopped by when they could. Amanda Misner worked and
lived in neighboring Prescott Valley, and she didn't get out of
work until ten at night. She then made the trip just to spend some
time with Sean. They sat in the back of his pickup truck and
talked deep into the morning about the baby growing in her
belly—a boy. Most of the guys slept in the backs of their trucks,
looking at the starry sky above, as if they were sleeping out in
the wild. Even though they were so close to home, they couldn't
commute back and forth from the line.

Grant McKee didn't like that. He longed to cuddle with his
fiancée, Leah Fine, on their twin-size bed. Leah made his overnight stays at Station 7 a bit more tolerable when she stopped by
every night, bringing him bags of gummy bears, cans of 5-hour
Energy drinks, and packs of Camel Crush, the menthol-flavored
cigarettes he smoked.

Stephanie Turbyfill came by every other night, bringing
along Brynley, who was one, and Brooklyn, almost three. The
girls ran around the dirt parking lot, picked rocks, and brought
smiles from the men, exhausted after a long day. Stephanie and
Travis sat on the tailgate of his white Toyota Tacoma, glad about
the life they had and its possibilities. "If you have dirty socks,
put them in a pan and leave them for me in the back of the
truck. I'll pick it up, wash them, bring 'em back, and put 'em right
back where you left them—your laundry fairy," she quipped. This
fire was closer to home than any other they had ever fought.
The visits from family provided a normality amid the chaos of
their work.

Steed, in command while Marsh nursed his injury, had proposed family barbecues on Saturdays when the crew wasn't busy fighting fires—lunchtime get-togethers open to all wives, fiancées, and girlfriends, children, and dogs. They gathered at Heritage Park, a short drive from Station 7. Warneke grilled the burgers. DeFord made jalapeño poppers, which were a huge hit. Juliann Ashcraft baked cookies, with different batches picked by different members of the crew. Wade Parker ordered chocolate chip and bacon. Brendan McDonough asked for peanut butter and jelly. For Steed, Juliann made orange dreamsicle cookies, his favorite and a specialty.

Children gravitated to Steed during the picnics, and he loved every minute of it. He took turns pushing the Ashcraft kids on the park's playground swings and laughed out loud zipping down the slide holding one of his own—Caden, four, or Cambria, three, as if he were a child, too. He strived to be a mentor to the other fathers on the crew, always wanting to teach them they could be great family men and also great Hotshots. He told the guys, "Family comes first."

Eric Marsh cared deeply about family, too, but it was different. He was on his third marriage. He didn't have children. His men didn't think he could understand what they were missing out on when they spent time far from home. But, in his own way, he could. He cared, so much—about his wife, Amanda, and about the women and children his men had left behind—that he bought a satellite phone and carried it with him on fires, so they could call home for birthdays, anniversaries, and other special occasions. After the end of their shifts, Marsh often peeled away from the rest of the guys, dialed Amanda, and talked to her about his day—the challenges he'd faced, the beautiful sights he'd seen. On Thursdays, Marsh had dinner with his own parents at the house they'd built in Prescott Valley to be near him.

Then, he kept going east on State Highway 69, to the AA meeting at the Kate Garber Activity Center in Dewey-Humboldt, the next town over.

Just a month before the Doce Fire, he'd voiced resentment, in his self-evaluation, about the challenges of running a Hotshot crew on a budget so lean he could barely fulfill the program's minimum requirements. The *Standards for Interagency Hotshot Crew Operations,* a federal document revised in 2011, called for at least seven permanent, or full-time, firefighters in leadership positions on Hotshot crews and listed the certifications required for each position. On paper, the Granite Mountain Hotshots met the second criterion, but not the first. Before the 2013 season started, Craig McConnell, the city manager, had authorized Willis to classify Ashcraft and MacKenzie as "full-time temporary employees." This acknowledged their year-round duties—they fought fires in the spring and summer and chopped brush or plowed snow in the wintertime—and conformed to the rules to preserve the crew's status. But that didn't give the full-time temporary workers employer-sponsored health insurance, paid holidays, vacations, or admission to the state's generous public-safety retirement system. The bureaucratic maneuver simply brought the Granite Mountain Hotshots in compliance, under a clause allowing nonfederal Hotshot crews to use "equivalent employment authority" to meet the qualification criteria.

By the time the Doce Fire came along, Ashcraft had worked sixteen months without interruption. He averaged fifty-five hours per week. Still, he had no benefits.

Marsh took the fights with the city personally. Willis warned him against it, telling Marsh he'd have to navigate the politics if he led the division someday. He had to learn to be tactful.

As the Doce Fire blazed in the Prescott National Forest, the

Granite Mountain Hotshots hiked, hacked, and sawed, drawing close to a huge alligator juniper, far bigger than usual. Hotshots don't often take time to think about the survival of trees they come upon, but this one was special. Alligator junipers—the scientific name is *Juniperus deppeana*—have rough, dark-brown bark, broken into small squares that resemble an alligator's tiled skin. They aren't towering trees, but have generous crowns and robust circumferences, typically about seven feet. The circumference of the alligator juniper the Hotshots had come across measured twenty-five feet. The tree rose fifty feet from the ground and spread across seventy feet. It was listed as a cochampion on American Forests' National Register of Big Trees as one of the country's largest alligator junipers, the longest-living tree species in the forest. The massive tree could be a thousand years old.

The men hiked up to the alligator juniper with the mission of saving it. A wilderness and trails manager at the Prescott National Forest had asked them to, and they complied, in selfish interest; after all, the champion tree was in their own backyard. Dried shrubs clogged its base, potentially a ladder of fuel for flames to climb. Branches hung close to the ground, an easy target for a moving fire. The Hotshots thought about sawing off those branches, but reconsidered. It felt like savagery. Instead, they chainsawed trees nearby. Swinging combis and Pulaskis, they broke and dug the ground, building a fire line that held the alligator juniper in a loose embrace. Then, they lit up the brush on the edge of the fire line, to deprive the approaching flames.

The following day, the men returned to see if the tree had made it. They found it singed but unharmed, a single flame burning on one of its branches.

Steed ripped out a page of the crew's unit log, the notebook where he recorded the day's assignments and activities on the fire line. A geocache was nearby (a prize in a GPS treasure-hunting game), so they signed their names on the page and left it inside the container, joining in on this modern version of hide-and-seek. Above the signatures, one of them wrote, "Granite Mountain Hotshots saved this World Record Holding Juniper Tree on 6-19-13."

Chris MacKenzie pulled out his cell phone and told the Hotshots to gather for a group picture. They assembled like a football team: some crouched, some standing, some sitting high up among the tree's sturdy limbs. Then, they formed a human pyramid in front of it, five stories high, the bigger guys lined up at the bottom, hands and knees on the rocky soil: Whitted, Turbyfill, Carter, Steed, and DeFord. Woyjeck, the smallest, knelt alone at the top, one knee on Warneke, another on Grant McKee, who looked ahead and smiled like a kid.

A BOLT OF LIGHTNING

J UST AFTER 5:00 P.M. ON FRIDAY, JUNE 28, 2013, A BOLT of lightning cracked the sky above the Weaver Mountains of Central Arizona. The ground smoked. A few puffs rose up from a jumble of parched manzanita trees west of State Highway 89, at the south end of Yarnell. Residents all over town soon spotted the smoke. Flames peeked out past a cluster of granite boulders impossibly angled along the rugged hillside.

The fierce energy released by this electrical force is beyond intense. It may heat the air around it to fifty thousand degrees— five times hotter than the surface of the sun. A bolt slamming to the ground in the parched wilderness is like a lit match dropping on a pile of hay: a big whoosh, then fire.

At dusk, Linda Ma's doorbell rang. She had been preoccupied that evening with organizing the Great Gatsby Dinner &

Dance at the Yarnell Community Center, a space with many purposes that also serves a popular lunch—fruit, salad, and a homemade main dish for $6, $5 for those over sixty-four, as four out of ten local residents are. At her door was a group of neighbors, worry written across their faces. They walked into her backyard, bordering the wilderness, the sky a lightly glow. Ma was happy for the distraction of the visit.

A little later, sipping a glass of chardonnay on her nearby deck, Karen Pattersen gazed at the lit mountaintop.

June is usually the driest, hottest month of the year in Yarnell, and that June had been no exception. The heat had been relentless, offering none of its usual breaks at night. An unforgiving heat wave held the entire southwestern United States in a sweltering embrace. In Phoenix, mesquite trees, staples of the desert, had closed their tiny leaves to protect themselves from the scorching temperatures. By month's end, dozens of Phoenix dwellers had escaped to Yarnell, "where a desert breeze meets the mountain air," as the town motto says. The town is a retreat from the city's noise and hubbub, a haven for retirees—but not the golf-playing type more common in Arizona. Second-home owners in Yarnell have retired from jobs teaching, reading gas meters, managing hotels, tending to government business. They're people looking to stretch their Social Security checks and savings, and Yarnell is just the place to accommodate thrifty living. The median income of its 638 year-round residents is just below $30,000.

In that sleepy place, the fire offered a spectacle.

Thirty-five miles away, in Prescott, dispatchers at the Yavapai County Sheriff's Office fielded seventeen 911 calls in twenty-four minutes from residents and passing motorists. The callers sounded more curious than alarmed—"Was this human caused or what?" one man asked. Their calls followed the fire's unsteady cadence—two calls in four seconds, no calls for three minutes, two calls in eight seconds.

At Station 7, the Granite Mountain Hotshots were readying for a different battle. East of a community called Highland Pines, in Prescott, where hundreds of cedar homes stood in the shade, and the air carried the sweet scent of ponderosa pines, a fire had been sparked by the same storm as in Yarnell. Prescott had just ducked trouble; crews, on foot and in the air, had beaten back the Doce Fire, so fire managers in the national forest played it safe and chose to engage the relatively small fire, called West Spruce. They didn't want to risk losing Highland Pines amid those tinder-dry lands.

The Hotshots gathered. Brendan McDonough had called in sick that day. But John Percin, his injured knee healed, was nervous about fighting his first fire, but also resolute. On his way out the door, he faced his roommate, Kirk Warren, and said, "This is gonna be nothing compared to what I've been through." That was his goodbye that day. Marsh, after working as a supervisor on the Doce Fire, a task that had taken him away from his crew at times, was back as the Granite Mountain Hotshots' superintendent, back on the fire line with his men, back in his element.

The Hotshots loaded up and departed the station for a blazing slice of forest nearby as the sun dipped behind the mountains.

In Yarnell, Barbara Kelso and her daughter, Kim, left their home around the same time, for a dinner of wood-fired pizza at the T-Bird Café, in neighboring Peeples Valley. Barbara was a sprightly ninety-three-year-old, and resident of Yarnell for nearly as long. She'd served for seven years on the fire district board, two as its chairwoman.

She and Kim stepped outside the restaurant and watched

the amazing electric storm exploding against the purple sky. Barbara's board experience had acquainted her with fire in the wild. She understood its dangers. She saw lightning clip a ridge to her left—south and west of the café. Alarmed, she called 911. "We're on it," the dispatcher told her. Barbara wasn't really sure what that meant—were firefighters on their way? She hung up anyway. She went back inside the T-Bird, sat down, and ordered dinner.

From his back porch on a hill overlooking State Highway 89, Bob Brandon watched the dark clouds gather and the lightning flash. Brandon was a founder and captain of the Peeples Valley Fire Department, an all-volunteer force. He swept his binoculars across the mountains, as he'd been trained to do whenever storms rolled in. The mountains were clogged with brush that hadn't burned in nearly half a century. He spotted a fire to his north, and then two more on the mountains. He grabbed his radio and summoned the volunteers available to work. Six men soon showed up.

In Yarnell, two firefighters were on duty at the station that night. The fire chief, a part-time employee named Jim Koile, lived out of town. He'd called in and told his firefighters to stand on the sidelines. Then he called Sally Foster, a volunteer captain at the department. Foster offered to work from home; she had no one to care for her ailing husband. She reached out to the Arizona Interagency Dispatch Center and notified it of the fire. The center was in charge of coordinating the response to wildfires such as the one in Yarnell, which burned on state land. One of its dispatchers contacted Russ Shumate, an assistant fire manager at the Arizona State Forestry Division. Shumate set about gauging the urgency of the situation and planning a first course of action.

Wildfires are classified by complexity on a scale of 1 to 5; the more challenging, the lower the number. Deciding the priority of fires to engage, with what level of commitment, and when, follows an established protocol, based on a series of questions.

How erratic is the weather?

How accessible is the area that's burning?

How dry is the vegetation?

How threatening are the flames to communities around them?

What else is burning out there?

It's a triage system for selecting effective use of limited fire-fighting resources. Thirty-seven fires burned in Arizona that Friday, including four of the eight large fires burning out of control in the entire Southwest. The largest of these, the Silver Fire, in southern New Mexico, had consumed more than one hundred thousand acres of the Gila National Forest, its smoke plume rising to thirty-nine thousand feet.

Shumate had worked for forty-three days without a full day off, answering calls when he should have been resting, before arriving in Yarnell. He'd driven out from the Prescott Fire Center, the regional hub coordinating governmental response to major state emergencies such as wildfires and floods. He'd been helping identify and rank the small fires ignited by the lightning storm that afternoon, including the West Spruce Fire and several others in the Prescott National Forest, where the Doce Fire still had a pulse. He knew he had to get his eyes on the flames so he could figure out what to do about the fire in Yarnell. And he knew that the fastest way was to find someone to view the fire from above. He pulled a single-engine air tanker assigned to the Doce Fire and instructed its pilot to veer southwest, swoop over the Weaver Mountains, and size up this new blaze.

The Doce Fire was 92 percent contained. A small cast of firefighters remained, clearing dying trees from fire lines, and extinguishing whatever still smoldered. The Granite Mountain Hotshots had been dismissed from Doce three days earlier. They'd kept busy cutting brush in town, eager for another run. That evening, lightning crackled and Marsh ordered them to stay put at Station 7. The decision paid off. They got a call, a fire right in town.

Above the Weaver Mountains, west of Yarnell, the pilot of the single-engine tanker circled, having trouble spotting fire amid the granite boulders and thick vegetation. Finally, he saw a wisp of flame in a corner of his view and banked toward it. The fire wasn't much. It covered a half acre near the top of Yarnell Hill, far enough from homes below—and hard to reach on foot. The pilot spotted an adjacent trail slicing the steep mountainside. The trail seemed wide enough for an all-terrain vehicle, though boulders and rocks would make a trip there rough. He told Shumate the difficulties in reaching the fire. Shumate wondered if such a small blaze justified the effort.

Shumate huddled with a range technician from the Bureau of Land Management (BLM) at the Yarnell fire station, since public lands in the area are managed by state and federal agencies, and it wasn't entirely clear at the time where the fire was burning. He consulted with Bob Brandon, the Peeples Valley fire captain, and others who'd also convened there, gathering information on the four fires they'd spotted. A quick burst of rain killed one, east of Peeples Valley. Bob Brandon's firefighters had already hiked three miles toward another, but Shumate ordered them back. Maybe the men knew the area well. But, he reasoned, that didn't make it safe for volunteers to go out, alone, fighting fires at night. Too much flammable brush was out there.

The two remaining fires got named. A team of BLM fire-fighters extinguished one of them, called the Oso Fire, quickly that night. They steered a four-wheel-drive engine truck into the wild, unfurled hoses, dragged them on a short hike, and drowned the flames. The other was the Yarnell Hill Fire. There was no way a fire engine could get near it.

•••

The peaks, canyons, and valleys around Yarnell hadn't burned since 1966. Back then, sparks from a train's wheels had ignited the brush on the west face of the Weaver Mountains, a chain of steep, jagged hills opposite Yarnell's humble homes and business district, between the town of Congress and the ghost town of Hillside. In 2013, thick, dry brush covered both sides of those mountains.

The oppressive heat wave that had descended on the Southwest was from a large high-pressure system over the region that trapped hot air. Temperatures broke records in California, Nevada, and Arizona. In Phoenix, meteorologists baked a tray of biscuits on the dashboard of their van. It was a worrisome start to summer, after one of the driest recorded winters. Temperatures in the region, already the warmest and driest in the country, had risen almost two degrees higher than historical averages. Its snowpack, meanwhile, had declined by 23 percent on average, compromising the vegetation's ability to stockpile water for the rainless months ahead, making it more prone to fires.

Wildfires need oxygen, fuel, and heat to burn. Yarnell had plenty of fuel, and not just on the mountains. Brush crowded the yards in town, in lots shaped like diamonds and trapezoids, wedged into Yarnell's hilly topography. The brush in both mountains and yards was overgrown, tangled, and tinder dry. Peter

Andersen, Yarnell's former fire chief, had pleaded in monthly meetings for help clearing it, but few residents took on the task. His wife, Judy, the town's fire safety officer, secured small state and federal grants and hired outsiders to do it. The work had fallen to a crew of inmates from the Arizona State Prison Complex at Lewis, one of eleven prison crews in the state trained to fight wildfires. Their labor came cheap—one dollar an hour for each man, and a modest stipend for wear and tear on their equipment. The inmates could only do so much, though. Some of Yarnell's residents were too old or too frail to hold the vegetation in check. Others refused. They liked the forest meeting their land.

The town hadn't received a good soaking in months. Only two inches of rain had fallen during winter and spring of 2013. The last measurable rain had come on April 7—a mere 0.11 inch. Daily relative humidity had averaged 22 percent since the beginning of the month. Gradually, the dry air had drained moisture from plants that already had so little of it stored, increasing the likelihood and speed with which they could ignite.

For the June 5 edition of *The Yellow Sheet,* a monthly newsletter for Yarnell folks, Sally Foster, the volunteer fire captain, had penned a prescient warning: "Danger of wildfire in the Yarnell area reached the maximum level (Extreme) on May 17 and is expected to remain at that level for the rest of the summer. We all love the wild beauty of our remote mountain environment, but the scrub oaks, pine trees, untamed shrubs, and dry grasses are all perfect fuel for a wildfire. Responsible residents in rural areas like ours should EXPECT a wildfire and plan ahead."

Foster had made her plans. On her dining-room table, in a basket holding bills and reminders of other chores, she kept a list of items to grab in a mandatory evacuation: laptop, family photos, jewelry, personal documents, prescriptions. In her closet, she kept paper file boxes, ready for quick packing.

• • •

That Friday evening, Shumate called the state's dispatch center at 7:19 p.m. He described the Yarnell Hill Fire as "inactive," and "not much of a threat." Standing by the town's fire station, on top of a hill called Looka Way and in front of the smoldering mountain, he had yet to see flames.

"Not taking action tonight," he announced to the dispatcher.

But Bob Brandon and other Peeples Valley firefighters had seen fire on the mountain. Brandon knew a path that led straight up there, one that tied to the trail the air-tanker pilot had spotted while flying over the blaze. Brandon had lived in Peeples Valley for two decades and had traversed those lands on foot and horseback, on hikes and cattle drives. He pleaded with Shumate, "I can go in through Glen Ilah. There's a little trail off of Candy Cane Lane that goes straight to where the fire's burning."

"No," Shumate had replied. He was tired and needed to get a good night's sleep.

So Brandon went home, too.

At 9:00 p.m., the Yarnell Hill Fire flared up. Shumate, still at the station, grabbed his binoculars. He decided it had been a single bush igniting. By then, it was too dark for him to pinpoint its location. He'd gone no closer to find out.

Right around that time, Barbara and Kim Kelso arrived home from dinner out. Barbara looked west, toward the mountains, and spotted smoke rising from a ridge that seemed far away. Unperturbed, she climbed into bed and fell asleep.

On a 1-to-5 priority list, state forestry officials had ranked the Yarnell Hill Fire number 4, low in the zero-sum competition for planes, helicopters, and crews qualified and available to fight wildfires. So Shumate let Friday plans go and focused on Saturday.

He directed a crew of inmates from the Lewis state prison to report for duty at the Peeples Valley gas station at 8:00 a.m. The inmates should bring a "double-sack lunch," he said—food for a full day of work out in the wild.

"Will you need water and Gatorade at all?" a state dispatcher asked him. An engine truck stationed outside Phoenix had been assigned to Yarnell on Saturday.

Shumate said it should bring Gatorade, yes, and water, too, as much as it could. "We will buy ice from the gas station," he said.

He ordered two single-engine airplanes and instructed BLM to add its Type 3 helicopter to the firefighting fleet, with seats for up to eight passengers and space to store a hundred gallons of water.

At 9:39 p.m., the Yavapai County Sheriff's Office got another 911 call on the fire, after a lull of three hours and forty-three minutes.

"I'm up in Yarnell and I'm looking sort of northwest at a fire," said the caller. "Just wondering if the authorities are aware of it?"

Three other good citizens phoned in—at 9:47, 9:48, and 9:49 p.m.

Shumate requested a spot weather forecast for Yarnell Hill.

From the National Weather Service's office outside Flagstaff, meteorologists pulled the readings from a remote weather station five miles away and typed up their findings: "Expect a warm night with poor relative humidity recovery and generally light winds. Another very hot and very dry day expected tomorrow with a slight chance of high-based showers and/or thunderstorms. These storms will have little chance of producing wetting rains. But may produce dangerous and erratic wind gusts." The air was so dry that the rain falling from these storms evaporated before it hit the ground.

Shumate left Yarnell at 10:00 p.m. He arrived home an hour later, to get the sleep he so needed. He probably hoped the fire would go to sleep, too, and die overnight, as fires sometimes do when the air cools and humidity climbs after dark in the wildlands.

At 11:35 p.m., the Yavapai County Sheriff's Office logged the last of the night's calls on the fire:

"Nine one one, what is your emergency—police, fire, or medical?"

"Fire," said the caller. "On top of the Yarnell mountain. I'm on eighty-nine north, coming from—"

"Okay, sir, we are working the fire."

"Oh, you know about it already?"

"Yeah, we are working the fire at Yarnell Hill."

At his home, Brandon couldn't fall asleep. All night, from his bedroom window, he watched the flames dancing in the dark. The fire burned freely. It showed no signs of dying out.

CALCULATING RISK

IN THE PRESCOTT NATIONAL FOREST, THE WEST Spruce Fire had been engaged, corralled, and tamed by 11:00 p.m., when the Granite Mountain Hotshots signed off for the day and headed home to rest.

Earlier, forest officials, pressured by flames nearing homes, had called up firefighters skilled in night missions on rugged ground. Two apt teams soon arrived. By chance, the forest's home crew, the Prescott Hotshots, and also their counterparts in the city, Granite Mountain, were around, not off working a fire in Idaho, Montana, or California. Both had geared up fast and easily reached the flames.

At that point in the season, Whitted and Caldwell, Granite Mountain's squad bosses, had firmed up seat assignments and chores for the men riding in the buggies—an expression of the Hotshots' set hierarchy. The buggies had ten seats, five along each side, one behind the other, a mini–school bus. The men sat by seniority and experience, not by choice or friendships. Rookies rode back, near the garbage.

DeFord and Percin washed the trucks' windows.

Misner and Woyjeck filled the coolers with water and Gatorade.

Warneke and McKee loaded in meals ready to eat (MRE)— individual rations, dinner for the night at the West Spruce Fire. MRE come sealed in sturdy plastic with a shelf life of three and a half years—if stored at under eighty-one degrees. Boneless pork ribs, chicken dumplings, beef enchiladas. They're rich in calories and nutritionally balanced. They sound more appetizing than they taste. Tabasco sauce helps—as Steed liked to say, "even bad food tastes good with Tabasco." En route to fires out of state, the guys walked out of restaurants with their pockets full of single-serve Tabasco packets and boxes of Cheerios. They did some serious damage at all-you-can-eat buffets.

Squad bosses and lead crewmen took turns behind the wheel. They talked shop, daydreamed, debated what had and hadn't worked on the fire line that day, and dozed. The buggies rumbled along—Whitted and MacKenzie in Alpha, Caldwell and Turbyfill in Bravo. Behind the driver's seat on Bravo, a DVD player taped to a board sat on an armrest, atop a slab of foam, a contraption to keep the movies from skipping while they played on a flatscreen TV hung behind the front seats. The guys had pooled cash and Turbyfill had bought the equipment. Together, the men of Bravo had installed it. Riding to the Thompson Ridge Fire, a long day on the road, Anthony Rose, who sat by the player, popped in the R-rated stoner comedy *Pineapple Express*. The West Spruce Fire was too close by for movie watching. Rose, short and wiry, with piercing blue eyes and a perfect smile,

listened to loud hip-hop on his iPhone. He had several nick-
names, all alluding to his penchant for singing and dancing like
a rapper. One was Tone Loc—after the gravel-voiced rapper of
"Wild Thing."

Marsh and Steed rode in the superintendent's truck to West
Spruce, as they'd done on the Doce Fire and every fire the prior
season, their first paired as Granite Mountain's leaders.

The crew and its Prescott counterparts worked in tandem,
building fire line in the wildlands off West Spruce Mountain, the
weather on their side: calmer winds, balmier temperatures, and
higher humidity at night than while the hot sun shone. They
felled trees, hacked brush, sliced and ripped roots from the
ground, carving a buffer zone between the fire and the Highland Pines subdivision. They worked into the night, delivering
another victory for Prescott homeowners against a danger that,
after years of dormancy, had threatened twice in a week.

The West Spruce Fire had crept through ten acres of forest
on the southwest side of Prescott, never posing much danger to
anyone or any home. Still, Marsh and Steed took customary pre-
cautions and wasted no time snuffing it out.

The Granite Mountain Hotshots had earned their reputation
as an aggressive crew. They pushed hard on the assignments they
handled and rarely turned one down. "Give us a tough one and
we'll make it happen," Marsh told his men. Marsh and Steed had
got good at offering smart alternatives to usual tactics, other ways
of accomplishing what a fire commander might have asked—
faster, safer approaches. They were mindful of danger. As outsiders, Marsh and Steed seemed to savor the respect and validation
that extrahard work—and calculated risks—had brought to them.

But sometimes, they felt that no matter how much they tried
to do what they felt was right, it wasn't enough.

One morning during the last wildfire they'd fought in 2012, in the Payette National Forest in Idaho, incident commanders had ordered the Granite Mountain Hotshots to switch strategies, from an "indirect attack," building fire line away from the edge of the fire, then burning back the vegetation left in between, to a "direct attack," physically separating the burning and unburned fuels by digging line right along the fire's edge, one foot on the black. Marsh and Steed had seen burned and weakened trees falling there, and many other trees threatening to do the same. They asked each other, "What's your comfort level?" They laid out the challenges and discussed them, gauging their ease, confidence, and concerns, as they often did. The crew's entire leadership chimed in, voicing worries and suggesting alternatives. In training, the Granite Mountain Hotshots had been free to speak their minds. In practice, though, inexperienced rookies deferred on decisions on safety and tactics to seasoned crew members. That was the case in most of the Hotshot crews out there.

Staging a direct attack on the Wesley Fire didn't sit well with Marsh. He assessed risk versus reward and didn't see a worthy payoff. He wasn't afraid of saying no. He told the commanders a direct attack "was too hazardous." The commanders disagreed. Marsh turned down the assignment.

The Granite Mountain Hotshots paid the price: they left that fire with a bad evaluation. A supervisor blamed the crew for the division's failure to meet its objectives for the day. Marsh was furious. The evaluation seemed a reprisal for judiciously saying no. There weren't exactly any consequences, but Marsh didn't like having it on his record, especially because he didn't agree that it was fair.

The West Spruce Fire, on the other hand, had seemed a perfect fit for the Granite Mountain Hotshots and got an instant yes from Marsh and Steed.

The men shuffled back to the buggies at the end of an overtime shift, knowing already that they'd have to come back by 6:00 a.m. on Saturday, June 29, 2013. A fire smoldered near Mount Josh, a few miles to the north.

The fire season had finally eased into a familiar rhythm. Money poured in from extra hours spent on the dirt, digging line, breathing smoke.

Percin was thrilled, but for a more fundamental reason. He was a wildland firefighter at last. Those hours on the fire line at West Spruce had made the Hotshot title real, and another fire awaited. He rode home to downtown Prescott that night, wrapped his arms around his roommate's neck, and screamed, "I did it! I did it!" Getting through that day, carrying his load on the fire line, had been the biggest victory Percin had scored in a while, validation of his worthiness, his moment of glory, at last.

Ashcraft, who also lived in town, drove home and peeked in at his children—his girl, Shiloh, in one room; his boys, Ryder, Tate, and Choice, in the other. They were all sound asleep in the wooden beds he'd made, kid-size. They were what he lived for. For them, he was willing to put up with Juliann's every demand and doubt.

Travis Carter had a home in Paulden, fifty minutes away, but he hadn't slept there much since separating from his wife. He had a harmonious combination of strength and agility, traits he'd developed since his days as an all-state, all-conference tailback in high school. His shyness could be charming, but it also kept him from sharing much about his personal problems. The guys didn't probe.

Carter had already arranged some of his clothes in hangers

and drawers in his childhood bedroom at his father's ranch. Too tired to go anywhere that night, he thought it best to sleep at Station 7.

Misner faced a thirty-minute drive, so he decided to sleep at the station, too. He called and checked on Amanda, who was seven months pregnant. Amanda had been awakened by contractions the previous night and they'd rushed to the emergency room, so he hadn't slept much.

"Do you feel ready?" Amanda asked.

"I'm tired. It's a lot of physical work," he told her. "But I trust the guys around me. I trust every guy working with me."

Misner had a tattoo across his chest, *Philippians 4:13*. It was his favorite biblical verse, "I can do all things through Christ who strengthens me." He was on the small side—five feet nine inches, and just 155 pounds. He'd played wide receiver on his high school football team, the Santa Ynez Pirates, and had a nickname, Mighty Mouse, because once he got his hands on the ball, he'd dodge and outrun the big guys on the field. From the stands, his mother, Tammy Misner, cheered and agonized. "There were times when he was hit, and you'd hear everybody go 'awwwww,' and I'd stand up, my heart racing, and he'd bounce right up, and it was, like, my boy is so strong, nothing's gonna keep him down," she said.

In high school football, the team's motto was "strong, competent, enthusiastic," and Tammy Misner said her son embodied all of that, which is why he fit in so well with the Granite Mountain Hotshots. "The coach would say, 'Hey, Sean, can you do this?' and he'd say, 'Yes, I can.' Eric Marsh would say, 'Can you do this, Sean?' and he'd say, 'Yes.'"

Like Percin, Misner looked forward to the next day's blaze, and he didn't want to risk being late. A fire beckoned in Prescott.

A SLEEPING FIRE AWAKENS

THE INMATES IN THE SUNRISE UNIT OF THE ARIZONA State Prison Complex at Lewis woke up full of anticipation on Saturday, June 29. On the Friday evening news, they'd heard of fires sparked by lightning, then they'd got their orders to go fight a fire burning high on a mountain in Yarnell.

The prisoners on the Lewis Crew were up at 5:00 a.m. Some stuffed cans of tuna they'd bought at the prison commissary in their backpacks before joining the others by the front gate of the squat cinder-block buildings, standing by the razor-wire fence. The buildings were dull gray. The ground around them, bare, orange-tinged dirt. The sun rose from behind the jagged peaks of the North Maricopa Mountains, above a wilderness where coyotes and bobcats roam at night. At the foot of the mountains, saguaros, arms bent, waved at the men.

They were dressed in orange shirts and pants, hardened men

trained and certified as wildland firefighters. Steve Parker had nine months left of a sixteen-year sentence for armed robbery. Andrew Williams was in the fifth of six years locked up for aggravated assault.

The gate opened. From an observation tower, a guard watched them. In single file, they walked to the prison's fire station.

They'd become the good guys.

Inmates of all sorts do their time at Lewis, one of ten state prisons. They're placed in specific units, cellblocks and dormitories, sorted by the severity of their crimes. Lewis has eight units. Six bear the names of fallen corrections employees. One of them is Sandra Bachman, a supervisor to an inmate crew assigned to the Dude Fire near Payson, Arizona. Bachman and five of the crew's prisoners had died when the fire suddenly grew in size and intensity and quickly spread out of control on June 26, 1990, a day of record heat. Another is Paul Rast, an ordained minister and Little League coach who'd been beaten to death by three juvenile offenders in 1975. The Rast Unit at Lewis houses some of Arizona's most dangerous criminals in 416 cells equipped with sliding doors and big windows, so officers can keep a good eye on the men.

Maximum-security inmates, murderers, and other violent felons generally move around in restraints and step out of their cells, into secured outdoor spaces, for only an hour a day. Inmates in minimum custody, with at most five years left to their sentences and clean disciplinary records, may work outside prison walls. They pick trash along the sides of highways and tame wild horses captured on federal lands. A select few fight fires. They get paid a dollar an hour, sleep out in the open. They work as if they were free, and the assignment is coveted. On the line, in gear, the prisoners aren't prisoners. They're firefighters. Lifesavers. Heroes.

In California, the Department of Forestry and Fire Protection—Cal Fire, for short—has the nation's oldest and largest inmate firefighting program—forty-three hundred men and women organized in two hundred crews. Prisoners dig line in orange jumpsuits, DEPARTMENT OF CORRECTIONS emblazoned in white letters on their red carriers. In Arizona, which has twelve crews, typically of twenty inmates each, prisoners on the fire line dress like everyone else.

When other crews asked the inmates on the Lewis Crew where they were from, they said they were from Buckeye, a fast-growing suburb forty miles west of Phoenix. They weren't lying. The prison occupies a desolate expanse of desert straddling State Route 85, between the wilderness and the drying Gila River, within Buckeye's limits.

Asked where in Buckeye, they'd joke, "A gated community," and leave it at that.

They'd had to qualify for their places on the crew; applicants with histories of escapes or arson were excluded. They had to get medical clearance for shoveling, climbing, running, sawing, hiking, pickaxing. They all had completed thirty-two hours of basic training, like other aspiring wildland firefighters. They'd had to walk three miles in forty-five minutes with forty-five pounds on their backs, a physical-aptitude exam known as a pack test, another universal requirement.

At the prison fire station that Saturday, Parker, Williams, and seventeen other inmates traded prison garb for fire-resistant shirts and pants, yellow and green—standard colors. They strapped on sky-blue helmets. They slung their heavy packs onto their backs. They grabbed their tools—adzes, pounders, shovels, rakes, chain saws, Pulaskis. They drove off in white buggies that had the state forestry division's seal on each side, and no other hint of the crew's origin. They turned north on Route 85, the first leg of their two-hour trip toward Yarnell.

Leo Vasquez and another corrections officer accompanied them on the ride, playing dual roles, as guards and teammates, bound by their shared commitment. On the fire line, they were equals.

• • •

Engines rumbled. The Lewis Crew's buggies labored up the twists and turns of Yarnell Hill, up an asphalt slalom course carved around chaparral and folds of rock. To their left stood giant slabs of granite, shaped like flat-bottomed eggs. To their right, a precipice.

The hill lies between Wickenburg, on the flatlands, and Prescott, in the mountains. In four windy miles, it rises thirteen hundred feet on State Route 89. It's a feat of engineering, a "miracle," drivers had said after it opened in the late twenties. Back then, it was a single lane of packed dirt sculpted on sweat and TNT blasts, zigzagging up a forty-degree slope. It was paved in 1933, widened by two feet in the early fifties. Still, school buses heading downhill lost many a side-view mirror to tractor-trailers driving up from Wickenburg. Route 89 was for decades the only connector between Phoenix and Prescott. The hill road stayed busy, day and night. Only in 1972 did it become a four-lane, divided highway, a serpent split in halves—one side leading down from Yarnell, the other leading up, toward it.

The inmates rolled past the Ranch House, a restaurant at the crest of Yarnell Hill that serves a generous breakfast of eggs and chili con carne. They pulled up to the town's fire station around 8:00 a.m., stepped out, and felt the morning sun baking their skin. The temperature was already at 83 degrees and there wasn't a single cloud in the sky.

From the fire station, Williams looked at the mountains ahead. He saw no fire, only a wisp of smoke. Parker didn't even see smoke, but he smelled it and wondered where the fire was hiding. He glanced at an American flag hanging listlessly from a pole out front and imagined the tough day they'd have out there—no wind, not a cloud in the sky. And the later it got, the hotter.

Russ Shumate greeted the prison crew members and their boss, Jake Guadiana, a state forestry coordinator who'd driven in from Prescott. Shumate knew a lot of people in the tight world of firefighting. He'd worked for the state forestry division since 1997, gradually climbing the ranks to the manager's role. He'd trained hard to earn certification as a Type 3 incident commander, qualified to run suppression activities on fires of relatively low complexity, such as the one in Yarnell. He remained committed to the plan he'd drawn up, convinced that the heat of the morning might stoke other small fires sparked by Friday's lightning storm, and that, with another storm in the forecast, new fires could ignite.

He had set up a command post at the fire station, a humble single office and parking area where crews assembled, supplies got delivered. Using his authority to mobilize state resources, he called up an engine crew based near Phoenix—four wildland firefighters and a huge truck with four hundred gallons of water in its tank. He activated a second prison crew, out of Yuma, in the faraway southwestern corner of the state, a few miles north of Mexico. He requested two single-engine air tankers, aiming to have them drop fire retardant, a mixture of chemicals and dye, around the fire's perimeter, to keep it in check until he could get boots on the ground up there. He counted on an old ATV trail to the fire's east as a natural line of defense between the flames and the town below.

Drought had cured the grass that lined the wilderness and sucked moisture from shrubs and trees. They'd browned and stiffened, perfect tinder. Specialists monitor and calculate the odds of ignition for vegetation in specific areas and mark their ongoing findings in the National Fuel Moisture Database. Two weeks earlier, the readings for the brush in Yarnell foretold catastrophe—odds of ignition stood at 60 percent for brush in shade, and 90 percent for brush in sunlight, where much of it was. On Friday night, the National Weather Service had warned of lingering low humidity in the hours ahead, and a blistering morning and afternoon on Saturday, with temperatures breaching one hundred.

On such days, it's best to catch a fire early. Whatever the complexities, the Forest Service had a reason for that decades-old deadline of 10:00 a.m. for aggressive, full-suppression attack on new fires, before they spread. Until about ten, meteorological conditions usually favor firefighters. The longer the delay, the more they favor the fire.

But the firefighters had fallen behind schedule. At 9:00 a.m., the crews gathered at the Yarnell fire station for a briefing, a late start. Shumate doled out assignments. The Yuma Crew would sit and wait—stage, firefighters call it, in case other fires popped up. Guadiana went off to figure out a way to move his Lewis Crew to the fire on the mountain. An hour later, he came back, saying he'd found no drivable roads up there, and no suitable hiking routes for the prison crew.

At the station, Shumate confronted the predicament. He

had two crew bosses, four corrections officers, one sergeant, and thirty-seven inmates, all trained, geared up, and eager to get to the fire. But, how? The Bureau of Land Management, which has jurisdiction over thousands of acres of land around Yarnell, had dispatched a helicopter to check the blaze. Shumate thought he could use it to fly some of the men up there. He just had to identify a safe landing site.

The helicopter's pilot had been looping over the fire, estimating its size—it was shaped like a cupped hand and covered about two acres. He'd spotted an opening, a distorted circle wide and flat enough for landing, and flew back to the station with the news. The spot was at nearly six thousand feet up the mountain. Taking off and landing at that altitude, on a hot day, was risky. Air is thin up high, less compressed, with fewer molecules per cubic unit. Add heat, and these air molecules pulsate and thin more, moving farther from one another. In aviation, that creates a dangerous condition called high density altitude. Pilots use charts of altitude and outside temperature to calculate the load their helicopters can carry. Too much weight and the helicopter drops out of the sky.

Guadiana rounded up some of his men. The helicopter's pilot added up the weight of tools, packs, fuel in the aircraft's tank, and bodies, including his own. He looked at his chart and saw that the helicopter could safely carry only three men at a time. Guadiana, Leo Vasquez, and four prisoners flew up in two loads. Nate Peck, a firefighter assigned to the helicopter crew, also came along. Up the mountain, Guadiana pulled out his smartphone and shot an eight-second video of the group's arrival. Noontime approached.

State dispatchers prepared for a long haul. They reserved sleeping space for firefighters at the old National Guard Armory, a fortress of sandstone and reinforced concrete in downtown Prescott. They preordered forty-eight dinners at the nearby Golden Corral. They called the Mountainaire Mini Mart in Peeples Valley and reserved bags of ice to chill warm Gatorade and water delivered to the station in Yarnell.

Bob Brandon and the other volunteer firefighters from Peeples Valley joined the remaining Lewis prisoners at the station. They watched the action through binoculars and listened to radio chats.

Two single-engine air tankers zoomed over the fire, turned, and did it again. Each pass, the tankers dropped eight hundred gallons of retardant, smothering what flames it hit. Seen through binoculars, the falling drops painted thick orange lines against a hazy sky.

The air tankers had taken off from Prescott. The municipal airport in Wickenburg, just down Yarnell Hill, also had a base for such planes, but operated as needed. Shumate had ordered it open at 6:51 that morning, but it took six hours for that to happen. Staff had to be called up, and the building had to be unlocked and prepared to receive and refuel airplanes. The base became active at 1:00 p.m., just as the planes returned to Prescott to refuel, reload, and wait for the next assignment.

The National Weather Service warned Arizona dispatchers monitoring wildfire activity that storm clouds were gathering northeast of Kingman, near the tiny community of Seligman (population 456), and blowing south, toward the center of the state. The area is a good 100 miles northwest of Yarnell. "Not too worried about what's going to happen near Seligman," Shumate told a dispatcher who'd relayed the weather information over the radio. He wasn't too concerned about the threat to those parts of Arizona. If it brought lightning, he said, it might just spark a couple of trees on open, sparse land populated more by cactus than people. It would be different if the storm hit Yarnell and the men from the Lewis Crew already fighting the blaze up on the mountain.

"Just wanted to give you a heads-up," the dispatcher replied.

The Lewis Crew was making good progress. The drops of fire retardant had calmed the blaze. The men set about boxing it. They dug the ground and scraped a rudimentary fire line from the southern tip of the blaze, its heel, toward the trail on the east. They extinguished smoldering brush. With their shovels, they stirred the charred soil. They touched the ground, checking whether it had already cooled, a technique known as cold-trailing. They chased flames that popped out of clusters of rocks, as if playing Whac-A-Mole. They did a little bit of a lot of things, and they thought for a while that they'd beaten the blaze.

The fire persisted.

Shumate had confidence that the firefighting prisoners could control the situation. He released the air tankers at 2:42 p.m. The fire seemed boxed in; a ridge on one of its edges helped hold its advance. An hour later, Shumate told Bob Brandon and the rest of the Peeples Valley volunteers to go on home. Brandon picked up his wife and drove her to a knoll east of Route 89. From there, they felt the winds pick up and watched the dormant fire come back to life.

Flames had crept along the craggy west side of the mountain and dodged past the prison crew. Shumate heard the news and dispatched six more firefighters. They were Nate Peck's comrades from BLM crews. Justin Smith, a trainee under Shumate, joined them later and directed the pilots striking the fire from above. The helicopter dropped off twelve bladder bags, backpacks equipped with hoses and pumps like trombones, spraying water with the push and pull of a piston. Each of the bags held five gallons: the men had sixty gallons in their hands—not much considering the reach of the blaze. They drained the bladder bags quickly. Smith arrived around 4:30 p.m. The flames hadn't abated.

Smith didn't like what he saw. Flames had put the prisoners into reactive mode—they were chasing a fire that kept surprising them, flaring up again where the prisoners thought they'd extinguished it. The head of the fire, its most active part, was advancing—north—and then to the east. Six Lewis Crew members and about as many reinforcements were giving their all, but there weren't enough of them, at least not in that heat, not with the steady wind blowing, and not on that challenging terrain.

From the fire station down below, Parker noticed the American flag dancing from the pole where it had hung earlier, rattling in winds blowing up from the west-southwest. Williams saw thick dots of smoke punctuate the sky. He worried. He said to the inmates next to him, "When are they gonna get us up there to help?"

In Phoenix, the thermometer reached 119 degrees, enough for one airline to cancel eighteen regional flights. Heat is a dangerous ally to fire—it dries up fuel fast and charges up the flames.

On the ridge, flying embers sparked brush on the far side of the trail—a slop-over, it's called. The fire breached the flimsy line of control along the eastern flank. The firefighters up there needed help, fast. Down below, Shumate needed help. A spot forecast for Yarnell, just issued, confirmed what he already knew: it was hot (105) and dry (11 percent humidity), with no relief on the horizon. At 4:00 p.m., he ordered the single-engine air tankers he'd dismissed back to Yarnell. At 4:15, dispatchers told him that lightning had ignited a parched field of piñon and ponderosa pine on the Hualapai Mountains, some ten miles southeast of Kingman. They could spare only one of the single-engine tankers, the dispatchers said. The other, they sent to this new fire, christened Dean Peak.

The tanker assigned to Yarnell eventually dropped forty-four hundred gallons of retardant on the mountain. The thirteen men on the ground swung their tools forever. This kind of coordinated assault is often effective against fire—but not that afternoon. Some of the retardant missed the flames. The Lewis Crew ran out of gas for its chain saw, and without a chain saw they found the gnarled chaparral impenetrable. The prisoners were rendered ineffective.

Two states to the north, in the bunkerlike headquarters of the National Interagency Fire Center, in Boise, Idaho, officials from BLM, Forest Service, and five other national agencies that oversee wildlife and public lands had yet to hear any concern about the fire in Yarnell. The center acts as the mother ship for a team that assigns priorities, coordinating the needs for crews, aircraft, and other fire-suppression forces for ten regional centers, when many complex fires burn at once in the country and the competition for resources is stiff. The team, organized as the National Multi-Agency Coordinating Group, meets every morning and analyzes what's burning, where, and how to distribute attention, manpower, and equipment to the regions with the most fires. The group sits atop a three-tiered system attuned to the shifting needs on the ground. At the bottom are local and state dispatch centers. They evaluate the demands of fires within their jurisdictions and assign resources accordingly. The regional "geographic area coordination centers," as they're officially known, are the middle tier and step in when local or state resources are nearly exhausted and extra help is warranted.

That Saturday morning, the coordinating group heard from Ed Delgado, the center's chief meteorologist, that a strong high-pressure system remained parked over the West, trapping hot air—a lid on a cauldron. They learned of scattered thunderstorms forming in the Northwest, and of mild temperatures in the northern Plains and New England ahead of an approaching cold front. They tallied the number of new large fires—three in Alaska and one apiece in Southern California and Utah—and analyzed older fires of significance that still burned: eighteen. They assessed the availability of resources after accounting for every interagency crew, every truck that carries water to fires, and every plane, helicopter, and incident management team already in use. They considered all of this and more and set the amount of strain on the nation's ability to fight wildfires—its "preparedness level"—at 3, halfway up a scale from 1 to 5.

Their situation report for that day listed the Southwest Area, encompassing Arizona, New Mexico, and West Texas, at preparedness level 4, tied for top place with the Rocky Mountain area. The report highlighted eight active fires that had burned through 179,000 acres of land in Southwest, an area about eight times the size of Manhattan. It also listed twenty-nine new fires, but named none because they weren't big or complex enough to qualify as national concerns. The assumption was that at least some would be extinguished on initial attack. The fire in Yarnell was in that group.

But by late afternoon on that Saturday, Shumate could tell he was losing the fight. The fire had defeated his initial offensive. He'd launched it too late in the day, giving fire and weather the opportunity to coalesce and conspire against him and his plans.

He tried to recapture the single-engine tanker he'd ceded to the Dean Peak Fire, but couldn't. He requested two other aircraft—a helicopter, housed in Prescott, and an airplane, stationed in Albuquerque, both equipped to drop hundreds of gallons of water or retardant. Neither showed up. At 5:43 p.m., Shumate heard they'd been grounded by thunder, lightning, heat, and erratic winds at their home bases.

He ordered more single-engine tankers, but got none. Dispatchers offered a DC-10, the mammoth of aerial firefighting, with a tank that holds twelve thousand gallons of retardant. Shumate decided that wasn't practical. It was getting dark, and firefighting DC-10s don't fly in the dark.

Late that afternoon, Shumate directed the rest of the Lewis Crew at the Yarnell fire station to get ready to fly up the mountain. He called Nate Peck, telling him to prepare the men he had up there to spend the night on the ridge. Together, Peck and Shumate settled on a list of supplies: MRE, fuel for chain saws, more water. The helicopter soon took to ferrying up the supplies. While making the delivery, the pilot noticed that fire was burning too close to the landing zone. That was the last flight he made that day. Shumate turned to the Lewis Crew members at the fire station and said, "Everybody stand by."

He could have sent crews up to the mountain on Friday. He surely could have sent them up earlier on Saturday. He'd given the fire an opportunity to gain strength and found himself trying to extinguish it under the most unfavorable conditions. The flames had turned on him, outwitted him, and forced him to plan bigger moves.

Shumate had been trained to visualize the big picture, and then to check his wants and expectations against the needs of other wildfire incident commanders. All day at the Southwest Coordination Center in Albuquerque, the region's base of operations, dispatchers had kept track of needs, requests, and requirements. They'd arranged and rearranged the pieces of an ever-changing puzzle.

Commanders at the Silver Fire, in southern New Mexico, ordered a replacement Hotshot crew. The Mount Washington Fire, in Mexico, had jumped into the Coronado National Forest in Arizona, and American firefighters needed permission to cross the border to help stop it. The newly ignited Willow Creek Fire in Nevada needed a Type 1 crew, and the center dispatched the Geronimo Hotshots, a unit of the San Carlos Apache Tribe, in eastern Arizona. They'd been next in the rotation for assignments beyond the Southwest Area's boundaries. The Fort Apache Hotshots had exhausted the maximum number of days allowed on the line. They'd be taking a mandatory "day off unavailable" on Sunday, June 30, to reset their clock.

At 7:25 p.m., those same dispatchers received a measured summary of the fire in Yarnell. It had grown to eight acres and crossed the ATV trail that Shumate had assumed as a safe line of control. The closest homes remained at a safe distance, though—three miles to the east, four miles to the north. "No values at risk," they noted in the day's log. The phrase is adapted from the investment-risk management business to indicate potential loss of assets—property—under given circumstances, during a specific time frame. They calculated that there was no reason to worry much just yet.

The center did approve a request for a Hotshot crew for Yarnell, a measure of precaution against a fire that could easily get bigger, given the weather and the terrain. It deployed the Blue Ridge Hotshots, out of Happy Jack, Arizona, a three-hour drive away. It declined sending an air tanker that was available, though, "based on no structures threatened."

On the mountain, the fire continued building. It fed on winds that blew steadily at ten miles per hour, with gusts twice as strong. Flames stretched up to twenty feet and advanced three hundred to four hundred feet an hour. The flames were moving straight north, away from Yarnell, toward Peeples Valley.

The Lewis Crew detachment and their peers from BLM felt helpless. The fire had taken on a life of its own, and they didn't have the manpower or energy needed to stop it.

By 7:38 p.m., the fire had grown to a hundred acres, fifty times its size that morning. The nearest structures stood a mile away, in Peeples Valley. There, Bob Brandon warned his wife to prepare for an evacuation that, he thought, seemed all but inevitable. Against the night's darkness, he saw the flames in frightful glowing glory. In Yarnell, Barbara Kelso and her daughter, Kim, packed their cars with documents, family pictures, prescription medications, and food for their dog, Katy, a poodle-terrier cross that Barbara had rescued from the pound years earlier. Mother and daughter drove to a knoll behind the Ranch House and joined neighbors gawking at the fire as it worked its way along a cascade of ridges.

From the fire station, Shumate told state dispatchers to cancel the dinner orders for the Golden Corral, and the sleeping space reserved at the armory in Prescott. He reached out to Justin Smith, his trainee, and told him to slow down, ease into a marathon pace up on the hill, and keep everyone safe while monitoring the blaze through the night. Shumate prepared to move the command post from the Yarnell Fire Department to the Model Creek School in Peeples Valley, empty during summer break. Parker, Williams, and the other Lewis Crew inmates who'd been left downhill slept fitfully on cots in a rear classroom. Other classrooms would soon turn into offices, operating twenty-four hours a day.

Shumate must have been drained, but still had much to accomplish. The Yarnell Hill Fire was his. He focused on its needs, and its needs only, drafting an ambitious wish list of resources: sixteen engine crews, three Hotshot crews, two Type 2 crews, one bulldozer, six helicopters, three large air tankers, four single-engine air tankers, and lead planes available to work all day mapping targets for retardant drops along the burning mountain. He figured these were the forces now needed to win a counteroffensive against the blaze.

That evening, state forestry officials at the Arizona Dispatch Center pushed hard on the Southwest Coordination Center to commit two more Hotshot crews to Yarnell, affirming the urgency of at least one element on Shumate's wish list. The coordination center agreed to release two crews from fires they'd been working on and placed them among a handful of crews available for a run on Sunday. One of these crews was the Arroyo Grande Hotshots, detached from the Los Padres National Forest, near Santa Barbara, California. The other was the Granite Mountain Hotshots, who'd spent their day away at the Mount Josh blaze. Because fire behavior can change overnight—and because some firefighters were committed to working overnight on new fires, such as Dean Peak—the regional dispatchers refrained from committing either new crew to a specific fire.

Granite Mountain got its orders anyway. A state dispatcher e-mailed Eric Marsh, summoning him and his men to the fire in Yarnell. The men were tired after 149 hours on the clock over twelve straight days with no break. Their last shift, at Mount Josh, had started seven hours after their prior assignment, at West Spruce. The work at Mount Josh that Saturday had been unremarkable: digging line against a feeble fire.

The crew usually had Sundays off, and Marsh knew they

were all looking forward to it. But he also knew that the guys could toil for two more days before maxing out their fire-line allotment. They might grumble about delaying their rest day, but they'd appreciate the overtime pay. Marsh knew how much they all counted on it.

Marsh wasn't a man to turn down work, and he wasn't about to refuse a call to a fire burning so close to home, run by people he knew well. In Central Arizona, longtime supervisors such as he were part of a tight group of fire commanders, individuals who had known one another for years, worked together for years, had the other's back. When Shumate realized he couldn't run the Yarnell fire alone, he phoned two of these commanders, close friends of his—Gary Cordes, a battalion chief at the Central Yavapai Fire District, and Darrell Willis.

Willis got his first call from a state dispatcher around 8:00 p.m. "I've been on a number of assignments," he said. "I wanted to go to church on Sunday."

Two hours later, the dispatchers rang him up again and patched him through to Shumate. "I really need some help down here on structure protection," Shumate told him. "Would you mind coming down?"

Willis relented. "I figured they really needed me," he said. He headed down around 10:30 p.m.

Shumate had asked him and Cordes to report for duty soonest and take charge of assessing which structures could be saved if the fire made a run for the towns. Cordes would be in charge of Yarnell. Willis, of Peeples Valley. When it came to knowledge and experience, they knew how to beat back the flames without much hand-holding or specific guidance. They also knew how to hit the ground running.

Willis—chief of the Prescott Fire Department Wildland

Division, which employed the Granite Mountain Hotshots—
got to Peeples Valley around midnight. He dispatched a group
of firefighters placed under his command to walk around
homes, ranch houses, stables, sheds, and the handful of businesses, checking how close they were to the wilderness and to
the fire, and if any stood a chance against the flames. He didn't
think the blaze would reach Peeples Valley overnight. But given
how close it was—and the forecast for hot, dry, and windy
weather overnight—he expected that it would get there in the
morning.

For Marsh, the technical challenges posed by the blaze and
the terrain where it burned weren't particularly daunting. His
Granite Mountain Hotshots had faced worse fires and had come
out on top. They were forceful. They were capable. They were in
control.

That night, after their work on the Mount Josh Fire, they returned home, to Prescott.

Marsh and his wife, Amanda, were taking a walk along
Courthouse Square after dinner together at a restaurant in downtown Prescott when Marsh's phone rang. He'd been telling her
about his work and the stress he'd had to endure from city officials who seemed intent on undermining him. He was calm, and
the call didn't faze him—"nothing out of the ordinary," Amanda
said, another day in the life of a man whose life, for years, had
revolved around fire.

On the phone, he accepted the assignment, then notified his
men to get ready for another day on the fire line.

PROMISES AND GOODBYES

THE GRANITE MOUNTAIN HOTSHOTS GOT THEIR marching orders hierarchically. The news spread from man to man, branching through a well-ordered and often-used telephone tree.

Marsh called Steed, his captain.

Steed called his squad bosses—Whitted, Caldwell, and Carter.

Whitted, Caldwell, and Carter each called the men under their command.

They delivered a clear directive: Report to Station 7 by five thirty the following morning, Sunday, June 30, 2013. We have a job to do.

The Granite Mountain Hotshots had come to live by a simple set of principles spelled out on page 1 of their standard operating guidelines: *Respond fast, solve the problem, be nice, go home safe.* "Be nice" was part of the crew's ethos, and one of the categories in which Marsh, Steed, and the other leaders were rated in annual performance reviews. Collectively, the men had come to believe in the importance of a positive attitude, and in the power of smiling while doing the grunt work their jobs required.

They'd learned that from Marsh.

Asked to shovel snow outside Prescott's City Hall in 2012, after a late-winter storm had buried streets and sidewalks under a fluffy blanket of pristine whiteness, they'd grumbled. Officials had again stuck them with a menial task, deflated their collective sense of worth. Marsh had turned to his men and said, in his characteristic twang, "Kill 'em with kindness." The men got the message and went out shoveling snow singing and goofing around. That's how closely they listened to, respected, appreciated, and obeyed Marsh. An unusual boss, he had a kind heart, firm hand, and a quirky sense of humor.

The cheery scene outside City Hall had surprised other municipal employees filing in to work past the shoveling Hotshots, climbing the concrete steps the men had cleared.

The Hotshots had thought they'd be home on Sunday, cuddling with their women, playing with their children, nursing hangovers after a night out. They'd planned time for cooking, making repairs, fishing, lounging around, watching movies.

They'd been dismissed from the Mount Josh fire early Saturday evening. By 8:00 p.m., their phones started ringing; Caldwell's phone blared like a fire alarm as Steed called him. A few of the men still reeked of sweat. They'd tussled from sunup to darkness with the Mount Josh Fire, breaking for only thirty minutes to gobble up lunch in the noontime heat.

Just before his phone rang, Anthony Rose had stood by the

front door and peeled off his dirt- and ash-caked White's, the dark lace-up boots that are the preferred footwear of wildland firefighters. Tiffany, his fiancée, had watched him from the rocking chair nearby, hands crossed over her bulging belly, six months pregnant. He looked exhausted. He walked past her, to the edge of the backyard. He unlatched his brown leather belt, removed his green fire pants, and shook the dust off them. He took off his socks and his grimy undershirt. He trudged off to the bathroom in his boxer shorts and jumped in the shower, lingering a while. "I've got to go back to work in the morning," he told Tiffany. She frowned, but didn't complain.

Rose returned from the shower, grabbed a bite to eat, and flopped onto the couch. Tiffany joined him. He lay on his back, a forearm over his forehead, exhausted. They watched *Sons of Anarchy*, the television series about an outlaw motorcycle club. The men in it also struggled balancing allegiance to one another and allegiance to their families.

Rose called it a night as soon as the show was over. Tiffany decided she should just go to sleep, too. Before she closed her eyes, she said, "I'm bummed you have to go in to work tomorrow."

"Eric wants us to get an early start in case we get called up to a fire," Rose replied. Lightning had sparked many small fires all around them in the past few days. Rose didn't know where the crew would end up, or if they'd go anywhere. Maybe they'd stage all day. He just knew that he and the other men had to show up prepared.

Steed knew exactly where the Granite Mountain Hotshots would be sent on Sunday.

A little after eight o'clock Saturday evening, he'd arrived home in Prescott Valley. He'd downed a cold Coors Light and some take-out Thai food. He'd sprawled on one of the new chairs on the patio and watched his children swinging on the backyard play set that some of the guys on the crew had helped assemble in exchange for beer, pizza, and their captain's warm embrace. His phone rang, and Marsh shared what he knew of the next day's assignment. Steed turned to Desiree, telling her that the fire he'd be going to, in Yarnell, seemed routine, almost insignificant. He said he might get back in time to sleep at home. He couldn't be away too long, anyway. Tuesday would be the first of the crew's two mandatory days off.

Kevin Woyjeck had planned to go fishing on Sunday. He'd grown up in Seal Beach, a surf town on California's Pacific Coast Highway, catching halibut and yellowtail from his weathered thirteen-foot whaler in the cold, sapphire-blue waters off Long Beach Harbor. He'd left the Mount Josh Fire, picked up his rod and reel at home, and steered his Jeep to a lake nearby, to camp overnight. Woyjeck had moved out of the studio he'd been renting and into a bedroom at the house McKee shared with his fiancée. His fishing rods were among the few prized possessions he had stored there.

Woyjeck and McKee, the youngest guys on the crew, were full of dreams for the future, drunk with the freedom of their exhilarating work, which seemed more like adventure. To them this was all a seriously hair-raising exploit, like dropping down the face of monster waves in Hawaii. They were healthy, strong, and vital, with plenty of years to work out the dreams they'd nurtured, and no worries clouding their todays. The night after Woyjeck had moved in with McKee, they'd had dinner at Texas Roadhouse, in a mall on the east side of Prescott, then driven home in the Jeep, singing Daft Punk's "Get Lucky" at the top of their lungs—"We've come too far to give up who we are . . ."

That Saturday night, Woyjeck got his call and turned the

Jeep right around. He headed back to his room to catch some sleep before setting out to fight more fire. McKee went to sleep too, curled up with Leah in the twin bed they shared.

Garret Zuppiger had rushed out of Station 7 after work on Saturday and returned to his old place, near Courthouse Square. He was moving out, so there was nothing left there, except a mattress pad he'd laid out on the floor. He slept on it. His clothes were packed in bags he'd stuffed in his car. His books—guides to fish and trees published by the National Audubon Society; *Desert Solitaire,* by Edward Abbey, lyrical defender of the threatened natural beauties of the West—were in storage. He'd already carried the Audio-Technica record player he'd bought with savings from his first fire season into a new apartment, along with his vast album collection—music by the Shins and the Decemberists; Paul Simon's *Graceland.* A friend vacating the apartment he was going to move into had given him the keys.

Zuppiger didn't own a lot of stuff. He didn't care for stuff. He was a free spirit, trying to live life responsibly on his own terms. He'd aced the Armed Services Vocational Aptitude Battery, a multiple-choice test on science, reasoning, word knowledge, verbal expression, and five other specialized subjects. The high score landed him at the top of a list of recruits for the Coast Guard—his mother said he could have gone in as an officer. But Zuppiger wasn't sure that's what he wanted to do. He feared the time he'd have to spend within four walls during his Coast Guard training would drive him nuts. He decided to spend his summers on the fire line, and he was first of his class at the academy, a distinction that earned him a free pair of White's, the wildland boots, which retail for at least $300. He told his grandfather Bruce Lindquist that if he couldn't chase drug smugglers on the rough seas off Florida, he could at least defend the country against forest fires. It was a noble vision. But it was the fellowship he'd found in the Granite Mountain Hotshots, and the discipline they shared that motivated him to work his hardest every day and to aim higher. He'd bought into the idea of an unselfish job.

He talked to his girlfriend, Emilee Ashby, at around 8:00 p.m. on Saturday. She'd traveled to Washington State for her family's annual Fourth of July pig roast. "I really wished I could make it," Zuppiger told her. But he had fires to fight, money to make.

"I'll be back soon," Emilee replied, and then she'd help him get the new apartment organized, arrange her clothes in the closet they'd share, nestle their toothbrushes side by side in a cup by the bathroom sink. That night, in his old place, he told her he was about to go grab a beer with the guys; McDonough and MacKenzie were meeting him at a dive on Whiskey Row. But he'd be right back, he said. He'd put off moving into the new apartment on Sunday because the crew had been urged back to work. He needed to get to the station early.

Dustin DeFord texted his brother Ryan Saturday night. They'd had a silly competition going since they were kids—I'm bigger, I'm stronger, I can lift more than you. Dustin wrote that he'd gained fifteen pounds. He'd tipped the scale at 195 pounds that day. He was stocky, with a red, bushy beard, and a generous smile, the fifth of ten children born to a preacher and a teacher who'd homeschooled them all. Ryan was a year older than Dustin, taller and slenderer. Both were wildland firefighters. Ryan didn't read Dustin's text until late that night, after the end of his own shift at the Jaroso Fire near Santa Fe, New Mexico; his team had rappelled from helicopters into a blaze. "Fatty," Ryan had responded.

Dustin lived in Ryan's house in Paulden, almost an hour's

drive from Station 7. That night, Dustin grabbed some supper, prayed, and bedded down to recharge.

Billy Warneke and his wife, Roxanne, shared a mobile home at the far end of a dirt road in Avra Valley, an arid farming town west of Tucson and three hours out from Prescott. Hotshots had to stay within two hours of their base during fire season, except on mandatory days off. That's when Billy was able to visit Roxanne. That Saturday, he stayed at an aunt's house in Prescott.

Warneke had last driven out to Avra Valley two weeks earlier, on June 15, 2013, the day before Father's Day. He'd seen the first sonogram of the baby girl Roxanne carried, their first child. The mobile home seemed forever under repair; Warneke fixed what he could whenever he came by. He'd taped a thick sheet of plastic across the master bedroom doorframe. Dark green mold grew deep down a six-by-three-foot hole in the en suite bathroom. The bedroom became mostly storage space and a hazard zone out of bounds to a pregnant woman. Billy stacked the old bathroom tiles there, the boards of insulation foam, and his tools—a drill, three different types of hammer.

On that Father's Day, he'd looked dispirited to Roxanne, gazing at all that needed doing at the house—and he had so little time to do it. "You're really tired," Roxanne had told him. "You just need to rest."

Roxanne had aimed to drive to Prescott on Sunday. She'd longed for some alone time with Billy, away from the chaos of home. But Billy's phone call came. "Don't come," Billy told her. "I've got to go into work."

At Andrew Ashcraft's house, the call to Sunday duty triggered bickering and disappointment. Juliann had looked forward to being with her husband at home for a couple of days, a spurt of normality during the unpredictable fire season that she could never get used to, though she tried. He had his own apron hanging in the kitchen and she'd already envisioned their Sunday together—church, burgers he'd make on the grill they kept in their tiny backyard, their house filled with his presence. He walked in, and she thought, "Now I get him back to me." She wrapped her arms around his neck and smiled at him playfully. She told him the kids were already in bed. He told her he'd have to get up early on Sunday and go back to the station. The news crushed her—"But you've just come in!" she said.

Andrew walked away in silence. He turned right on the hallway off the living room and peeked inside Shiloh's room; she was asleep. He'd thought a lot about Shiloh during the long, lonely rides in the buggy to and from faraway fires. He'd lose himself in his thoughts, eyes closed, music playing in his headphones—maybe Ted Nugent, or maybe a country ballad he'd had stuck in his head about a homeless father watching his daughter, a waitress, who had no idea who he was. Halfway through his first fire season, Juliann had given Andrew a blank journal, to record fire stories their children could read when they were older. Andrew lived for his kids, but he had distinct affection and concern for his girl. He called her Shy. While riding to a fire in New Mexico, in July 2011, he wrote, "I won't be able to protect her forever but the truth is I'm gonna try. There is something about having a daughter that is different than a son. I know my Boys will grow to be men and be strong and be better than I am. I have no doubt about that. I just want to be there for Shy to keep her safe."

He'd stepped out of Shiloh's bedroom, walked to the other end of the hallway, and entered the boys' room. Ryder, the oldest, lay awake. Andrew sat next to him and told Ryder to take care of Mommy while he was gone—"You're the man of the house." Andrew always said that to Ryder before leaving for a fire.

As Andrew made his rounds with the kids, Juliann sat on the living-room couch, staring at an *Arrested Development* rerun, frustrated at his leaving again. His job demanded so much of her.

"I'm exhausted," she said to him as he entered the room.

"I have to be up at five," he replied drily. "I have to go to sleep."

He trudged upstairs. They lived in a cozy town house in an old subdivision, among mostly older neighbors. Her grandparents, Jim and Nelda Crockett, had died there, months apart, after a placid sixty-five years of marriage. Juliann and Andrew's union was of a different kind—a roller-coaster ride—thrilling, full of ups and downs. They'd just snapped out of a particularly trying period. Andrew had left home. Juliann had asked for a divorce. They'd drafted papers and turned them in at court, resolved to end it all. Then, they'd reconsidered. Marital counseling had helped, but what really kept them together was the love they had for each other—it couldn't be broken. A month into the 2013 season, Andrew drafted a document, "Team Ashcraft Contract." It listed nineteen commitments to his wife.

I promise to always take out the trash.
I promise to always be honest with you.
I promise to always be your best friend.
I promise to always be your biggest fan.
I promise to always take care of you.
I promise to protect you with my life.
I promise to hold you.
I promise to show my love for you.
I promise to be someone you're proud of.

I promise to show how thankful I am for you.
I promise to always put your needs first.
I promise to take you away and be with you.
I promise to love you for time and all eternity.
I promise to be the father our family deserves.
I promise my decisions will make our family strong again.
I promise to never ease up and coast.
I promise to be mean if it means helping you and our family.
I promise I will rise above my environment.
I promise to love you.

That Saturday night in June, Juliann fell asleep on the couch, still stewing, the TV still on. Andrew's handiwork surrounded her: a bookcase he'd crafted to resemble the one she'd seen at IKEA, frames he'd made for family photos so perfect they looked like pictures from a catalog—matching outfits, radiant smiles. Shiloh, four years old, has her mother's half-moon dimples in her cheeks. Tate, three, has his father's broad smile. Ryder, six, is the old soul, his mother's protector, the enforcer of house rules—when he wasn't the one breaking them.

Choice is the baby, the one who shouldn't have been. Twenty weeks into Juliann's pregnancy, her doctors had told her and Andrew that something was wrong with the boy she carried—that he had no lungs. The doctors had tried to nudge them toward an abortion; the boy didn't stand a chance of surviving, the doctors had said. Juliann and Andrew said no. They'd chosen to keep the baby and deal with whatever happened, as they'd always done. Choice arrived on the same day as Andrew's twenty-eighth birthday, small at four pounds and fourteen ounces, but healthy.

Andrew and Juliann fought and had their differences, but they always found ways past their problems. They had a powerful connection, carnal and spiritual. The trick was figuring out how to keep it going when he was away.

Travis and Stephanie Turbyfill were schooled in the art of being apart. They'd been dating for five months when he joined the Marine Corps in December 2007. Eventually he got stationed in its Air Combat Center at Twentynine Palms, in the Southern California desert. At a good clip, it took him five hours to drive from there to Prescott, where she was committed to a nursing program. Every Friday night, he'd made the drive, speeding along desolate roads through a national park, an Indian reservation, and miles of sand and hills, to be with her for the weekend. He wrote to her every day that they couldn't see each other or speak on the phone.

He had a goal of becoming a machine gunner and deploying to Iraq, a conflict whose purpose he saw through a prism of selfless patriotic duty. Turbyfill wasn't the type to be easily afraid; he'd borrowed from *Catch-22*'s Joseph Heller for his quote in the Prescott High School class of 2002 yearbook—"I have decided to live forever or die in the attempt." The rising death toll among American troops—4,003 by the end of the month of his boot-camp graduation, March 2008—never dissuaded him. But fate intervened. During a training exercise, a fellow marine lost his grip while helping Travis lift a .50-caliber machine gun off his shoulder, and the weapon dropped on his head. His cerebellum swelled. In coming days, he started blacking out. He passed out while driving to Twentynine Palms from Prescott, wrecked his truck, climbed out from the rubble, banged up but alive. Transferred to light duty, Travis left the Marines three years into his five-year enlistment and moved back to Prescott in time for the birth of his first daughter. Together, he and Stephanie shared the early challenges and discoveries of parenthood.

He joined the Granite Mountain Hotshots the following year, resuming the gone-and-gone-again routine he and Stephanie had gotten used to. Before the fire season started in 2013, they'd interviewed a few candidates for a babysitting job, and Travis had insisted on asking all of them a question he used during crew interviews—"What's your definition of integrity?" For Stephanie, his persistence felt at once amusing and annoying; "Why does it matter so much?" she'd asked him. Simple. The answer reveals character, and character matters when it comes to hiring a person to watch our kids, Travis had told her.

That Saturday, as soon as Travis got home from the Mount Josh blaze, the family eased back into a comfortable routine, trading morsels of ordinary news from the hours he'd spent away.

Stephanie grilled him a ham-and-cheese sandwich. It looked so small in his big hands—hands that were so gentle to her, and to their girls.

He'd dangled the girls by their feet after dinner, swaying each in turn like a clock pendulum, the girls shrieking with delight. Stephanie called him Energizer Bunny. His pep seemed endless. "He never complained about being tired, never complained that he needed to get up early," she said. "When he came home from a fire, he'd jump right into helping out with the kids, playing with them, taking them out to do things, and I sort of envied that. I envied that Travis had no need for any type of recovery time." He'd go from firefighter to daddy without missing a beat.

At home that Saturday night, she looked at him and their children and felt an overwhelming sense of completeness. The scene was perfect: Travis, Brooklyn, and Brynley, laughing and absorbed in an absolutely great time. Stephanie considered getting up, grabbing her phone from the kitchen counter, and snapping a photograph, or recording a video—it would make a great

Facebook post later on. But she didn't. "Just sit there and enjoy the moment," she told herself. "Just enjoy life, don't always be so busy, don't always be in such a rush."

Later, after the girls had gone to sleep, she and Travis lay in bed. He cradled her in his arms and asked, "If anything ever happened to me, you would just get remarried, wouldn't you?"

The question caught her off guard. They'd never spoken about the dangers of his job, never discussed the possibilities, or contemplated an ending to their story. Theirs was a mature love. They were intentional about making it work and centered on the goals they'd set for their family.

Stephanie said, "I don't know. I've never thought about it, but I don't think that I would. Why? What would you do?"

"I would just focus on being the best dad that I could be without you here." Then he added something so youthful and un-abashedly honest, so Travis: "I would probably sleep around a lot, but I would never get remarried because you're the love of my life and I could never replace you."

Eric Marsh had met Amanda for dinner, then returned to Station 7, where he slept. He wanted to be ready when his men arrived the next morning to fight another fire by his side.

• • •

The Granite Mountain Hotshots arose before the sun on Sunday, following the marching orders they'd received by phone.

Thurston picked up Rose, who lived near him in Prescott Valley. On Rose's way out the door, he kissed Tiffany's rotund belly and said to the baby girl, "I love you."

Zuppiger folded his mattress pad, stuffed it in with the bags of clothes in his car, and drove to Station 7. He called Emilee after he got there. "We're about to leave on a fire," someplace nearby, he told her. "If anything happens to me, you can keep my albums and my record player." Not that he had any reason to think anything would happen, and Emilee knew that. It was just his way of showing her how much he loved her. The player and the albums were cherished possessions. So was a red-and-black Honda Proline XL motorcycle that his grandpa Lou had given him for Christmas in 2010. After hanging up, Emilee called Joe Crockett, Juliann Ashcraft's brother and a college buddy of Zuppiger's from Prescott, and asked him to check if Zuppiger had moved the motorcycle out of the garage of his old building. She worried that it might get towed while he was away.

Steed planted a kiss on Desiree's lips and clomped out of their bedroom. She stayed under the blankets, hearing the echoes of his footsteps on the tile floor.

Ashcraft approached the couch and tapped Juliann on the shoulder. He'd shaved off the mustache she loved. "I gotta go." He gave her a kiss. Outside, he underscored the kiss with an instant message: "i love you juliann."

At the other end of town, Stephanie told Travis, "I'll get up quickly and make your lunch." That's what she normally did—got up and packed him a good meal. "I'll make your lunch real quick, make us coffee."

"No, we're on a fire today, so our lunch will be made," Travis told her.

"Oh, okay."

She watched him tread out of the bedroom, rolled onto her side, and fell back asleep.

•••

One by one, as they got to the station that morning, the men revealed their moods and energy levels in words and numbers scrawled in red marker on a big whiteboard, under GRANITE MOUNTAIN HOTSHOTS DAILY PERCENTAGES, as usual.

They joked; Ashcraft wrote "stache-less" by his name, and Turbyfill, who hadn't had a haircut in a while, jotted down "Fro-Tastic." They hinted at their exhaustion—"37.6 and dropping," scribbled DeFord; "moderate day," Caldwell noted. Zuppiger remarked, "YEAH BUDDY!" Warneke, sounding ambiguous, put down, "35 or 50%." (On the board, his name read War-neke.) Marsh said, "68%." Steed, "76%." Woyjeck marked, "87%." Donut, starting his first day back after being sick, and a night out, exclaimed, "HELL YA."

In the ready room, Marsh told them they had an assignment in Yarnell, on a fire working through a jungle of chaparral along a rocky ridge. He picked up the phone and called Willis, telling him the Hotshots were on their way to Yarnell. Willis said he was already there and wished Marsh and his men a safe day on the fire line.

The crew set out from Station 7 in their buggies a few minutes past 6:00 a.m.

At 6:08 a.m., Billy sent Roxanne a message: "Off to Yarnell Arizona. Temp of 116."

She replied, "Stay hydrated."

Billy wrote right back, "And cool!"

Billy's was the last in a file of single seats behind Caldwell, who rode shotgun that day. Percin sat next to Billy. From his iPhone, he typed a post to his Facebook wall, a little prayer: "Lord, watch over us as we go into battle. Amen."

At 6:09 a.m., Rose texted Tiffany, twice: "we're going to a fire out in yarnell; its supposed to be 116 er so its just outside wickenburg."

6:09 a.m., Tiffany: "wheres that?"

6:10 a.m., Tiffany: "116 what? ok."

6:11 a.m., Rose: "degrees, but its 500 acres."

6:11 a.m., Tiffany: "geez well keep cool as best you can and stay hydrated."

6:12 a.m., Tiffany: "does this fire have a name?"

6:12 a.m., Rose: "yeah for sure and not that i know of."

6:22 a.m., Tiffany: "ok, have you taken off or not for a bit?"

6:24 a.m., Rose: "yeah we just stopped at frys to get breakfast but now were on the road."

6:31 a.m., Rose: "imma lose service for awhile though baby, were driving through skull valley. i love you and hope you have a good day baby."

She could picture Skull Valley, a tiny, rural town of maybe five hundred people. All it had was a gas station, a church, a post office, and a diner open for breakfast and lunch every day but Monday, and sometimes also for dinner. It sits on the edge of Iron Springs Road, the less windy route between Prescott and Kirkland, another tiny, rural town. In Kirkland, the road veers left, changes its name, and goes on straight to State Highway 89, which leads right into Yarnell.

6:32 a.m., Tiffany: "i love you too babe, text or call when possible . . ."

PART II

...

A TREACHEROUS COMBINATION

T HROUGH MUCH OF THE YEAR, A FRESH, DRY AIR mass caresses the southwestern deserts under a dome of blue sky. As days lengthen and summer approaches, the sun sears the land, hot air rises, and air pressure at ground level drops. Then, high pressure drifts eastward. The wind switches direction. The evolving current brings moisture-rich air from the Gulf of California sweeping over arid ground—first Mexico, then Arizona. Humidity rises. The wet and warm wind climbs to higher elevations, where it cools. Storm clouds form, cluster on the horizon, and march south. Rain falls, thunder roars, and lightning pounds.

Air rushes from high to low pressure zones, and from colder to warmer areas. The change of season prompts a significant shift in the wind that flows in Arizona, and similar shifts in other hot parts of the world—West Africa, Southeast Asia, Australia. Ancient traders plying the Indian Ocean and the Arabian Sea called it *mausim,* an Arabic word meaning "season," the period we call monsoon. The traders timed their journeys accordingly, sailing west in the winter, with favorable winds to their backs. Vessels departed from India and Sri Lanka and glided to ports along the Red Sea. On the way out, they carried pepper and sugar for flavoring, indigo for coloring, and ebony for furniture making. They returned after the wind had reversed, loaded with Egyptian linen, sheets of copper, and olive oil and wine made by the Romans.

In Arizona, the moisture travels in from the ocean and interacts with the Mogollon Rim, a geological marvel of tall cliffs carved by tectonic fractures and erosion, extending for two hundred miles across the center of the state, at the southern edge of the Colorado Plateau. Thirty to 50 percent of Arizona's annual rainfall pours down from monsoon storms, powerful forces of destruction and restoration. With the rains, groundwater sources, such as the overtaxed Colorado River basin, supplying seven states in the West, receive needed replenishment. Green grass grows in arid pastures. Prickly-pear fruit, red, sweet, and tangy, springs from thorny leaves, feeding a homegrown industry of candy-, syrup-, and jelly-makers. Cacti drink in the moisture supplies that sustain them after the wet season. Wildflowers sprout. Butterflies and migrant birds fill the air.

The downpours also turn dry washes, canyons, and arroyos into fierce rivers. In minutes, they swell, knocking down walls and bridges and dragging cars, trees, and homes—whatever is on the way.

But that's after moisture permeates the surface air, usually in July and August. Before then, there is lightning, but no rain—a treacherous trigger for fire in the wildlands.

The Southwest's biggest fires occur in the late spring and early summer, as monsoon season's opening act. In June of 2013 in Arizona, wildfires devoured tens of thousands of acres of forest and brush stressed by a hotter, drier climate—the years since 1950 had been warmer than any other period of comparable length in at least six hundred years, rainfall patterns had ranged from "severely dry" to "exceptionally dry" since April, and harsh drought conditions prevailed throughout most of the state.

By Sunday, when the Granite Mountain Hotshots arrived in Yarnell, clusters of clouds had been rolling over the area in rhythmic succession, ushered in by salvos of thunder and lightning. The rain they dropped evaporated midfall, in the still-dry air that hung high above. As the crew rolled into town that morning, this familiar pattern was already taking shape, its outline clear on the images captured by Doppler radars.

Doppler radars look like giant golf balls perched atop squat buildings or steel towers. They're pearly white spheres, their surfaces carved in a pattern of elongated triangles. Inside them, the antennas rotate, beaming microwaves far into the atmosphere—reflecting them off tiny particles up to 250 miles away. Each time a wave strikes a raindrop, snowflake, or hailstone, it transmits a signal back to the radar. The signals translate into images on forecasters' computer screens, color-coded to indicate the intensity of the precipitation—green weakest, red strongest. The National Weather Service based the code on a theory by the Austrian mathematician Christian Doppler, who'd argued in 1842 that the pitch of sound emanating from an object falls or rises if the object is moving away from or toward a stationary observer, respectively—think of the waning of a fire truck's siren as the truck speeds on past you. The principle, the

Doppler effect, allows meteorologists to chart the movement within the clouds, measure wind speed, and observe the ongoing evolution of storms as it happens.

Forecasters approach their job like documentarians, registering the elements of their narrative from wide angles to tight close-ups. They're resourceful and act quickly to keep up with changing conditions. They begin their work shifts by inspecting soundings reported by weather balloons launched at least twice daily from weather stations around the world. Brian Klimowski and his team near Flagstaff release theirs from a dome in a meadow east of the office at four in the morning and four in the afternoon. The synthetic rubber balloons are inflated with hydrogen or helium. They're equipped with sensors that register temperature, humidity, and air pressure as they rise far above the clouds. Tiny radio transmitters broadcast the findings, providing vast moment-in-time cross sections of the atmosphere. These are the starting points for meteorological predictions and models: Will a layer of warm air up above keep storm clouds from expanding? Will significant variations of speed in the winds blowing aloft perhaps turn ordinary thunderstorms into beasts?

These changes in the weather help determine the magnitude and course of wildfires. Rain quenches fires. Wind fans them. Humidity soothes fires. Roiling thunderstorms stoke them, building sparks into flames. Forecasts offer firefighters some advantage. The most complex wildfires have their own assigned meteorologists, who work on the ground, side by side with the leaders calling the shots. The United States has eighty-five of these meteorologists, trained in the artful science of microscale forecasting, the peculiar needs of firefighting operations, and the caprice of fire. They interpret upper-air soundings, radar images, and computer-generated weather models and consider the lay of the burning land: What could happen when the wind hurtles against these tall trees or eddies around those hills or funnels through that box canyon? How different are the temperatures at the foot and at the crest of these steep slopes? Incident meteorologists—they go by their acronym, IMETs ("eye-mets")—work with fire-behavior analysts to decipher the movement and rhythm of the flames.

On the fire line, understanding the ways weather and fire interact is a universal responsibility. Every time Eric Marsh taught beginners at the academy in Prescott, he took them outside and coached them, pounding in the notion that knowing the weather sharpens their "situational awareness." Together, Marsh and his students read the clouds dotting the sky: Do they look like outsize cauliflowers? That's a sign of an unstable atmosphere, and reason for concern, he said. Without an upper layer of warm air, or a cap, clouds, wandering masses of ice and water, ascend, thicken, and strengthen, amplifying the intensity potential of thunderstorms.

Saturday night, Russ Shumate had called up an experienced team of commanders to take control of the blaze in Yarnell, having already realized that corralling it would take longer and require more effort than he'd planned for—and that he was coming up against the maximum number of consecutive hours he was allowed to work. The team had its own fire-behavior analyst, Byron Kimball, a veteran of the US Forest Service who had joined Arizona's Forestry Division a year earlier as a planning and preparedness officer. On most days, Kimball's job consisted of evaluating dried and overgrown pieces of state land, and managing them to minimize the danger of fire, when the division's squeezed finances allowed.

Between fiscal years 2007 and 2011, the budget had shrunk

by 26 percent, reflecting the crash of the housing market that helped support Arizona's economy. A slice of the cuts had been offset by hiring prison crews, which cost less than civilian crews. State forester Scott Hunt wrote about the cuts' "significant impact on public safety" in his budget request for 2013. He highlighted the devastating drop in the number and availability of personnel and resources to manage the lands and fight wildfires.

Kimball checked in at the Model Creek School at 8:00 a.m. that Sunday and met with Shumate, who'd spent most of the night awake, facing the obvious—the Yarnell Hill Fire had dodged all of his attempts to catch it—and preparing for the change in leadership he had requested. Such changes are common in the dynamic world of wildland fires.

Shumate's replacement, Roy Hall, a Type 2 commander, was already at the command post situating himself when Kimball arrived that morning. With a new boss comes a new team of supervisors. Often, they all take charge at once, as a unit. Not Hall's team. Some of its members had received their orders the night before. Others who'd missed calls got them through voicemail messages they'd heard when they'd woken up that morning. At first, Hall didn't seem too concerned, mostly because the fire didn't seem to be too much of a threat. He was glad to have Kimball there, though. He could use someone like him, a knowledgeable fire-behavior analyst who'd keep a close eye on the flames, anticipating their moves.

Kimball swung by the fire station in Yarnell. He could see the flames well from there. The fire covered about three hundred acres and was advancing north toward Peeples Valley. He watched it for about forty minutes, then drove back to the school. On the short trip north on Highway 89, he glanced at the ridges to his left, a wavy ledger along the west side of Yarnell. He noticed the brush, thick and bone-dry, and the homes set so close to it. The scene reminded him of the hills in the Angeles National Forest, in Southern California, where he'd worked, and where drought and development have turned wildfires into year-round events. It seemed to Kimball that things could go bad real quick.

In the control room of Bellemont's National Weather Service office, an unremarkable single-story building off Interstate 40 in Arizona, the radar tracker and another meteorologist gazed at a row of computer screens arranged side by side. They had to translate complex concepts and data sets into six-line weather statements that would be read over the radio for everyone working the blaze to hear.

These meteorologists also worked with geo-mapping computer programs—everything from topographic charts to Google Earth—to grind out place-specific, made-to-order assessments of the weather on Yarnell Hill, their "spot forecasts." Incident commanders rely on these forecasts often; in Yarnell, Shumate got one Friday night, then three on Saturday—early in the morning, at midday, and late in the evening. State dispatchers had ordered them specifically, online, as such forecasts are often commissioned wherever a fire of some significance is burning. They used standardized forms that stored the fire's name, so no one had to take the time to reenter it.

Officials requesting spot forecasts punch latitude and longitude coordinates into a form on a Web page that automatically updates itself every minute. The result is closely monitored by meteorologists, who combine that information with other data, such as the type of fuel that's burning and the size of the conflagration. They narrow their predictions to a two-square-mile grid. The information guides firefighters adjusting their action plans. But that's not what happened in Yarnell.

TROUBLE IN THE SKY

O N THE MORNING OF SUNDAY, JUNE 30, 2013, THE soundings from Brian Klimowski's National Weather Service office north of the fire looked as expected—a normal monsoon day. They depicted an unstable atmosphere and a warm, dry layer of air near the surface. Forecasters deduced that scattered thunderstorms were likely, with a risk of strong winds near any that formed.

The designated storm-watcher took notice. He kept up with the fires burning in Yarnell and near Prescott. He understood the growing danger. Rain from those early-season storms would evaporate in that dry layer below the clouds. The rain-cooled air would rush downward, and, after hitting the ground, spread out in all directions, at dangerous speeds, like flour dropping onto a table from a hanging sack. That's what "downdraft winds" do.

The storm-watcher turned to the radar and searched for more signs of trouble.

The fresh team of incident commanders trickled in. Shumate's replacement, Roy Hall, had first glimpsed the fire on his way in to Peeples Valley, from a rise on Iron Springs Road. The flames swayed with the placid morning, burning near their point of ignition two days earlier, and still very much alive. He'd pulled over to make a call. Green buggies carrying the Blue Ridge Hotshots had passed him. Hall had followed the buggies, turning right off Highway 89, the main road in the town, toward the command post at the Model Creek School. He noted the time—seven forty-five—and stepped inside.

An information center occupied a classroom usually shared by first- and second-grade students in the tiny rural school. Big men sat on child-size chairs; adult furniture hadn't yet arrived. Barbara Kelso, the longtime Yarnell resident who'd served for years on the town's fire board, had packed her bright-blue Ford Focus, shut the front door of her house—but forgot to lock it—and joined the men at the school, at the Yarnell fire chief's request. She knew a lot of people and just whom to call to get things done. In no time, she'd mobilized the school's secretary, who'd come in and reprogrammed the telephone system, opening direct access to lines from classrooms as more of them became offices, dormitories, and conference rooms.

Darrell Willis was in the field already, surveying the structures—owner's and guest houses, caretaker quarters, and four other buildings on the Double Bar A Ranch, one of the oldest in Peeples Valley. The buildings stood amid dry brush at the end of a bumpy dirt road west of the school, abutting the burning wilderness. Shumate had assigned the Yuma Crew to Willis, and Willis had instructed the inmates to fire up their saws, swing their Pulaskis, and thin the vegetation ringing the property. He sought help from fire departments in Prescott and Groom Creek. Each dispatched a trailer equipped with sprinkler heads, miles of hoses, and a pair apiece of foldable water tanks and portable pumps. Willis's plan was to install a giant sprinkler system around the ranch that would keep its buildings wet, in hopes of warding off the fire.

In the Yarnell neighborhood of Glen Ilah, Gary Cordes, in charge of protecting homes and other structures in Yarnell as part of the new team of commanders, hiked along a thin trail with shoulders of high grass and chaparral. He clambered over rocks and mounds of dirt, and climbed a gentle slope that brought him to a burned-out clearing. He found the area challenging, but figured he could get a bulldozer to carve some fire line there. The place was full of dried, dying, and overgrown brush. "If fire hits this town," he said, "we'll lose it."

Cordes stopped by the fire station on Looka Way. He met with Shumate there, and also Hall and Kimball and an old friend of theirs, Todd Abel, a captain at the Central Yavapai Fire District. That morning, Abel and another man, Paul Musser, had taken charge of managing ground and air teams for the Yarnell Hill Fire—a crucial post formally called "operations section chief," also part of Hall's new leadership team. As the fire grew in size and complexity, from a Type 4 to a Type 2 blaze, so did the number of qualified commanders needed to fight it.

Shortly after 7:00 a.m., the Granite Mountain Hotshots wheeled into the Yarnell fire station parking lot in their buggies. Marsh, who knew Abel and everyone else pretty well, greeted them with his slow *good mornings* and *how are yous*. The fire burned visibly in the distance. They huddled around an iPad, looking at Google Maps satellite images of roads into and out of the wild. They debated which were still passable after decades of unrestricted vegetation growth. Cordes had traveled along some of these roads already, assessing what might be saved. He pointed to a gap in the knotty coat of withered green on a hill ahead of them, a ranch called Boulder Springs. It had a thick band of dirt around it, and a house, barn, and some sheds in the middle, far enough from anything that burned—Cordes described it as a "bombproof" safety zone, so well protected was it from an approaching fire. And Cordes said to Marsh, "Of course, you still have the black," referring to a patch of about two hundred acres scorched over the past two days on the southwest side of the ridge where the crew would be working.

At the meeting, Abel picked Marsh as supervisor of Division Alpha, one of two geographic sections of the fire. In his new post, Marsh would oversee crews working the rear of the fire—its heel, the least active of its borders, but a crucial point of defense. Steed would then fill in as superintendent, guiding the Granite Mountain Hotshots on the ground.

Abel pulled Marsh aside and said he was worried about the chaparral lining the hills, ridges, gorges, and mountains in the fire zone. It dried quickly with heat, he said, and that June had seen plenty of heat already, even in a cooler place such as Yarnell. The town had been tested by years of drought, its wilderness overloaded with trees that fire hadn't pruned back. Fires start easily in that kind of terrain, and they aren't easy to stop. Abel stressed that and reminded Marsh of the thunderstorms meteorologists had predicted, and the lightning and wind gusts these storms would bring. He made sure Marsh had the air-to-ground frequency programmed on his radio and asked him to rush his guys up the mountain soon, before the weather turned.

Marsh and Abel agreed that the firefighters lacked an advantageous anchor point and knew the cardinal rule that no wildfire should be fought without a solid anchor. It's firefighters' best assurance that flames won't double back on them. Building an anchor would become the Granite Mountain Hotshots' first mission on the mountaintop, and the only clear task they'd be given that day. Abel figured that once the new team of commanders got settled, they'd assign more crews to Marsh's division, and these would join Granite Mountain on the fire line.

At 8:59 a.m., shortly after Granite Mountain had begun its trek into the wild, the Southwest Coordination Center, in Albuquerque, released the day's priorities to dispatch centers in its jurisdiction. The fire in Yarnell was now number one on the list, ahead of seven other troublesome fires burning in the region, out of seventeen in all of the western United States. The Dean Peak Fire, at number two, was eating through brush at the mouths of narrow canyons, also a reason for concern. Managers at the center decided to assign a third specialized team to Yarnell, the Arroyo Grande Hotshots. In turn, they diverted two air tankers they'd dispatched to Yarnell over to Dean Peak, figuring the tankers would slow the flames before they entered the canyons, raced uphill, and exploded.

Shumate, Abel, Hall, and Kimball left the Yarnell fire station, bound for the school and the last formal briefing Shumate participated in as incident commander. On his way to the school, Shumate noticed two single-engine tankers swooping down over the wild, dropping orange retardant on the blaze. Measured at only two acres the previous morning, the fire had consumed five hundred acres by then.

At 9:18 a.m., a hiker snapped a picture of the Granite Mountain Hotshots passing by her and a friend. The men trudged along a path of stone and cured grass. They were at fifty-four hundred feet; from up there, Yarnell looked like a toy village. Steed, in his red helmet, led the line. He looked stern and purposeful. Marsh was up ahead as a scout, tying pink plastic ribbons to bushes every hundred feet or so, marking the way as he climbed to fifty-six hundred feet.

The men were trudging along the southern edge of the blaze as the fire marched north, toward the Double Bar A Ranch in Peeples Valley, which Willis was struggling to protect.

Conrad Jackson and Mark Matthews, Prescott firefighters, had parked a red fire-department pickup truck by the main house of the Double Bar A Ranch, deep inside the property. They were part of the reinforcements Willis had summoned to help him. Jackson and Matthews rushed around, laying out hoses and sprinklers, inflating pumps, and unfolding a water tank they'd set at the end of a slanted driveway. Jackson had a bad feeling about the spot they were in. The roads were precarious, tough to drive on, and the brush around them looked like tinder. Where could they escape to if the fire came too near? They settled on a house they'd passed maybe a quarter mile back. It was sur-rounded by land that cattle had grazed—the safest place they could find.

By the time they'd assembled their equipment, the flames were closing in a half mile away.

Willis looked ahead. The height and width of the flaming wall amazed him. It rose twenty feet high, moving fast, un-deterred by twenty-four thousand gallons of fire retardant dropped across its path from the belly of a DC-10. He directed the Yuma Crew to light up the brush west of the road they'd been enlarging. That might deprive the incoming fire of the fuel it needed to keep charging ahead.

Guided by the ranch's caretaker, Jackson and Matthews's structure-protection team tapped into the ranch's ninety-thousand-gallon reservoir and filled up the water tanks that fed the sprinklers. Suddenly, clouds of ash and smoke wafted their way. The firefighters coughed. Blue skies darkened. Willis ordered the caretaker to leave the property. It wasn't prudent to risk a civilian's life.

At the command post, Byron Kimball sat at a computer, requesting a spot forecast through the National Weather Service Web interface. He entered the elevation of the mountain where the fire blazed (fifty-three hundred to fifty-five hundred feet), and the vegetation it consumed (brush, unsheltered). He defined the parameters that the spot forecast should include: cloud coverage, temperature, relative humidity, level of lightning activity, and the Haines index, which estimates a wildfire's growth potential by measuring the stability and dryness of the air circulating over the flames. It ranges from 2 to 6; the drier and more unstable the lower atmosphere, the higher the index. By 9:45 a.m., he got his response: "Strong high pressure over the Southwest will maintain the heat spell for the next several days. Limited moisture will result in isolated thunderstorm activity today and Monday. These storms will produce lightning and strong gusty winds . . . but little or no measurable precipitation. The temperatures will decrease slightly and minimum relative humidity will slowly increase over the next few days." The spot forecast called for wind gusts of twenty miles per hour in the afternoon. Meteorologists put the Haines index at 5, nearly at the top of the scale, all the way through Monday.

An hour later, the fire had swallowed a thousand acres of land.

Volunteers working for the Yavapai County Sheriff's Office sprang into action, going door-to-door telling residents of the Model Creek subdivision, a development northeast of the Double Bar A Ranch, to evacuate. Flames would soon reach their doorsteps. The blaze threatened that whole side of town.

People grabbed their pets and dropped them at Kate McCullough's Muleshoe Animal Clinic, on the east side of Highway 89 in Peeples Valley, figuring to reclaim the animals in a few hours. Kate and Gerry, her husband, had been watching the fire from the clinic, but soon got busy caring for twenty-eight cats, several dogs, and a pig named Waffles.

At the command post, Shumate finally said his goodbyes. He had stuck around to update Roy Hall on the fire's overnight movements, the crews and assignments he had doled out since Friday, a hurried explanation that underlined his lack of progress in controlling the flames. Now, with Hall officially in command, it was time for Shumate to go home.

It was just past 10:00 a.m.

●●●

Hall was a veteran of thirty-nine fire seasons, four as a Type 2 incident commander for the State of Arizona. Partial to plaid shirts and cowboy hats when not in firefighting gear, he'd been in Yarnell for only a handful of hours and was already annoyed. His team members had arrived piecemeal, forcing him to repeat himself again and again until all of them had learned about the fire's behavior, his concerns and strategies. He had misgivings about their ability to handle this complex fire, not because they couldn't, but because there didn't seem to be enough of them. Hall rang Jim Downey, Arizona's district forester. He told Downey that the flames were increasingly active, increasingly menacing—to homes, and also to the incident command post at

Model Creek School. Hall suggested calling a full Type 2 team to run the show, with a full complement of twenty-seven members, almost twice as many as he had at hand. He wanted a local Type 2 team, which could get to Yarnell fastest. The fire was moving at a good clip.

Hall hadn't received specific instructions from Downey or any other of his superiors. They'd had no detailed debate about goals or tactics. His mandate was simply to take on the fire and put it out.

Hall organized the best offensive he could muster, while pressing for more help from above, more boots on the ground, more power to tame a stubborn fire. He asked managers at the Southwest Coordination Center for three additional Hotshot crews and another DC-10 air tanker.

In Yarnell, Cordes picked three "trigger points," geographic features aligned from north to south that would each prompt a certain reaction from him and his troops if the fire reached them. Best to stay ahead, he figured, and prepare in case the wind shifted and the fire changed direction—always a possibility. He kept a close eye on the flames from a rise on Highway 89, tracking their migration toward the school and structures in Willis's territory. In the distance, he picked out a narrow peak—it looked like an index finger pointing at the sky—and decided that if the fire got there, he'd evacuate the town. Then, he chose a rounded hilltop and told his firefighters over the radio that if that hill started to burn, they should prepare to leave the wild. Finally, he selected a long ridge line stretching east and west, about a mile from his vantage point. He named it his "aw-shit ridge." If the flames got there, everyone better be up by the Ranch House already, out of harm's way.

Up on the hill, the Granite Mountain Hotshots had begun

to dig a fire line toward the bulldozer track that Cordes's team was starting to lay out way down below, a rudimentary barrier to the fire's spread toward Glen Ilah. They strained under searing sunshine and huffed as they whacked their way through the mesh of chaparral. They advanced frustratingly slowly. Marsh called on his men to burn some of the brush. From the old grader, the Blue Ridge Hotshots saw Granite Mountain wield their drip torches, dousing a small slice of brush in diesel and gasoline, then lighting it with ignition sticks.

At 11:36 a.m., a single-engine air tanker whirred overhead, opened a door in its fuselage, and spilled a stream of retardant on the fire Granite Mountain had just set. Nine minutes later, another tanker made another drop. Two useless and mistaken drops, the crew's hard work undone. The flames petered out. Marsh got frustrated. He summoned Air Attack on the radio— that's not what he'd asked for. The planes returned to their base and reloaded. Marsh went back to the drawing board. He saw no point in attempting a backfire again.

With McDonough and a few other Hotshots, Marsh followed the charred hem of the fire to the side of the mountain opposite Yarnell. They stopped on a burned, barren piece of ground. From there, they began to scrape the soil, shaving a trail about three feet wide heading back in the direction they'd come from. They'd found their anchor, a launching pad for their line, tied to cold, black ground.

Marsh told everyone to start digging along the fire's eastern flank.

Brian Frisby, superintendent of the Blue Ridge Hotshots, radioed Marsh, asking him about the fire. Frisby complained of the poor briefing his men had received. Marsh alerted him to dead zones and other problems with portable radios. At times, firefighters had had to share radios and call or text one another on personal cell phones to communicate. Frisby's captain, Rogers Trueheart Brown, mentioned that even firefighters who'd been working in Yarnell since the day before still weren't sure what they were supposed to do. Shumate hadn't been clear about it, and neither had any of the newly arrived commanders on Hall's team. Some of these firefighters had been thrust into the wilderness with only a real estate agency's road map. Blue Ridge had been assigned no specific task and hadn't been placed in any division since arriving. They'd parked their buggies next to Granite Mountain's that morning, not far from the Shrine of St. Joseph, in Yarnell—an obscure pilgrimage site that drew Catholics from around the world. They'd found a way to make themselves useful.

A Blue Ridge squad leader sat behind the wheel of the bulldozer Cordes had requisitioned, replacing a driver who didn't have a supervisor directing his work, wasn't clear about his assignment, and didn't have a working radio of his own. The squad leader powered the dozer uphill, toward the old grader. Frisby drove to the anchor point. He discussed strategy face-to-face with Marsh and Steed. Everybody on the team was annoyed— who was calling the shots? Noon approached and Marsh had no more crews assigned to his division than he'd had when his day had started and no new directions about the mission he'd been asked to fulfill with the Granite Mountain Hotshots. Still, Marsh seemed to have made no particular effort to update his commanders on the conditions his men faced in the wild.

The Granite Mountain Hotshots had already excavated a hundred yards of solid fire line, parallel to Yarnell—a start. Down below, the bulldozer strained to carve its own piece of line. Marsh and Frisby decided that the Blue Ridge Hotshots would work to connect the dozer line to Granite Mountain's line. The terrain was steep and rugged; the job would take a lot of sweat, skill, strength, and time. It was exactly the kind of job for Hotshots. There just weren't enough of them to get it done in one afternoon.

They needed a lookout who would keep eyes on the fire while the rest of the men worked. Marsh and Steed often alternated in that role, but neither could do it that day because of the responsibilities they had—Marsh was running his division, Steed was running the crew. Marsh assigned the post to Brendan McDonough, a digger in the third month of his third season as a Granite Mountain Hotshot.

McDonough boarded Frisby's ATV, and the pair drove off northeast until they reached an outcropping, with a view of the men cutting line and the flames in the distance. McDonough thanked Frisby for the ride and radioed Marsh to tell him where McDonough was. They could see each other, and McDonough could see the flames.

Marsh got a call on his radio from Rance Marquez, a BLM employee with twenty-five years of experience. Marquez had been appointed supervisor of Division Zulu, the other geographic section of the blaze, but had no crews to work with because none were available. Still, Abel instructed Marquez to work out the boundaries between the Zulu and Alpha Divisions with Marsh. They argued; Marsh felt that Marquez was attempting to encroach on Division Alpha's territory—Marsh's territory. The conversation ended without a resolution. Marsh told Marquez to move farther north and find a way into the wild from there.

Marquez considered the terrain—its rough ground, thick vegetation, the lack of an appropriate place for a safety zone. It was no country for an engine truck, he thought, no country for vehicles of any kind. He'd need hand crews if he was to make any progress with his division, but there were none.

At noon, at the school in Peeples Valley, Hall gathered his field commanders in a corner of the gym. The fire was burning so close out the window that he saw retardant raining on the brush.

The region had run out of Hotshot crews; all twenty-one were committed to the fire in Yarnell and fires elsewhere in Arizona and New Mexico, were traveling, or were on mandatory days off. Dispatchers at the Southwest Coordination Center agreed to try elsewhere, maybe Northern California, but made no promises. They did promise another air tanker, and a helicopter—the Arizona dispatchers had requested two of each for Yarnell. The fire got back the two heavy air tankers it had been forced to give up to the Dean Peak blaze. They buzzed low over the area, bombarding the flames.

At 12:27 p.m., Hall gave David Geyer, Arizona's fire management officer, a full assessment of the magnitude and potential of the Yarnell Hill Fire, a complexity analysis he'd prepared to bolster his demands for more—much more. Flames rushed through ever more acres of heavy chaparral, and along a forest floor covered in dried grass and shrubs. The blaze burned a half mile from the closest homes in Peeples Valley. Unless it slowed, it would reach them in an hour. It threatened 25 businesses and 578 homes there and in Yarnell; four out of five of these homes were someone's primary residence. None of the roads, not even the four wide lanes of pavement along certain stretches of Highway 89, were any longer considered barriers.

The fire had now almost doubled in size since midmorning, covering nearly two thousand acres.

Hall paused and considered the precarious situation of their school turned command post. Flames approached fast, threading through a thicket of cactus and scrub oak four hundred yards away. Looking south from the school building, he could see shades of red smeared against swirls of gray smoke—a painter's palette of flames coloring the sky. The fire hissed, whooshed, and roared. The sounds made Barbara Kelso anxious, but she kept her worries to herself.

Hall walked into and out of the school, eyeing the approaching blaze. He decided to keep everyone where they were; the fire stood far enough away, and the building's concrete frame offered good protection. But he rounded up drivers and had them move every parked vehicle away from the fire's likely route. Barbara's daughter, Kim, who had accompanied her mother to the command post, ran outside through the smoke and repositioned their cars. Then she ran back inside, out of the acrid air and heat belching from the inferno.

From a ridgetop east of Yarnell, the Granite Mountain Hotshots followed the overall pattern of the fire. They understood now that they couldn't count on getting additional help; all forces available were concentrated on Peeples Valley. They made their way back along the line they'd just built on the heel of the fire and reinforced the rough anchor point they'd carved. They were on their own.

At 12:57 p.m., the coordination center heard good news about the Dean Peak Fire: retardant had thwarted the flames entering the canyons. It was a small victory at a time of trials and defeats.

Hall, meanwhile, spoke by phone to Downey again, and Scott Hunt, the state forester. Downey and Hunt told Hall the blaze looked challenging enough to justify calling a Type 1 team, instead of the full Type 2 Hall had suggested. Type 1 commanders form an experienced group, well prepared to handle the demands posed by a complex fire. Hall would have to hang on just a little longer. With its members scattered across several states in the West and beyond, the Type 1 team needed time to assemble and travel to Yarnell.

By one o'clock, the fire was expanding too fast for accurate estimates. It pushed north, and it slogged east, fanned by winds and fueled by the dry ground. It had won every round so far and had the upper hand.

• • •

State fire officials advised the Yavapai County Sheriff's Office to launch its reverse-911 system and notify residents of Yarnell that they had four hours to pack up and leave. The fire threatened them, and no one could guarantee their protection if the town started to burn.

At 2:02 p.m., a meteorologist at the National Weather Service office near Flagstaff rang up Byron Kimball, the fire-behavior analyst, with an alert. On the radar, he'd spotted a loose chain of clouds stretching from north to east, an early warning of a gathering thunderstorm. A storm moving toward the fire, with potential downdraft winds of thirty-plus miles per hour. Winds such as these could wreak havoc on the fire line, turning the resilient Yarnell Hill Fire into a monster.

At the command post, Barbara and Kim Kelso heard more about the storm, but the warning carried no hint of dread. The storm sounded like just another early-season monsoon disturbance, a normal high-desert occurrence. It was coming in from Prescott, where it had brought thunder, lightning, and a lot of rain. Rain was not likely over the Yarnell Hill Fire, though. Still, as soon as they'd received the recorded message from the sheriff's office on their cell phones, mother and daughter had asked for permission to leave. They'd stay the night at a friend's house in Chino Valley, an hour's drive away. The road there led straight across the storm's path. It was the only route to their destination.

Linda Ma stood by the side of Highway 89, looking north and thinking, "Those poor people in Peeples Valley." She stuck around, in no rush to get back home. Several others stood with her, and no one was hurrying. Ma never got the sheriff's warning and had no idea about the fierce weather brewing not far from where she was. It was 2:15 p.m. She'd packed some possessions in her car—personal documents, a computer, African drums, her favorite moisturizer. But she left others on top of her bed. "I'll just come back and get them later," she thought.

In Prescott, Juliann Ashcraft's cell phone buzzed. She'd sat with her four kids in church that morning, then they'd all gone to the pool to swim, cool off, and burn some energy. She'd put the younger ones down for naps—finally. She enjoyed her rare moments of relative quiet at home. She picked up the phone and noticed a message from Andrew. He'd sent her a picture of the Hotshots sitting in a field of rocks, watching flames that burned in the distance. "This is my lunch spot," Andrew had texted her. "Too bad lunch was an MRE."

At about the same time Andrew Ashcraft had texted the photo to his wife, two crews, of four men each, converged at the end of a road past the Shrine of St. Joseph. Bob Brandon ran one of these crews of volunteer firefighters. Darby Starr, a captain with the Sun City West Fire District, ran the other. The bulldozer had come up to a deep ravine that it couldn't cross. Gary Cordes had asked Brandon, Starr, and their men to go in there and finish the fire line the bulldozer had started. They had to hack and saw through a quarter mile of steep ground choked with scrub oak and manzanita, some of it eight feet tall.

Starr had received the Yarnell assignment late on Saturday. He was the officer on duty for the night. In 2012, Arizona's Forestry Division had split the state into areas, and the areas into groups, for easier activation of local resources during large wildfires. Starr's group has firefighters from communities west of Phoenix, such as Surprise, Goodyear, and Avondale—suburbs developers had built right out in the wild. Their fire departments have Type 6 engines, four-wheel-drive pickup trucks equipped with tanks that hold up to 150 gallons of water. Starr drove the Sun City West truck to Yarnell on Sunday. He'd rolled in around 7:00 a.m., checked in at the Model Creek School, then hooked up with Cordes, who asked him and his men to triage the homes in Glen Ilah—which ones could they save? Starr took a look and wrote most of them off. He estimated that it would take his firefighters a half day to clean up the brush around each of the houses. There was no time.

Starr had caught the warning about the approaching thunderstorm on the radio not long after his crew was dispatched to the dense wilderness northwest of the Shrine of St. Joseph. The warning was vague—it said a storm was moving in from Prescott. Nothing more. He wasn't conversant with the geography of that part of the state. He wondered where Prescott stood in relation to Yarnell. (Twenty-eight miles, northeast as the crow flies.) He didn't make much of it. He didn't think supervisors would send crews into the wild if the storm posed dangers.

Working from the state Dispatch Center seventy miles south of Prescott, Glenn Joki, the fire's new deputy incident commander, called up Tony Sciacca, who'd just finished a successful run managing the Doce Fire. Joki had realized that orders for

two safety officers for the Yarnell Hill Fire had never been fulfilled because they'd been lost somewhere in the electronic system that governs the assignment of crews and commanders—a
bureaucratic mess. Safety officers perform crucial tasks, in charge
of assessing and mitigating risks on the fire line, and keeping an
eye on crews working on the blaze. He wanted Sciacca to take
on that role.

Sciacca pulled up to the command post at the school a few
hours later and encountered a startling scene—flames advancing toward the building. He greeted Hall and asked him for his
assessment. "Well, look it," Hall replied, "I got a mess." Hall, the
Yarnell Hill Fire's top commander, "had a lot of distractions going
on," Sciacca recalled. Hall told Sciacca he was busy, and that
Sciacca should reach out to Paul Musser to figure out how he
could be useful.

Sciacca found Musser and presented himself for duty. Then,
Sciacca left the mess at the command post behind and joined
Willis by the ranch, to get his "situational awareness"—a feel for
the action.

Sciacca used Willis's radio to "clone" his own, copying all the
frequencies in play. He was on the side of the blaze opposite from
where the Granite Mountain Hotshots toiled alone on a ridgetop.
He looked up and saw an air tanker dropping fire retardant on
Willis's territory. His phone rang. It was Marty Cole, an old friend
and a crusty veteran of many fire seasons, two supervising
Prescott's wildland crew, back in its early days. Cole was driving
west from his home in Chino Valley, through rain and hail, bound
for the school command post. Joki had mobilized him, too—a
second safety officer as the inferno evolved.

"We got a hell of a rainstorm, hailstorm up here," Cole told
Sciacca. "Anybody call any weather?"

No one had just yet.

The Yarnell Hill Fire closed in on the school. It bumped right against a last obstacle, Model Creek Road, and leaped over it to a brush field that bordered the school. Smoke drifted inside the building through air-conditioning vents. Parker, of the Lewis Crew, stepped outside; he was stunned by the flames' proximity. Hall ordered everyone to leave the building and take shelter behind it. He guided Parker and other Lewis Crew members to beat back the flames that had slopped over the road, directing engine crews to spray water on those flames and also the unburned fuel, cooling it off.

Chaos reigned at the Double Bar A Ranch also. For hours, the blaze had teased Willis, testing his patience and skills. It had slowed down and perked up, hidden and shown its face, in a game of peekaboo. The fire was getting even with them—a dangerous bully. Willis worked to contain the flames, dispatching some crews to ignite the chaparral around the ranch, fighting fire with fire.

But the blaze kept growing and spreading. Willis realized that a ring of fire surrounded the buildings. If he didn't act fast, he and the firefighters on his team would have no escape. He had to get them all away.

"Everybody out!" he commanded.

Jackson and Matthews immediately pulled back. They left the sprinkler system they'd set up running, to give the ranch house a chance against the flames. They'd seen the fire rush uphill, slide into a basin, catch a ride with the wind the basin funneled, and sprint toward the command post. A firefighter looking for an alternative escape route spotted a road to the north, and everyone followed it. Engine trucks filed out, chased by fire. They lined up side by side along a rise. The men had a front-row view of an unfolding disaster. From a knob nearby, Jackson turned to Matthews and said, "We're going to lose Peeples Valley."

Near the shrine in Yarnell, Brandon, Starr, and six other firefighters felled manzanita trees, hewed shrubs, and dug and scraped the ground, slowly building more fire line.

At home in Prescott, Juliann's cell phone buzzed again with another message from Andrew, a picture of the fire line, smoke rising in the background.

"It looks like the inferno," she replied.

At 3:19 p.m., he wrote, "We could really use a little rain down here."

The Granite Mountain Hotshots had gathered by a field of boulders atop a ridge southwest of Yarnell, watching from a safe distance as the fire burned. They had received no clear directions from any of the commanders down below, so they watched, waited, and weighed, on their own, what to do next.

CHANGE IN THE WINDS

T ODD ABEL RADIOED MARSH: HAD HE COPIED THE weather report?

"Affirmative," Marsh replied.

At 3:26 p.m., a meteorologist working near Flagstaff had phoned Byron Kimball with a second warning. A storm was approaching from the north, on a collision course with the fire, which was already out of control. Threats of a downdraft had materialized on radar. The meteorologist wanted to be sure Kimball knew. The winds might be fierce and erratic, might spray down on the flames at forty or fifty miles an hour.

Danger lurked in the darkening skies.

Dutifully, Kimball had raised Abel on the radio and relayed the news, reminding him to watch out for those downdrafts. Abel transmitted the information to Marsh, telling him about the twin storms building to their north and, it seemed, to their south.

"Do you have eyes on both of them?" Abel asked him.

"Yep, I got eyes on both," Marsh replied.

Marsh was high up on a ridge, and Abel thought, "He can see the world from up there."

"You can see the one to the north, through the smoke?" Abel said.

"Yep."

"That one's making me nervous," Abel cautioned him. "Make sure you keep eyes on that thing."

"Affirmative," Marsh responded. "We got eyes on it."

Bob Brandon, working west of the Shrine of St. Joseph in Yarnell, overheard parts of some other radio warning about the storms, but not the bit about those downdraft winds. Nearby, Darby Starr heard something about a storm near Prescott, nothing else. Then, he got back to work.

At 3:33 p.m., the Yavapai County Sheriff's Office, through its emergency-alert system, ordered the immediate evacuation of every home west of Highway 89 in Peeples Valley. The homes stood within range of flames that were still on a northward path.

But then the winds began to change, moving erratically, swirling this way and that in different parts of the fire, at varying intensities. The dueling storms had crashed. The one that had approached from the north quickly won the battle. It pushed the fire south, toward Yarnell. That would lead to disaster.

In Peeples Valley, the fire that had devoured part of the Double Bar A Ranch suddenly lay down. Smoke that had fogged a dirt road on the ranch's border dissipated. Flames quit. It seemed like magic, a miracle. "Puff," Willis thought. "No problem." He sighed, glad that at least four of the ranch's seven buildings might survive.

Jackson and Matthews high-fived each other and danced a happy dance on the rise where they'd sought refuge, thanking Mother Nature for her timely help. Game over—on their corner of the fire, at least.

The shifting winds had thrust the fire in the opposite direction.

In Yarnell, Marsh had been scouting ahead of the rest of his crew, as he often did. He was on a ridge northeast of Steed and the seventeen other Granite Mountain Hotshots, who had busied themselves for a while reinforcing a piece of line they'd dug—a brutal task. The mountain offered them no shade, and the sun, no mercy. Wade Parker had texted his mother, Michelle, telling her that he had a headache; "pray for rain," he wrote.

"Lord please put this fire out!!!! Send rain. I love you son," Michelle wrote back.

On the radio, Marsh and Abel discussed the pair of monsoon storms closing in on the fire—from the north and from the south. Abel asked if Marsh could see both. Marsh said yes.

The storm approaching from the north made Abel nervous. When the wind blows from a single direction, as it had through much of the day, flames lean one way. The structure of a blaze is clear—its head, or flaming front; its heel; and its flanks, left and right. But Abel felt the wind flopping around and noticed that the fire column had stood up straight, as if shored up by invisible blocks—a sign of an impending shift.

The right flank, energized, gradually became as active as the fire's head.

Marsh told Abel on the radio, "The winds are getting squirrely over here." He said flames were about to challenge a strip of fire retardant painted on the brush ahead of him, skip over the line sliced by the bulldozer down below, and move toward the northern edge of Yarnell.

"Are you guys in a safe place?" Abel asked.

"Affirmative," said Marsh. "We're in the black."

Moments later, Marsh relayed to Abel, "I'm trying to work my way off the top."

"Okay, copy, just keep me updated," Abel responded. "You guys hunker down and be safe, and then we'll get some air support down there ASAP."

From his lookout perch, below Marsh and 120 yards from the old grader, McDonough scanned his surroundings. Glancing north, he observed the flames leaning toward him—opposite the direction they had tilted all day.

McDonough had established a trigger point, a ridgeline to his north, as he'd climbed the knoll. If the fire reached it, he'd retreat. Soon, his trigger point got breached. Flames whipped the hilltops. Fat embers danced in the air, traveling through heavy smoke to spots the fire hadn't yet burned, and setting them ablaze. He notified Marsh and Steed that he had to reposition. They acknowledged the fire's proximity and told McDonough to go on, hike down from the knoll, and make the best choice for himself—leave, if he had to.

At the foot of the knoll, McDonough looked over his shoulder. A menacing plume of smoke filled the horizon. Flames pulsed behind it, tinting the smoke amber and purple. He weighed his options. He could move to a lookout spot farther up. But Marsh had taught him always to play it safe, and he followed Marsh's lessons closely because he trusted Marsh, respected his knowledge, valued his judgment.

McDonough had to get out of there. That was the safe way

to go. He was about to call Frisby, the Blue Ridge Hotshots' superintendent, and ask him for a ride out of the wild, when Frisby zipped by in his ATV and stopped. McDonough hopped aboard. Steed radioed McDonough and said, "I've got eyes on you and the fire, and it's making a good push."

Frisby stomped on the gas, zoomed past the old grader, and made a beeline to the spot where Granite Mountain had parked its buggies on a patch of yellowed grass.

High on the mountain, Scott Norris, a sawyer on the Granite Mountain Hotshots, fired off a text to his mother, Karen: "This fire is running at Yarnell!!!"

It was 3:54 p.m.

• • •

The wind unleashed in stages. It hooked and shoved the flames away from a steady northern track, directly to the east, then, to the south, feeding on the unburned brush that lined the expanse from Peeples Valley to Yarnell. With each dive into a chasm, each swing upslope, the fire gained strength. The winds fanned it. Flames stretched sideways and fused, burning through mountains and valleys at sprinter's speed. The fire howled and bellowed as it moved.

Human beings take shelter from hurricanes, flee tsunamis, keep their distance from tornadoes, move indoors when dust storms roll by. Wildfires, they choose to fight. They feel a certain familiarity with fire, have a sense they can control it. Fire burns in campfires and fireplaces, flames on stove tops, flickers from candles that light up the darkness, a warming and comforting presence. It provides nutrition. It sparks romance. It protects.

In the wild, fire bullies and teases firefighters. Even in difficult situations, modern firefighters almost always come out on top. Even if they make a bad decision, they might reach a good outcome. That's the unspoken reality behind many of their victories. Triumphs made for danger because they inspired confidence.

The fire hurtling toward Yarnell that Sunday had made a U-turn in the sky, mesmerizing bystanders. From his cockpit, a pilot in charge of guiding airplanes on fire-retardant drops noted the flames' growing strength and speed and alerted Marsh that, at the pace the fire was going, it would reach Yarnell in one hour, and that Granite Mountain's buggies appeared to be on its path. Marsh told the pilot not to worry, that he had a plan.

Shortly after his exchange with Marsh, the pilot called it a day. On his way out, he gave his replacement, a two-men crew that used the designator *Bravo 33*, a quick update, making no mention of the locations of crews on the ground.

Musser, one of the fire's operations section chiefs, reached out to the Granite Mountain Hotshots—he spoke to Marsh, or maybe Steed—and asked if some of the crewmen could come off the mountain to help down below. He heard back that the men were committed to their position, but that he should try the Blue Ridge Hotshots. They were closer.

NO ANSWER

MARSH CALLED FRISBY ON THE RADIO—"I WANT TO pass on that we're going to make our way to our escape route."

Frisby asked, "You guys are in the black, correct?"

"Yeah, we're picking our way through the black." Marsh mentioned a road off the bottom of the mountain and said his crew was "going out toward the ranch."

Cordes listened in on the conversation and deduced that Marsh and his men had in mind the Boulder Springs Ranch. That was the bombproof safety zone that had been singled out on a map after the briefing that morning. It stood at the mouth of a box canyon, east of the fire line Granite Mountain had been building. Cordes had tried to get hold of Marsh minutes earlier to talk about the changing weather, but was having problems being heard from his radio—and a backup, mounted in his truck, wasn't programmed with the frequency he needed.

Cordes didn't try to stop Granite Mountain. He thought they would have plenty of time to get to the ranch.

The fire had hit the first of three trigger points Cordes had set, the hill that looked like an index finger, so he instructed dispatchers to give folks in Yarnell an hour to pack up and leave. That's how long he thought the fire would take to reach the town.

Bravo 33 looped around the fire, straining to fulfill its dual roles that afternoon—scheduling and tracing routes for air-tanker drops, and managing air-to-ground communications. Its crew told dispatchers that flames threatened six hundred structures on the north and southeast sides of Yarnell. The now erratic winds were pushing the fire all over the place.

An air attack supervisor pleaded with the Southwest Coordination Center for six more tankers, more water and chemicals to drop on the flames. The center granted one and dispatched it from Southern California, hours away, but the closest still available. Flying toward Yarnell, the tanker experienced engine trouble. It dumped its full load of two thousand gallons of retardant where none was needed, turned around, and flew back to base. Mission aborted.

In Prescott, Juliann Ashcraft enlisted her older kids to shut the windows. Powerful winds banged at their front door like an angry visitor. Rain poured. She hoped the storm would bring rain to Yarnell, too, quench that fire, and free up Andrew to come home that night. She and the kids missed him.

At 4:04 p.m., she picked up her smartphone and typed a question to Andrew: "Are you sleeping down there?"

Frisby had enrolled two drivers to help McDonough move

the Granite Mountain Hotshots' buggies over to the dirt parking lot at the Ranch House Restaurant. McDonough turned the key, started the superintendent's truck—Marsh's truck—and the radio crackled. He heard Marsh's and Steed's familiar voices. The carriers' radios were always tuned to the crew's frequency, which only they used.

Marsh and Steed were apart, but keeping in touch, as they had through much of the day.

Marsh had trudged across a ridge northeast of Steed and the rest of his crew, then hiked down, in the direction of the Boulder Springs Ranch. He could see his men up above. Cordes had told him the ranch was safe, absolutely safe. Others had asked him to bring the men to Yarnell to help protect the homes there, be in position to lend a hand once the fire passed through.

Incident commanders, overwhelmed by the fire's escalating threats and their own shifting priorities, had left the Granite Mountain Hotshots to make a lot of their decisions on their own. But Hotshot crews were trained to do just that. After hours of heavy toil, Steed and his seventeen men were momentarily idle—*disengaged,* as they would have explained it, a military term that means much more than doing nothing. They were carefully considering what to do next.

By radio, Marsh and Steed discussed choices and comfort levels.

As division supervisor, Marsh had checked the terrain and judged the best route for the assignment the crew had been handed when it arrived in Yarnell, the ideal spots to build an anchor point, cut line, and corral the fire, bit by bit. He was an overseer that day, a post a notch above his own official title in the chain of command. On paper, Marsh's supervisory role testified to his abilities as a leader. In practice, it reinforced the authority he already had over his own crew.

Steed, as acting superintendent, had turned Marsh's instructions into action. He'd earned his place at the top with his charm, smarts, and sheer resolve. He'd steered the Hotshots, guided them all day, and they did as he said to them. Steed was a man of principle—a marine through and through. He had the firmness to implement orders, the confidence to question orders he disagreed with, and the discipline required to yield to superiors, if he trusted them.

Marsh had taken one route to the ranch, but a shorter one, a straight shot, cut through dense, unburned brush and along a slope angled like a skateboarder's half-pipe. The Granite Mountain Hotshots could handle the slog. He was confident of that— perhaps too confident.

That afternoon in Yarnell, they marched, together, into a bowl, down the mountain. Marsh joined them at the mouth of the canyon, a funnel for the flames that barreled their way.

Firefighters often talk about the *Swiss-cheese model*, a risk-management term adapted to their realities. That's when a hole poked by a mistake, a bad call, a screwup on the fire line, is subsequently filled by something that's done right and goes right. In the case of the Yarnell Hill Fire, all the holes aligned into a tunnel that led straight toward catastrophe, as if someone had lit the tip of a trail of powder that ended on a stack of dynamite.

No one had erred on purpose. No one had been malicious. It is quite possible that one person's bad call had gone unnoticed or unacknowledged by the next person who made a bad call, and then by the next. Those were the ingredients for the disaster that was about to unfold.

Eric Marsh and Jesse Steed would have wanted nothing but to bring their men back home to their families, their lives. They would have wanted nothing more than to go back to their own lives. But they were annoyed, and under pressure from forces in and outside of the fire. The 2013 season was supposed to mark an end and new beginnings: Darrell Willis would retire, Marsh would take his place, and Steed would, in turn, permanently ascend to the superintendent's perch, opening a vacancy for the ambitious men under him.

Marsh knew the leadership team he had been working for in Yarnell well. Some had been his mentors. He respected them, and they respected Marsh. Besides, his Granite Mountain Hotshots were problem solvers. It's safe to say that pretty much all the Hotshot crews out there are—men and women well versed in the chess game of fighting a fire while protecting themselves and others, and protecting property and land.

When a commander—a friend—asked Marsh to bring his men to Yarnell, Marsh would have listened attentively and measuredly considered the request. He had been frustrated all day—with the air tanker that had twice dumped retardant on fires his men had calculatedly set, with the argument he'd had with the appointed supervisor of a neighboring division over the boundaries of their territories, with the lack of direction and resources he and his crew had had to endure. When the fire turned and it became clear that Yarnell stood squarely in its path, Marsh was making his way down the mountain on his own, along a circuitous route to the north of Steed and seventeen Granite Mountain Hotshots, toward the Boulder Springs Ranch.

He and Steed may have argued over the radio, presumably after Marsh directed Steed to lead the Granite Mountain Hotshots down toward the ranch, too, but to take a different route

The Granite Mountain Hotshots pose in front of the alligator juniper tree they saved during the Doce Fire in Prescott, Arizona.

FRONT ROW: Chris MacKenzie, Andrew Ashcraft, Brendan McDonough, Garret Zuppiger, Joe Thurston, Sean Misner, Travis Turbyfill, Billy Warneke, Scott Norris, and Travis Carter *(hanging from branch)*.
BACK ROW: Jesse Steed, Robert Caldwell, Dustin DeFord, Grant McKee, Kevin Woyjeck, Anthony Rose, Wade Parker *(hanging from tree, left)*, and Clayton Whitted *(on tree, right)*.

Anthony Rose and his fiancée, Tiffany Hettrick, celebrating the impending arrival of their first child, a girl she named Willow Mae.

Billy and Roxanne Warneke, doing one of the things they enjoyed doing most together: fishing.

Andrew Ashcraft, his wife, Juliann, and their four children *(left to right),* Shiloh, Tate, Ryder, and Choice, posing for their Christmas portrait in 2012.

Garret Zuppiger had a degree in business management, but couldn't stand to work within walls. He was in his element here, on the Colorado River banks.

Jesse Steed, his wife, Desiree, and their children, Caden and Cambria, on a sunny fall day in Prescott in 2012.

Travis and Stephanie Turbyfill and their girls, Brynley *(on Stephanie's lap)* and Brooklyn. He used to read *Goodnight Moon* to his girls over the phone while out fighting fires.

Sean and Amanda Misner on their wedding day. Her bouquet matched his corsage, and she had on black cowboy boots under her princess gown.

Eric and Amanda Marsh in Malibu in 2010.

Wade Parker waving and smiling inside Squad Alpha's buggy. He was a sawyer for the Granite Mountain Hotshots in 2013.

Kevin Woyjeck as a young EMT with his father, Joe, a captain of the Los Angeles County Fire Department. Like father, like son.

A selfie of Chris MacKenzie while on night duty with the Granite Mountain Hotshots.

John Percin, wearing his Granite Mountain Hotshots cap while riding a mountain bike in Prescott at the start of the 2013 fire season.

Lunch break for Eric Marsh
on a fire in Idaho in 2007.
On the menu: Stagg Chili.

From their
mountainside
lunch spot, the
Granite Mountain
Hotshots watch
the Yarnell Hill
Fire burn down
below.

Andrew Ashcraft, lugging his pack
and chainsaw moments before
the men were trapped by the fire.

The disorderly devastation of the Yarnell Hill Fire, which swept through Yarnell, Arizona, as if playing a game of drunken hopscotch.

Coming home: The body of Christopher MacKenzie is carried from a C-130 transport at the Joint Forces Training Base, Los Alamitos Air Field on July 10, 2013, in Los Alamitos, California.

Vice President Joe Biden speaking at a memorial for the Granite Mountain Hotshots on July 9, 2013.

Seated behind him are *(from left to right)* Gov. Jan Brewer of Arizona; Marlin Kuykendall, mayor of Prescott, Arizona; Prescott Fire Chief Dan Fraijo; and Darrell Willis, chief of the Prescott Fire Department Wildland Division.

Makeshift memorial on the fence around Station 7, the Granite Mountain Hotshots' base in Prescott.

from the one Marsh was taking, that straight path through a box canyon choked with tall, parched, and unburned brush. People who had been around Marsh and Steed long enough knew that it was sometimes tough to distinguish a heated conversation from an argument. In challenging circumstances, they didn't necessarily talk like gentlemen. They didn't mince words.

Ultimately, Steed led seventeen men into that canyon— because they agreed it was the best next move, based on circumstances, prospects, and the information they had, or because they simply trusted their leaders.

They were strong.

They were fast.

They knew it wouldn't be easy, but they must have trusted that they could make it to the ranch before the fire got to them, optimally positioning themselves, perhaps, to reengage once the inferno had roared through.

They were not on a suicide mission.

No one—not Marsh, not Steed, not the men under them or those above them—expected the flames would beat them in this race.

• • •

Linda Ma was unsure if she should leave her home in Glen Ilah. She looked out at the skies and spotted flames licking a ridge under a half mile away. She walked to her neighbor's and lent a hand with packing. A friend, Cheryl Remmerde, pulled up, dashed out of her car, and screamed, waving her arms, "Get out now!" Remmerde had worked for the Forest Service years back and had learned about wildfires. She lived in Congress, at the foot of Yarnell Hill, but had driven up to the Ranch House to watch the fire. She saw the winds turn and the flames reverse, and smoke and ash fill the air. Remmerde had raced to her car and run to fetch Ma.

Air traffic intensified. The pilot, Tom French, and John Burfiend, right-seat crewman, on Bravo 33 monitored a handful of radio frequencies and their own communication channel. Burfiend had planned a sequence of fire retardant drops over Yarnell and attended to questions from Abel and others on the ground. French offered directions to air tankers, including a DC-10 that had finally arrived in Yarnell.

In the hubbub of the cockpit, Burfiend heard someone talk about a safety zone and asked Abel, "Do we need to call a time-out?"

"No, they're in a good place," Abel said. "They're safe and it's Granite Mountain."

Burfiend then asked Marsh, "Is everything okay?"

"Yes," Marsh assured him. "We're just moving."

At 4:08 p.m., the sheriff's office unleashed a series of text and voice messages to residents who'd signed up for its emergency alert service, CodeRED: "This is a mandatory evacuation notice for the Yarnell and Peeples Valley areas. All residents need to evacuate immediately."

Cordes surveyed the homes in Glen Ilah. He realized he couldn't even try to save them. He directed the firefighters in his structure-protection group to gather their gear and get out. If Yarnell was going to burn, so be it.

From the edge of a field west of the shrine, Bob Brandon took a minute to evaluate the changes around him—shifting winds, air tankers' altering flight patterns, thickening clouds. Frisby and his captain, Brown, were riding an ATV up the mountain, along the trail they'd crossed for a meeting with Marsh. Embers landed on the brush. Spot fires flashed around them; no time to waste. They steered the ATV back down through Armageddon, along the trail they'd climbed. They ordered their men to jump into the Blue Ridge carriers and head over to the Ranch House.

Brandon watched them go and pondered, "They're professionals. We do this on a volunteer basis, so what aren't we seeing?" He wanted to get the hell out of there, too, but couldn't. A handful of fellow volunteer firemen were still in the wild. There was no way he would leave them behind.

He grabbed Matt Keehner, a Peeples Valley firefighter working as Brandon's lookout, and got into their truck. A fireball dropped from above, and suddenly the land around them was aflame. It grew dark. At the Boulder Springs Ranch, a security camera switched from day mode to night. Brandon turned on the truck's emergency lights so he could guide his guys toward safety. "Start driving very slow," he told Keehner, screaming over the whistling inferno—like a jet engine seconds before takeoff.

The truck slogged toward the shrine. Brandon kept looking back, terrified he'd never see the guys again. Suddenly, they emerged—apparitions in an apocalyptic scene. One of them, Ron Smith, had the hair on the back of his neck singed as he ran, chased by leaping flames. He had thought he wouldn't make it.

They passed Darby Starr on their way out. Starr kept telling everyone to get out, sounding urgent. He stood like a chaperone, making sure no one had been forgotten in that slice of wilderness near the shrine, where stone-carved statues arranged on granite boulders portrayed the crucifixion of Jesus Christ. Starr gripped the big hoe he'd used to split the ground. He ushered Brandon and Keehner out, and also firefighters from suburban Phoenix who'd accompanied him to Yarnell. He told them to follow the trail carved by the bulldozer and hook left, skirting a small ranch through a flat field of grass, where their trucks were parked. Wind and fire wailed. Firebrands rained on them. The fizzle and boom of exploding propane tanks echoed against the mountains. For the first time, some of the men panicked and dashed away wherever their legs took them.

Starr gave little thought to running. Fighting fire is a physical undertaking and a mind game. He'd fought too many fires to lose control. He walked with purpose and didn't look back. Smoke swirled like a slow-moving tornado above his head. He felt the hot breath of flames close behind him. He barely saw the path ahead.

With a *whoompf,* patches of grass ignited to his right. He kept striding, picking up his pace. A ridge burned to his left. A drop of rain landed on his hand, triggering a memory and a warning. Starr recalled Sciacca mentioning a raindrop that had fallen on him during the Dude Fire, on June 26, 1990. Thunderstorms had been forecast for that afternoon. Sciacca, on the fire line, had noticed the wind quieting down, and the smoke dissipating—the calm before the tempest, he'd thought. When the single raindrop struck him, he realized he was under a thunderhead and ordered his men out.

Starr reached his truck. His firefighters were already in their seats. The engine was running. He slipped out of his pack and tossed it inside. Then he stepped back and looked at the field he'd just crossed. It had been overtaken by fire. Gone.

"Shit," he said, "that was close."

Starr and his men drove through Glen Ilah, to the Ranch House. They joined a line of cars packed with people and their belongings inching along Lakewood Drive, bound for Highway

89, to escape. McDonough and the Blue Ridge Hotshots were already at the restaurant. Sciacca had ended up there, too, and also Cordes and Musser. Cole was on his way, driving south from the command post in Peeples Valley along Highway 89. He peeked in his rearview mirror and spotted the wall of fire devouring the wild. Spatters of rain mixed with ash muddied his windshield.

On the radio, a voice asked, "Granite Mountain, what's your status right now?"

Marsh replied, "Well, the guys, uh, Granite, is making their way out the exact escape route from this morning . . . and it heads, ah, south."

After a brief pause, Marsh continued, "Midslope, cutting over."

At 4:18 p.m., the storm's fierce winds blew against the northern edge of the inferno. Flames doubled in height and tripled in speed, to sixteen miles per hour, fourteen hundred feet per minute. Six minutes later, radar images measured the height of the smoke plume at 31,500 feet.

Cordes understood that he had underestimated the fire's potential. The ferocious flames had reduced to minutes the hour he had set aside for evacuation, following their arrival at the northernmost of his trigger points. The flames had reached his second trigger point far faster than he'd anticipated.

By 4:33 p.m., the smoke plume had soared to 38,700.

The advancing fire ate whatever stood in its way. Barbara Kelso gazed at it and drove out of the command post, turning north on Highway 89. "There goes Yarnell," she thought.

A mountain split the slab of fire in half. The fire carried on, its destructive power doubled. One half entered a drainage and swung east, into Glen Ilah. The other burned along the base of

a ridge, rounded a knoll, and entered a box canyon, face-to-face
with the Granite Mountain Hotshots.

• • •

Steed and seventeen other crewmen had been stationed at the
southeast end of the fire. More than four hundred acres of
torched land and brush extended westward, away from Yarnell,
away from the flames. When the fire changed direction, it nulli-
fied the usefulness of their anchor point and fire line. All the
work they'd done was wasted and offered no protection to the
little town of Yarnell. They'd made plans, adapted them, scrapped
them, started again. Veteran Hotshots such as Steed were well
versed on the games fire played.

The men had left their safe spot—the black—together,
heading south. They had traversed an old trail, a rough road used
by the occasional hiker and all-terrain vehicle. They had
reached a dip, a break along the path that sliced the ridgeline—
a saddle, they called it. Higher ground was behind them. They
could see the fire to their left as they walked and the Boulder
Springs Ranch ahead of them, out beyond a bowl-shaped canyon down below. The ranch seemed so close.

Together, they'd dropped down a steep slope scarred by
water from long-ago rains and pawed by deer and bear. They'd
fought their way through an entanglement of manzanita and
scrub oak, brush and mountains fast blocking their view of the
flames. Halfway down, the incline softened, though unburned
fuel lined the path. They pressed ahead, toward the ranch.

Suddenly, the monster loomed from behind a hill to the
northeast.

On the radio, a desperate cry—"Breaking in on Arizona 16,
Granite Mountain Hotshots, we are in front of the flaming front."

Fourteen seconds go by, and no response. Musser chimed in, "Bravo 33, Operations. You copying that on air-to-ground?"

Five seconds later, Bravo 33 responded, "Granite Mountain, Air Attack. How do you read?"

In Yarnell, flames towered over trees and knolls. Winds tossed embers far ahead of the fire. The air turned the color of caramel.

Musser, on the radio: "Granite Mountain, Operations on air-to-ground."

Marsh: "Air Attack, Granite Mountain 7. How do you copy me?"

Chain saws buzzed. Sawyers and swampers worked, probably harder than they'd ever worked before: Carter and Ashcraft; Thurston and Norris; Zuppiger and Parker; DeFord and Rose. The fire rushed at them. They gave up on reaching the ranch. They couldn't run faster than the flames. They'd clear the ground around them. The place was thick with brush. They had to get rid of it. They'd clear the area as best as they could, then dive inside their shelters. It was the only option left.

Calling on Musser, the Air Attack crew, Bravo 33, said, "Operations, Bravo 33. I was copying that traffic on air-to-ground."

A moment later, Bravo 33 continued, "Okay, I was copying a little bit of that, uh, conversation, uh, on air-to-ground. We're . . . we'll do the best we can. We got the Type 1 helicopters ordered back in. We'll see what we can do."

One of the Hotshots screamed on the radio, "Air Attack, Granite Mountain 7!"

Bravo 33: "Okay, uh, unit that's hollering on the radio, I need you to quit."

Musser, to Bravo 33: "Okay, Granite Mountain 7 . . . sounds like they got some trouble, uh, go ahead and get that, he's trying to get you on the radio. Let's go ahead and see what we've got going on."

Bravo 33: "Okay, copy that. I'll get with Granite Mountain 7, then."

Marsh: "Bravo 33, Division Alpha with Granite Mountain."

"Okay, Division Alpha. Bravo 33."

"Yeah, I'm here with Granite Mountain Hotshots. Our escape route has been cut off. We are preparing a deployment site and we are burning out around ourselves in the brush and I'll give you a call when we are under the sh—the shelters."

"Okay, copy that. So you're on the south side of the fire, then?"

"Affirm!" A fierce gust of wind blew into Marsh's microphone. The escape route he had mentioned wasn't quite an escape route—it was lined with brush.

"Okay. We're going to bring you the vee-lat, okay?" *Vee-lat* is the pronounced acronym for "very large air tanker"—VLAT—the DC-10. It carried twelve thousand gallons of retardant in its belly, and it could fly in that weather. It could find the Hotshots.

Seventeen seconds of silence, then Bravo 33 jumped on the radio again: "Division Alpha, Bravo 33 on air-to-ground."

A radio squelched, its transmission unclear.

"Is that Division Alpha? Bravo 33 on air-to-ground."

Twenty seconds of silence.

"Division Alpha. Bravo 33 on air-to-ground."

Seven seconds.

"Okay, uh, we're working our way around there. We've got, uh, several aircraft coming to you. We'll see if we can take care of business for you."

Fourteen seconds.

"Division Alpha. Bravo 33. I need you to pay attention and

tell me when you hear the aircraft, okay? 'Cause it's gonna be a little tough for us to see you."

The radio squawked.

"Division Alpha, Bravo 33. Do you hear a helicopter?"

Two minutes and fifty-five seconds.

"Granite Mountain 7, Bravo 33 on air-to-ground."

No answer.

GONE

At 4:47 p.m., Bravo 33 contacted state dispatchers and confirmed the deployment—but only that. No one knew where the Hotshots were, how many of them lay in their shelters, if they were injured, or dead.

Abel phoned Willis and asked, "Did you hear what's going on with Granite Mountain?"

Willis was still in Peeples Valley, checking that the fire that had half-destroyed the Double Bar A Ranch was under control. He'd followed the chaos on the radio, unable to focus on it much while working. But Abel was talking about his crew. Those were his boys. He felt dizzy for a moment, thinking of Marsh and his aspirations for himself and his men, the faith they had in one another, the bond they shared. They couldn't all be gone like that. The ideal they embodied—they were a righteous army, doing an honest job—couldn't be gone. Willis had invested time, political capital, and emotion molding Marsh, and guiding him as Marsh in turn molded the crew. The Granite Mountain Hotshots were a big part of Willis's legacy. He loved those boys. And he loved Marsh as a father loves a son who tests his patience but also makes him proud.

Willis turned to two of the firefighters who'd been working with him at the ranch and said, "Keep mopping, keep watching this. I'm gonna drive around."

Willis drove straight to Yarnell.

With so much smoke and ash in the air, he could barely see the road. A pair of horses dashed in front of his truck. Willis almost hit them. He slammed the brakes, his heart racing. He looked toward the mountain and saw it ablaze.

Willis pulled up to the Ranch House. The parking lot was choked with fire trucks from many crews, all fleeing the inferno. Todd Abel and Paul Musser stood off to a corner, on the radio and on the phone, making plans—and waiting. The Granite Mountain Hotshots' white buggies stood out in the sea of red and green vehicles. Willis spotted them right away.

"What's going on?" he asked.

The crew had run into trouble and gone silent, Abel replied. He'd put ambulances and medical helicopters on standby. Dispatchers were calling every hospital in the state, reserving their stockpiles of blood plasma for treating severe burns.

Willis called his wife, Judy, and said, "You gotta pray for these guys." His anchors were his faith and his wife, who'd known some of the Hotshots for a while and knew one of them very well, Clayton Whitted. She'd prepared Whitted to mentor teenage boys and girls at Heights Church, where Granite Mountain

Hotshots past and present filled the sanctuary's front-row seats on Sundays. That's where Willis had planned to be that Sunday. Instead, he was in Yarnell, confronting the unthinkable.

He phoned Dan Fraijo, chief of the Prescott Fire Department. Fraijo had been hired as interim chief in the spring of 2012 and was asked to fix the financial and organizational mess that budget cuts imposed by the city during the recession had visited upon the department. He'd come out of retirement for that. He had reluctantly agreed to take on the job full-time only four months before fire devoured Yarnell. He barely knew the Hotshots.

"Our guys have deployed," Willis told him. "I hope they're just out of radio communication. We haven't been able to contact them."

"What do you think?" Fraijo asked.

"The worst-case scenario is we just lost nineteen guys."

McDonough sat inside one of the Granite Mountain's buggies, listening to the crew's internal radio, hoping for signs of life. He heard only the unsettling sounds of static. Willis approached and softly asked McDonough if he was okay.

Gary Cordes had lost his connection to the air-to-ground frequency. He didn't know much about the Granite Mountain Hotshots' troubles, their deployment, or the unanswered calls on the radio. He'd left the wild after Starr and his crew, who had escaped with fire on their backs. A firefighter from the Central Yavapai Fire District assigned to one of the engine crews on Cordes's team filled him in on the details.

"Bullshit," Cordes fired back. "They didn't need to deploy. They were in their safety zone and it was bombproof."

But Cordes pushed the thought aside. He and the rest of the command knew that nothing about the Yarnell Hill Fire was routine. The odds of everything turning out well had plummeted. Cordes focused on the urgent task before him, his firefighter's hat always on. He drove into the Glen Ilah neighborhood and rescued residents trapped there. Safeguarding the area had been his responsibility. Minimizing the damage there was work still open to him.

The fire had swerved southwest after reaching the northern tip of Yarnell. It had followed a ridgeline, burning through the Shrine of St. Joseph and the slice of land from which Brandon and Starr had escaped. It had incinerated much of Glen Ilah, hopscotched along Ridgeway Drive, Lakewood Drive, and Westward Drive, where it destroyed all but one home.

On Manzanita Drive, Cordes drove between burning houses and burst propane tanks, looking for stragglers. A lot of people had been fooled by the fire, as he had, and had delayed their departures. An elderly couple, Bob and Ruth Hart, emerged from the thick haze. They held hands. He had on pajamas. She wore a light-pink robe, her hair as white as cotton.

They had been married for sixty-seven years. He was ninety-four, she was eighty-nine, and they had that kind of measured love that longtime companionship teaches couples. They'd moved to Yarnell some ten years earlier, enjoying the cool air, the tranquillity, and neighbors who kept an eye on them, but also let them be.

The Harts had been watching television at home, unaware of the approaching fire; they'd heard no warning call from the sheriff's department. Bob had finally looked out their kitchen window and seen trees ablaze right in their backyard. They had only the clothes on their backs, and each other, left.

They'd driven their Honda Ridgeline out of their garage into flames and darkness. Bob had made a wrong turn, then tried to turn around. One of the wheels of his Honda had caught in a ditch. The tire had blown out. He and Ruth had abandoned the vehicle and walked about five hundred feet before they came upon Cordes.

Inside her slippers, the soles of Ruth's feet had burned.

Cordes stepped out of the truck and helped Ruth climb in. He exchanged no niceties or introductions with her or Bob. He drove the couple to the Ranch House only a few hundred feet away, dropped them off, and returned to Glen Ilah.

On Ridge Way Drive, a woman and her daughter refused to turn their backs on their elderly neighbors—or on the neighbors' thirty-five cats and dogs. Cordes told mother and daughter they could die if they stayed behind, but they weren't persuaded. So he drove back to Manzanita, angry at their stubbornness, angry at the fire. He saw a man waving at him. His name was Bryan Smith and he said that his cousin Pearl Moore was on the side of the road up ahead, waiting for someone to come get her. Smith was sixty-three and ailing; he had chronic lung disease. He hadn't been able to carry Moore, who was eighty-five, after she could no longer walk.

Cordes looked up the road. All he could see was fire.

He found Moore on the ground, picked her up, and placed her on the rear seat of his truck. She had some burns. Smith had opened the truck door to let his cousin in. Embers flew in and blistered his face. They were the last people Cordes rescued. It would have been lunacy to head into that inferno again.

At the Ranch House, Cordes waited for a lull in the fire so he could begin to assess the damage in Yarnell. But most of all, he waited to hear from the Hotshots.

Paul Musser had notified Roy Hall of the Hotshots' reported fire-shelter deployment, and Hall had called every fifteen minutes—"Any word?" An hour, four phone calls, and nothing. Hall grew steadily more worried. He called the state forester Scott Hunt and prepared him for the worst. Hall authorized a search party to leave from the restaurant parking lot and go find the Hotshots and help them if help was needed. That was the now-unlikely result everybody hoped for—a search party finding nineteen men in need of help.

Brian Frisby, the Blue Ridge Hotshots' superintendent, was one of five firefighters who set off on the ground search. Another was Trueheart Brown, his trusted captain. The remaining three were Prescott-based firefighters assigned to the Central West Zone Type 2 management team. Hall had considered giving the team command of the fire. The team members had heard about it, and some had made their ways to Yarnell, just in case.

The searchers had to find a route around the flames and fallen trees to reach the mountains and the Hotshots. They veered north on Highway 89 and turned left on Shrine Drive. They passed the Family Diner, where locals dance to live music on Fridays. They passed the post office and its bulletin board, where a handwritten room-for-rent sign hung next to the coming week's menu at the community center. They passed the entrance to tiny Flora Mae Park, named after a girl who'd ridden a wagon mule bareback into town, chasing thieves who had stolen her father's horses.

Deer sometimes frolicked in the park. That afternoon, there was only fire.

They forged ahead until the blaze halted them. They retraced their route—back past the park, the post office, the diner, then south on the highway onto Lakewood Drive, the main road through Glen Ilah. But that route was also dangerous. They warned engine crews dispatched to put out house fires in the area to turn back and wait some more, as awful as waiting might be. Firefighters aren't trained to wait while houses burned. They'd rather work and distract their minds from an unfolding tragedy.

They returned to Shrine Drive. They had to find a way to punch through the conflagration. Among them, they had a medical kit, a few oxygen bottles, and a backboard—not much to aid nineteen victims, but it would have to do. They sensed that they were running out of time.

"Fuck it, let's go for it," Frisby said, and they all barged through fire, weaving past hanging branches and power lines in their off-road vehicles.

By then, Eric Tarr, the police officer–paramedic with the state's Department of Public Safety, was already scanning the smoldering mountains from a helicopter. The pilot, Clifford Bursting, had offered the chopper's aid with the search, and Bravo 33 had green-lighted the mission. Bursting put minimal fuel in the tank—enough for an hour or so in the air, to keep the chopper light and safe in heat and high altitude. He took off toward the center of the fire, following a trail that veered south off the bulldozer line. Frisby and Brown raced below on their ATV along the bulldozer line. It was where they had last seen the Hotshots. There was no one there.

The Yarnell fire still burned. To the east of Tarr, tankers dropped gallons of retardant on the flames. Below, through breaks in the heavy smoke, they saw blackened dirt, blackened boulders, blackened cacti, and blackened tree skeletons that looked like spent matchsticks. The air crackled with an unbearable heat.

As Tarr and Frisby searched, news of the Hotshots' disappearance started to make the rounds. A handful of reporters had driven up from Phoenix to cover the fire—an ordinary story, until it wasn't. At 6:08 p.m., one of them, Michelle Ye Hee Lee, of *The Arizona Republic*, tweeted:

"BREAKING: 20 firefighters unaccounted for. State forestry is trying to verify that. 200+ firefighters on scene currently. #Yarnellfire."

With that hashtag, the fire began to spread online.

Along a ridgeline, with a sinking heart, Tarr spotted a cluster of bright yellow backpacks close to where he had seen the Hotshots earlier. Frisby, Brown, and the rest of the ground searchers sped uphill, toward the spot above which the chopper had hovered for forty-five minutes, signaling the location. The trail became impassable. The searchers abandoned their off-road vehicles and hiked the rest of the way, three hundred yards across a moonscape of blackened soil and pulverized brush. When they got to the backpacks, disappointment. The packs were bladder bags the Lewis Crew had used late Friday night while trying to put out the flames.

There was still no sign of the Hotshots.

Bursting steered the helicopter closer to the chain of mountains by the crest of Yarnell Hill. He kept his eyes on the fuel gauge. Tarr kept his eyes on the land. The buildings of the Boulder Springs Ranch came into view. Bursting aimed the aircraft toward it, the tank nearly empty. At the bottom of a canyon, the Hotshots' fire shelters blended with the terrain around them—ashen and still. Bursting dipped low and circled the shelters. Tarr stared at them. Nothing stirred.

At 6:19 p.m., Lee filed another tweet: "Fire officials got word that a helicopter flying over fire saw firefighters down. Crews going in to verify. #Yarnellfire."

Still aboard the helicopter, Tarr relayed the shelters' coordinates over the air-to-ground radio frequency. Musser passed them on to Frisby, who punched them into his handheld GPS and set off.

Bursting finally landed the chopper, on a clearing he'd spotted not far from the ranch, five hundred yards from the shelters. Tarr jumped out and the chopper took off, hurrying back to base four miles away for refueling.

Tarr walked uphill.

At 6:35 p.m., he deadpanned over the radio: "We have nineteen confirmed fatalities."

At the Ranch House parking lot, Willis turned to Abel and asked, "Did I hear that correct?"

Willis called his wife again and shared the devastating outcome. He was then silent as the news washed over him. He took a seat and for an hour, maybe more, maybe less, was lost in thought. He couldn't run a sequence of events through his mind to explain what had happened because no sequence of events made sense to him. Nineteen Granite Mountain Hotshots were doing what they always did—fighting fire. Then, they were gone.

The crew's manifest, turned in when the Hotshots had reported for duty at the Yarnell fire station that morning, contained nineteen names. If McDonough was alive, who was the nineteenth fatality? John Percin's name had been left off. The second fire he ever fought was his last.

At the regional dispatch center, a fortified building of red brick and concrete across from Prescott's City Hall, Wade Ward, a firefighter who had occasionally filled in with the crew, was on double duty as the fire department's public information officer. In its 128-year history, the fire department had never logged a fatality. It fell to Ward to handle nineteen that day. Calls poured in, from reporters in faraway places—New York, Ireland, Hong Kong. "We can't confirm it," he told them in a calm monotone.

He asked Tim Wiederaenders, city editor at *The Daily Courier*, Prescott's hometown newspaper, for time: "Please, let us tell the families first."

It was too big a story, in too competitive a news cycle, to risk letting outsiders scoop the local paper. At 7:20 p.m., an article went up on the Web site of *The Courier:*

"PRESCOTT—The Prescott Fire Department lost nearly its entire crew today—the Granite Mountain Hotshots—with 19 firefighters dying."

• • •

The families of the Granite Mountain Hotshots had communicated with one another throughout that evening through a telephone tree, sharing what they'd heard. Mostly they asked questions. Their telephone tree had none of the order, hierarchical structure, or predefined purpose of the Hotshots' well-established tree. It started out of despair. Until that evening, the families weren't a unit, although the Hotshots had been. They were familiar with one another, but they weren't family. Shared grief soon bonded them.

Amanda Marsh was working, as she usually did when her husband wasn't around, leading a horse named Honey on exercise laps around her ranch in Chino Valley to help heal its sore feet. That's what Amanda did for a living: She got horses used to walking barefoot and trimmed their hooves to maintain their natural shape. Her phone rang. It was a Prescott Fire Department dispatcher she knew, telling her the Granite Mountain Hotshots had gone missing in the wild: "Nobody knows where they are."

Amanda hung up and frantically dialed her mother: "Eric's missing, Eric's missing, the crew's missing."

"Just calm down," her mother told her. "It's going to be okay."

Stephanie Turbyfill had gone to her parents' home in Prescott for dinner. She hadn't heard from Travis in a while, and his silence had started to nag at her. He usually called right after the end of his shift. Her mother had cooked a Thai pasta dish and set some aside for Travis.

"I don't think Travis is coming for dinner," Stephanie told her mother. But Stephanie texted Travis anyway, asking if he was.

No reply.

"I miss you," she wrote to him later on.

No reply.

Dinner over, Stephanie drove home, Brooklyn and Brynley strapped into their seats. Stephanie spotted a DC-10 flying over Prescott, and due southwest—toward the fire, she figured. She reached out to Travis again after she got home. Nothing.

A friend texted her, "What's going on?"

"I don't have any idea what you're talking about," Stephanie responded.

The friend told her that she'd heard of nineteen firefighters trapped by the fire in Yarnell. Stephanie's hands started to shake. Her body trembled. The phone rang. It was Travis's adoptive mother, Colleen, and she spoke about the trapped firemen, too.

"Where did you hear this?" Stephanie asked.

Colleen said someone she knew had read it on *The Daily Courier*'s Web site.

Stephanie opened her laptop, and there it was, in big bold letters, a headline reporting the deaths of the Granite Mountain Hotshots—her husband's death.

Stephanie called her mother, sobbing. Brooklyn stood by her side, as tall as Stephanie's midthigh, and said, "It's okay, Mommy. It's okay."

Though Stephanie read that one of the Hotshots had survived, she felt sure that it wasn't Travis.

Clayton Whitted's wife, Kristi, called her. Stephanie broke down and cried, "It's them. They're gone. They're all gone."

Kristi had already gotten a call from Anthony Rose's fiancée, Tiffany. A disturbing alert from the Fox News affiliate in Phoenix had popped up on Tiffany's phone, and Tiffany wasn't sure what to make of it. Kristi assured her that if anything had happened to Anthony, Clayton, and to the rest of the Granite Mountain Hotshots working in Yarnell, someone would surely have let families know.

The alert, relayed at 7:30 p.m. through the station's smartphone app and on Twitter, read:

"BREAKING: Prescott Fire Department confirms 19 firefighters have died while battling the #YarnellHillFire."

Back from a shopping trip with her mother, Jesse Steed's wife, Desiree, answered a call from a good friend: "Have you seen the news?" Desiree grabbed her iPad and looked it up online. No way they were dead. If they were, she would have been notified before the reporters. Jesse and the guys must be injured; "I wonder what hospital they're at," she thought.

Desiree contacted the Prescott Fire Department, and a dispatcher directed her to the Mile High Middle School, where the families were gathering. Right then, Desiree knew. Why make everyone meet at a school if not to notify them of the deaths?

Juliann Ashcraft and Amanda Misner learned about it on TV—unwitting spectators to their own personal tragedies. Their worst fears were now a reality, broadcast across the country for millions to see.

Juliann ran to her bedroom and cried alone, away from the

curious eyes of her four children. Amanda called Tim McElwee, Sean's uncle and leader of the wildland crew that had preceded Granite Mountain. She also sent a message to Sean: "If you get this, you need to text me right now."

Silence.

She touched her stomach, a nervous habit she had developed, and a new wave of anguish washed over her. She was due in September. Sean would never meet the child she was carrying.

In Seal Beach, California, Joe Woyjeck tapped the Find My Friends app on his phone, trying to locate Kevin. He'd checked earlier in the day, a habit of his since Kevin had started fighting fires, and the app had placed Kevin in Yarnell. That evening, Joe waited for Kevin's spot to pop up on Joe's iPhone's screen. Instead, he got a message: "Location Not Available."

He watched his wife's eyes well up. Anna Woyjeck had got a call from their younger son, Bobby, telling her a friend had heard on the news that Kevin's crew had "deployed."

"What does that mean?" Anna asked Joe, again and again and again.

Joe was a firefighter. He knew. The men had deployed their fire shelters. Never a good thing.

In the buggy, McDonough heard the beeps, rings, and buzzes of calls and text messages to the cell phones the men had left behind.

The families who lived in and around Prescott wandered into Mile High. Amanda Marsh arrived with her neighbor Duane Steinbrink, who'd hired Eric for the Wildland Division and molded him into a leader. She'd packed an overnight bag for Eric, thinking he might need it—his cowboy hat, his favorite jeans, his boots. She stepped out of the car and tried his cell phone again. He didn't answer. She called the clients she had scheduled for Monday, telling them she wouldn't be able to honor their appointments, but that she'd call back in the days ahead so they could pick another time. Someone invited her inside the school, but she said no. She sat on the curb instead and waited.

Stephanie Turbyfill stepped into the school's band room, where Andrew Ashcraft, class of 2003, had learned to play the trumpet. Stephanie saw men wearing the Prescott Fire Department uniform, some of them friends of Travis's. "He's gone, right?" Stephanie asked. They told her to come inside, take a seat. Why did she have to wait? Everybody else seemed to know the answer. On Twitter, strangers were already asking for prayers for the families and calling the men heroes. Her Travis had died doing a job he'd signed up for; a job whose risks he'd understood and accepted. His death wasn't heroic. It was a catastrophe, her entire world collapsing.

It took Desiree Steed a while to get to the school. She lived in a remote corner of Prescott Valley, and she couldn't find anyone to stay with her kids. She brought them. A close friend met them in the parking lot and kept the kids entertained in the car, watching movies and playing games on a cell phone. Desiree walked by Tiffany's silver Jeep Compass, with a BABY ON BOARD sign hanging from its rear window.

Dan Bates, a Prescott firefighter, carried a list of nineteen confirmed fatalities to the front of the room, a place of utter sadness. He read their names—Andrew Ashcraft, Robert Caldwell, Travis Carter, Dustin DeFord, Christopher MacKenzie, Eric Marsh, Grant McKee, Sean Misner, Scott Norris, Wade Parker, John Percin Jr., Anthony Rose, Jesse Steed, Joe Thurston, Travis

Turbyfill, William Warneke, Clayton Whitted, Kevin Woyjeck, Garret Zuppiger.

Stephanie walked up to Bates when he was finished and yelled at him: Why did nobody tell us? "This happened hours ago," she said. "Why did we have to find out from the news?"

Moments later, an older man hurried past the families. He stopped to greet no one. He stepped in front of a fireman and announced, "I'm Travis Carter's dad." The man, Tripp Carter, wanted to know if his son was okay. He'd missed the announcement.

The fireman looked at Tripp. Tripp looked stupefied. The fireman held Tripp's hands and told a father his son was dead.

Outside, Amanda Marsh asked a stranger who'd just left the school building, "Did they read the name Eric Marsh off the list?"

"Yes," the stranger replied.

At Joe Woyjeck's home, a firefighter and a police officer pulled up together outside. Joe stared at them as they walked up to his front door. Before they could say anything, Joe asked, "Confirmed?"

For Roxanne Warneke, who lived in Avra Valley, a rural enclave in southeastern Arizona, three hours away, confirmation came late, really late. She'd tried hard for hours to get answers. She'd called Billy's cell phone, and Steed's cell phone, and the phone at Station 7, where she left a message: "I saw in the news that Granite Mountain deployed. It's Roxanne Warneke and I'm looking for information on the whereabouts of my husband, William Warneke." She'd called the Red Cross, and her mother, who told her to pray that Billy would be okay.

It was well past midnight. She was in bed, wide awake. Her dogs barked. Someone knocked on her door. She lived out by a swath of federal land, a travel corridor for immigrants who'd crossed from Mexico into the United States.

Roxanne grabbed a handgun and approached the door. "Who is it?"

"Fire Department."

She cried out, "Billy's dead."

TWO THOUSAND DEGREES

A FIRE SHELTER'S SKIN IS ALUMINUM FOIL FUSED TO silica fabric, which seals in air that is cool enough to breathe—an imperfect shield that reflects the radiant heat from a fire. An inner layer of foil laminated to a mesh of fiberglass toughens the fabric. This shiny envelope is the firefighter's final line of defense.

Shelters reflect radiant heat well, but aren't designed to resist direct contact from flames, nor the searing convective heat fires blast. If the sack heats to 500 degrees, the glue bonding the shelter's layers comes undone. The foil, unhinged, flaps in the turbulent fire winds. If it rips, game over; without the foil, the shelter loses most of its protective qualities. If it lasts, it is good until the temperature reaches 1,220 degrees. Then, aluminum begins to melt.

Fire shelters are credited with saving more than three

hundred lives, but the design trades portability for additional security. A shelter is not a magical force field; it is a last hope.

Survival depends not only on the resistance of the materials, but also on the shelter's deployment and the occupant's positioning within. Firefighters must hold the sides and ends of the shelter closed with arms and legs to keep it from flying away, keeping their feet toward the flames and face into the ground to protect nose, throat, and lungs from scorching air. Helmets and gloves must be kept on.

Still, polycarbonate, the durable plastic from which firefighters' helmets are made, softens at 375 degrees. The gloves, made of processed leather, shrink by half at 600 degrees. At 300 degrees humans can barely breathe. Once over that threshold, they suffocate.

The Granite Mountain Hotshots had been fighting their way through the maze of thorny chaparral when a wave of flames and scorching heat closed in on them. They dove into the shelters. Most of the men had made it under their shelters. The temperature in the bowl climbed to 2,000 degrees, as hot as lava from a volcano. The shelters offered no relief. The men had no time to get to the ranch, no time to clear brush from a large enough area to protect themselves.

They'd lain in the shelters, trapped.

•••

Tarr, treading uphill on burned, hot dirt almost two hours after the Granite Mountain Hotshots had last been heard from, came upon a scene that revealed the shelters' limitations, the Hotshots' haste, the fire's ferocity, and the absolute horror of the final moments.

The Hotshots had about 120 seconds to carve out a deployment site. Donning chaps of nylon and Kevlar, Carter, DeFord, Thurston, and Zuppiger had picked up their Stihl chain saws and cut as much brush as they could, as fast as they could. Eight charred stumps formed a rough V off the eastern corner of the deployment site, facing the fire. The stumps ranged from one to two inches in diameter and stood about twenty to forty-five feet from the men. The sawyers may have sliced off other brush that hadn't withstood the flames.

Some of the men had worked to burn back the vegetation around them.

They'd had too little time.

The men had clustered inside a lopsided oval, twenty-four feet by thirty feet. They'd been trained to fling the ignition sticks, gas, and oil they carried away from where they'd deploy their shelters; to hurl their backpacks far from the cocoons of their shelters—in case anything in the packs might flare up or explode. They'd been trained to toss away the tools they carried before entering their shelters, and to keep helmets and gloves on while inside.

Ten of the nineteen men had gone in with bare hands.

Twelve had found the few seconds needed to point their feet toward the fire. Two pointed their feet in the opposite direction. Tarr found no sign of the two men's helmets and not a shred of clothing on their bodies.

Seven of the nineteen rested facedown, properly situated inside fully deployed shelters—the backs of shirts and pants charred, the fronts mostly preserved, yellow and grimy, as they must had been just before fire set upon them.

Tarr saw the darkened soil, and a granite boulder that had heated and flaked. Other boulders had cracked. The fire had tinted them brown and gray. Nothing green was left.

He saw that chain-saw engines had dissolved into dull silver clumps of metal. Stuck to the lumps were the saws' twenty-eight-inch steel guide bars, unscathed. He saw that tool handles, made out of wood and fiberglass, had disintegrated, while tool heads, made out of sheet steel, had endured.

Travis Carter and Andrew Ashcraft lay side by side, face-down, bottles of saw gas and oil wedged between them.

Sometime during the winter, Andrew had started coming to work wearing a white silicone band on his right wrist with the words BE BETTER engraved on it. Andrew had grown up in a Christian home, but joined the Church of Jesus Christ of Latter-day Saints to please Juliann, a lifelong member. She had told him that she wanted to raise their children in her church. One of the church's traditions is called home evening, a weekly gathering meant to strengthen faith and family bonds. One home evening, Andrew had given his wife and their four children white bracelets just like his. He told them this would remind them to be good to one another, to strive for greatness, and to always stick together.

Juliann and the kids put on their bands, but most of the bands came off one by one in the ensuing days.

Not Andrew's. "I'm going to wear it until it falls off my wrist, or until I die," he'd pledged to Juliann.

He'd kept his promise.

Fire had destroyed his pocketknife and compass, but not his wristband. It had turned deep brown, and gotten a little thinner. But it hadn't crumbled or broken.

Stephanie Turbyfill got back Travis's black carbon-fiber wedding band, intact, and the brass Granite Mountain belt buckle he wore, melted and cracked.

Tiffany Rose got Anthony's iPhone 3G stuck to a piece of his green fire pants, smeared in ash. The back of the phone, made of plastic, had melted and fused with coins or keys that Anthony carried in his pocket.

Claire Caldwell got Robert's wallet, singed a bit around the corners.

Desiree Steed received Jesse's sunglasses, melted, and a pack of cobalt-flavored 5 gum, unopened and unblemished.

Amanda Marsh got a clump of plastic and metal that had been Eric's flip phone. She got the pocket-size mirror he'd used to signal air tankers to the spot where he'd wanted them to drop fire retardant. It had cracked. There was the wedding band they'd bought together at a silversmith's in Ouray, Colorado— hammered yellow gold, $200 for the his-and-hers set. Eric had not removed it since the day Amanda slipped it on his finger at the idyllic chapel by Fain Lake in Prescott Valley on April 3, 2010, almost four months after they'd met at an AA meeting in the same town. Marsh, a guest speaker at the meeting, had talked about the crew he'd built. Amanda had been in the audience, an alcoholic logging her 206th day of sobriety.

She slipped his ring on her finger, lodging it under hers.

Mike MacKenzie got his son Christopher's belt buckle— the Granite Mountain Hotshots' logo, a prized possession for several members of the crew. It had blackened, but hadn't burned. Mike polished it, attached it to a brown leather belt of his own, and got to wearing it, always, taking Chris with him everywhere.

COMING HOME

THEY SHUFFLED ABOUT OUTSIDE THE MILE HIGH
Middle School amid a serenade of wails and sobs. A dozen
men in navy-blue Prescott Fire Department T-shirts had been
handpicked to bring their brothers out of the mountain. They
gathered under a lamppost and listened to their instructions:
Report to Station 71, down the street, on White Spar Road, by
1:00 a.m. Have your wildland gear ready—pants and shirt,
helmet, gloves, insulated boots. The fire still raged in Yarnell.

At the station, three fire department trucks and many boxes
of pizza awaited. Each man took a piece and sat on a bumper of
a fire truck parked in the bay. Not all of them ate.

The trucks pulled out, warning lights flashing. J. P. Vicente,
a captain, departed in his own Chevy crew cab, hazards on. He
picked up Danny Parker across from the Sonic hamburger joint
on the north side of town. Danny's oldest son, Wade, was one of

the fallen Granite Mountain Hotshots. He wanted to carry Wade home.

Danny Parker and his wife, Michelle, had married in high school, and that's as much schooling as they were able to get. They had worked hard to make a living, support a family. Their first child, a girl, came within months of their wedding. Danny enlisted and served five years at Chase Field, the naval air station in Beeville, Texas, fifty miles from the sea. Afterward, he thought his only option would be construction, though he dreaded the instability of the trade, its moods dictated by the economy and the weather. Then, he heard about openings in the reserve program at the fire department in Chino Valley, his hometown, a rural community carved out of farmland just north of Prescott. He applied and was chosen.

Danny and Michelle cherished family dinners. Gathered around the table, their children—two boys and two girls—fell under the spell of Danny's stories of fires and rescues. One evening, he told them about a kid whose horse had got a hoof stuck in a cattle guard. Danny and a few other firemen had been walking back from a store, with soda and sandwiches they'd bought, when they'd spotted a kid tugging on a horse by its reins. They took off running; Danny's captain threw a coat over the horse's head to keep the horse from jumping and kicking. Danny and the rest of the firemen lay on the horse while they waited for a vet to arrive. They didn't want the horse to break its leg. The vet calmed the animal with a tranquilizer. The firemen used a hydraulic Jaws of Life tool to pry apart the bars of the cattle guard. The tool usually released people stuck in mangled-car wrecks. That day, it freed a horse.

After his story, Danny saw the smile on Wade's face, the twinkle in his eyes. Danny knew that expression well. His son had fallen in love with Danny's job. From that moment on, Wade talked about what he'd be when he grew up: a baseball player or a firefighter.

Wade had a wholesome childhood—school followed by baseball and football games, ten o'clock service at Word of Life Assembly Church on Sundays, occasional rides with his father on a fire truck, backyard target practice with a bow and arrows his father had crafted. In 2009, he enrolled in a community college in Lamar, Colorado, not far from the Kansas border, on a baseball scholarship. A year later, he was back home. He wanted to be a firefighter and marry his high school sweetheart, a petite, hazel-eyed brunette named Alicia Owens. He wanted to be like his dad.

"I'm fifty years old," his father told him. "I'd go play baseball every day if I could."

Wade was determined. He had it all planned out.

He wanted to spend a couple of years on a Hotshot crew, fighting big fires and "camping for a living," his father used to say. Then, he'd apply for a job as a structural firefighter. He and Alicia would have children, be happy. He'd watched his parents. Happiness was what he'd known about marriage. In Christian books—*The Five Love Languages: How to Express Heartfelt Commitment to Your Mate, Wild at Heart: Discovering the Secret of a Man's Soul*—he'd studied the steps to becoming a good husband.

Danny had driven Wade to Station 7, in a neighborhood of factories and warehouses north of Courthouse Square, Prescott's modest industrial district. Danny urged Wade to go in and talk to Marsh. "Call me when you're done," Danny told him. "You have to get this on your own. You have to put in the effort, do the work."

Father and son had had many conversations about the duty and honor of being a firefighter. "We're the front line," Danny had told Wade. "On September eleventh, 2001, they didn't call the navy. They didn't call the Marine Corps. They called the policemen and the firemen. We are the soldiers of our community."

Wade applied to Granite Mountain in December 2011. In the employment-history section, he listed a handful of prior jobs—at In-N-Out Burger ("I left for college"), at a truck-repair shop ("I was laid off"), at a valet service that paid $4.37 an hour, plus tips. As reason for leaving, he wrote, "Was spending more in gas than I was making."

He was hired for the 2012 season and earned the coveted Rookie of the Year award. His rise on the crew was relatively fast. Following Darrell Willis's advice, Wade had picked a veteran Hotshot to emulate—his model was Brandon Bunch, a skilled sawyer—and asked him all sorts of questions, got Bunch to teach him a lot of what he knew about felling trees and building fire line. By the end of the season, Wade had mastered the use of a chain saw. In 2013, after Bunch left the crew, Wade and Garret Zuppiger joined up as one of Granite Mountain's four sawyer-swamper teams. "I believe I have the responsibility, and the leadership quality to fulfill this position," Wade wrote in his paperwork that year.

Wade still lived with his parents when he died.

Danny had to go to Yarnell. He had to pick up his boy.

J.P., at the wheel of his crew cab, drove west on Iron Springs Road. Danny sat by his side. A young firefighter named Matt Demenna joined them, seated in the back.

The road snaked through the Prescott National Forest. The truck rolled past guardrails melted by the Doce Fire. Matt looked up at the stars above and at a waning moon that cast a soft light over the vastness around them. He saw the looming silhouette of Granite Mountain. He thought about Wade, and how proud he'd been to have helped stop the Doce Fire. Matt hadn't realized until then how close to Prescott the flames had come.

Matt Demenna and Wade had tried out for the Granite Mountain Hotshots together and got in together. In their deep Christian faith, they'd found an instant connection. They'd hiked Thumb Butte before their first day at work, and Wade told Matt that he wanted to start going to church more often and read the Bible more often, "for grounding."

In firefighting, Wade said, he'd found his path.

After meeting for the first time, they'd easily agreed to become each other's motivator, to hold the other accountable—"What have you read in the Bible today?" they'd ask the other, then discuss how it applied to the uncomplicated lives they led. They'd never been uncomfortable talking about God in front of other Granite Mountain Hotshots. Often, the conversations included others—sometimes Zuppiger, who nurtured a respectful curiosity about religion, and Clayton Whitted, who'd also chosen religion as his guiding force.

Wade and Matt used to half joke about joining the Navy SEALs someday. They knew that SEALs were another breed of warrior, with tougher standards and requirements beyond the forty hours of classroom training and the physical tests that wannabe Hotshots had to take.

Matt had ended up injuring his Achilles tendon on grueling hikes and toil on the fire line, so he had to skip the last two fires of the season. He'd stuck around through the fall, helping out however he could. The following year, he landed a job on the structural side of the fire department.

Wade set a date for his marriage to Alicia, October 19, 2013, so it wouldn't interfere with fire season. He wrote down the goals he had for work: "make the season enjoyable," "keep us safe," "help keep our squad together as a unit"—and tucked the piece of paper inside his Bible. That's where his parents found it.

In the crew cab truck, rumbling toward Yarnell, Matt, Danny, and J.P. crossed Skull Valley, its homes darkened, the tiny town asleep. It must have been three in the morning. Matt heard the click-clacking of hazard-light blinkers. The fire department radio was off, the FM radio was off. Danny whispered, from time to time, "He was such a good boy. Wade was such a good boy."

The truck stopped at a roadblock, then another. "We're from the Prescott Fire Department," J.P. said, and officers waved the truck through.

J.P. turned right on Lakewood Drive, into Glen Ilah. Matt couldn't see the stars anymore, only smoke and fire. Homes were burning. Some had burned up. Flames had torched one-half of a tree and left the other half intact, its leaves green. In a lot, a charred refrigerator stood near a stone fireplace and a chimney, still erect in the rubble. Flaming vehicles stood under collapsed carports. A house had been reduced into ashes, but the flames had spared the irises growing on the front yard. Water still gushed from a fountain outside another house.

The fire was still on the move, and many structures were left for it to consume; flames were licking front yards. Matt wondered if it was safe to drive through town without water and a hose handy. J.P. had seen a lot—he'd served as a flight medic in the US Army before becoming a firefighter—but had never witnessed as much destruction as he saw in Yarnell. It looked as if a bomb had exploded in the middle of town.

They drove in through an open gate at the end of Ridgeway

Drive, up along a winding dirt driveway over to the Boulder Springs Ranch. They parked outside the stable; a donkey and miniature horses. Darrell Willis approached Matt, Danny, and J.P. and hugged them, looking exhausted. He could barely stand. Willis tried to explain what had happened to the Granite Mountain Hotshots, though he couldn't quite understand it. He said that a bulldozer had been working to build a road up to where they lay, and that they hadn't been alone for a minute since they'd been found; two sheriff's deputies stood guard.

Matt looked toward the mountain, but it was too dark to discern anything except the red taillights that lit when the dozer driver braked. Danny saw headlamps glistening on the hill, where firefighters worked extinguishing hot spots. He nearly lost his mind listening to the beep-beep-beep piercing the silence as the dozer backed up. The beeps reminded him that his son lay somewhere past the edge of the line the dozer was digging.

Danny and Matt sat on the bed of the Chevy, joining J.P. and another fireman. Unsure what to say to one another, they didn't say much. Matt had worked a full day and night before ending up here. He was so tired. He got up at one point, snuck into the backseat, and tried to sleep. He woke up after a half hour, his heart racing.

The new day dawned at last. The swish of a helicopter's blades turned everybody's eyes skyward. The air above the deployment site had been declared a no-fly zone—who'd dare defy it? Someone grabbed a pair of hunting binoculars, intent on making out the chopper's tail number. The firefighters were sure it was a news helicopter.

The helicopter hung way up there for a bit, then flew away.

Deputies from the Yavapai County Sheriff's Office arrived, trailed by forensic investigators in unmarked Chevy

Tahoes—white, their windows tinted dark black. They drove past Matt, past J.P., and past Danny. The white of Danny's eyes had reddened from so much crying. The deputies drove up the bumpy road the dozer had carved overnight and parked at its end, where newly dug-up caramel dirt met the scorched land. The investigators got out of their vehicles, walked around, stopped, crouched, took pictures, took notes, all engaged in the bureaucratic choreography of processing the scene through which they walked. Matt noticed the body bags they carried, bright orange—dollops of paint on a wrinkled sheet of carbon paper.

Matt lost track of time. The investigators got all the nineteen men inside those bags, then tagged and numbered them.

Matt, down by the ranch, jumped into the back of a pickup truck that was about to ride uphill, to the nineteen Hotshots. Willis took the wheel. Danny was in the passenger seat. The truck bumped up the same road the investigators had driven, parked where they had parked. Throughout the ride, Matt turned his back to the mountain; he didn't know if he was ready for what he would see. He looked at Yarnell instead. He smelled fire, but didn't see flames.

The truck stopped, its tailgate turned toward three rows of orange bags. Two more trucks lined up. It was 8:00 a.m. on Monday, maybe later. Matt hadn't bothered to check the time.

Willis joined Danny Parker, whose son lay with his brothers on the mountain, and Matt Demenna, who'd joined the crew with Danny's son, outside. Others were already there—Conrad Jackson and Mark Matthews, the veteran Prescott firefighters; Cory Moser, a battalion chief. They draped American flags over each of the Hotshots, then walked around them, as the investigators had asked them to, so as not to disturb the scene. Matt made out the outlines of the fallen men underneath flags and body bags. On the ground, he spotted the twisted metal frames of fuel containers called banjos, a water bottle, and the head of a Pulaski. He saw a radio, its label still legible—CHRIS, it read. The radio had belonged to Chris MacKenzie.

Matt pointed out the radio to Willis, who bent down and touched it. Just then, the radio crackled, startling everyone. It still worked.

Willis gathered everybody by the trucks. The men stood in a circle. Willis had a Bible in his hands. He opened it to Psalm 23:

"Yea, though I walk through the valley of the shadow of death, I will fear no evil; for You are with me. . . ."

A gentle breeze caressed the mountains. The ground had cooled, but the air was still hot and carried the smell of burned logs. Wispy clouds covered the sky, shielding the sun. Out in the distance, Danny spotted the bright yellow shirts worn by firefighters who were at work extinguishing spot fires that still smoldered.

"Is it okay if I say something?" Danny asked the men around him. They nodded. "I want to thank everybody for being there, and for the opportunity to help carry my son out of this place. Wade loved being a firefighter and he really loved the firefighters he worked with. He made me so proud." Danny squeezed his eyes shut. Tears flowed. He bowed his head and recited a prayer.

Matt believed that firefighters were fixers. They go and put out fires, help injured or sick people, make things better. He gazed at the bags and thought, "That, no one can change."

Moser got his attention. It was time. He split twelve men into three groups of four. Eight men lined up along the sides of a tailgate, saluting. Four men picked up a bag, one man at each corner. The four men carried the bag to one of the trucks, past the twin rows of saluting firemen. They slid the bag onto the back of the pickup trucks, headfirst. They did so again, and again, and again. The trucks carried two Granite Mountain Hotshots at a time to the Maricopa County Medical Examiner's Office vans that waited down by the ranch. The Hotshots never traveled alone.

Matt made three or four of those trips, crouched between the two bags on the truck's flatbed. He talked to the guys as they rode; he had no idea what else to do. "It's over," he said to them. "You're not in pain anymore. We're going to take care of you."

Danny Parker didn't look inside the bags. No one did. The bags had been tagged and numbered, but they had no names. Danny didn't know which held his son Wade. He didn't want to guess and risk missing him. So Danny held a corner of each of the nineteen bags the firemen brought out.

"To me, they were all Wade," he said. "They were all my son."

"WE TAKE CARE
OF OUR OWN"

S HARON KNUTSON-FELIX CLOSED THE DOOR TO HER
home in Phoenix that Monday morning—a checkbook in
her purse, a mission to fulfill. She was executive director of the
100 Club of Arizona, a nonprofit offering practical and emotional
support to families of firefighters and police officers killed or injured in the line of duty. This delicate process often yields last-
ing relationships. The group has hired someone to mow the lawn
of a fallen police officer's elderly mother, as the officer used to
do. It has paid off debts, helped build homes, provided scholar-
ships to children interested in a career in law enforcement,
planted seeds of hope that grief and pain will someday become
tolerable.

Sharon had lost a son, Ricky Knutson, her firstborn. A car
had jumped a curb and hit him, knocking him out of his shoes.
He was six. Fifteen years later, she'd lost her husband, Doug

Knutson, a motorcycle officer for the Arizona Department of Public Safety. He'd been standing inside a triangle of asphalt where a highway and an off-ramp joined, waiting for a tow truck he'd summoned to cart away an abandoned car. The driver of a pickup truck crossed over the solid white lines at forty miles an hour, slamming into Doug's bike, then Doug. He was forty-three.

The experiences schooled Sharon in the slow progress of grief, beginning right away with questions and scrutiny by the media, the inevitable, unwanted spotlight that comes with public tragedies. She knew the things well-meaning people told young widows because she'd heard them, too—"You'll meet somebody else," "What a shame for such a good-looking guy to die."

She had remarried and understood that a new husband wasn't a replacement, but was a chance at a new beginning. She also understood that nothing could patch the hole left by a child's death.

On Sunday, Sharon had heard about what happened in Yarnell the way most families of the Granite Mountain Hotshots had: through phone calls and text messages from friends. She heard from people who knew that she cared, and that caring was her job. She'd been at home, and after the first messages came, she asked her husband, David Felix, to turn on the TV.

May had been a rough month. In one day, a Phoenix firefighter and a police officer had died—Brad Harper, pinned between two fire trucks at the scene of a blaze, and Daryl Raetz, struck by a passing SUV while making a drunk-driving arrest.

Then came the nineteen deaths in June.

"I don't know if I can do this," Sharon had said to David, with news of the Hotshots flashing on the television screen.

But she did. She had nineteen families to comfort and

nineteen checks to write, each for $15,000, initial assistance for immediate needs, no strings attached. Sharon hadn't been sure enough money was in the bank to cover nineteen times $15,000—$285,000. She'd called the chief executive of the credit union holding the group's accounts. He assured her that he wouldn't let the checks bounce.

On Monday morning, Sharon stopped by the 100 Club office in West Phoenix before heading up to Prescott. What she found there stunned her. Donations for the nineteen families had poured in all night, many of them $5 and $10 contributions from strangers. In twenty hours, the group had gathered $800,000 in cash gifts through its PayPal account; the club's connection to the site had frozen three times, overwhelmed by the flood of donors.

In Prescott, sad, urgent meetings had commenced at daybreak—at the Mile High school, at fire department headquarters, in the basement at City Hall, and at the Hampton Funeral Home down the street. Unions had put out calls to members, asking if they'd give a day off or a vacation day and staff the fire stations in Prescott, so local firemen—the department had no female firefighters—could attend memorials and burials and tend to the families that their friends had left behind. Soon, fire trucks from all corners of the state—Chandler Fire Department, Globe Fire Department, Flagstaff Fire Department, Lake Havasu City Fire Department, Sierra Vista Fire Department—rolled along local streets, answering calls for the local firemen.

The Prescott fire chief, Dan Fraijo, helped set up an incident command system like the one used to run wildfires, with groups handling planning, logistics, financials, and operations—folks who got things moving. They planned a dignified memorial ceremony to honor the nineteen men. They also found housing for the men's out-of-town relatives during one of the busiest times of the year in the city. It was Independence Week, with Frontier Days festivities including a popular rodeo and a big parade. Thirty-five thousand visitors were expected in Prescott, about as many as lived in town.

By the time the sun rose on Monday, handmade signs had appeared in storefronts around Courthouse Square, and a spontaneous memorial materialized on the chain-link fence around Station 7. Purple balloons and American flags and nineteen flying discs, one for each of the men, hung on the fence—they'd loved playing ultimate frisbee. The memorial had votive candles and flowers of many kinds and water bottles arranged in the shape of a heart. A couple whose house the Doce Fire had threatened posted a note: "You saved our home and now you're gone. We wish we could turn it all 'round."

Cans of Coors and Copenhagen, the chewing tobacco, lay among stuffed teddy bears. So did a copy of the picture book *Love You Forever*. Inside, Anna Woyjeck had written for the son she'd lost:

> My Kevin,
>> My memories of you I will forever cherish. Those keep me going. A piece of me is missing but you will forever be in my heart.
>> I'll love you forever.
>> You'll always be my baby.
> Love,
> Mommy

In Yarnell, the fire still burned. Eighteen fire crews, eighteen engine companies, four bulldozer teams, and five water-dropping helicopters worked to stop the flames from spreading east and burning what was left of the town. A Type 1 incident command team, the most qualified, took control of the blaze by early evening. But the damage had been done.

Sharon signed check after check for the families, handing them over for delivery to firefighters who'd volunteered to serve as liaisons. She also signed a check that paid for blankets, pillows, and sheets for beds in the Yavapai College dormitories, where many of the Hotshots' relatives stayed. Tourists cleared out of booked homes voluntarily, turning them over to mourning families. The area had only so much lodging space.

The donations kept coming in. On Tuesday, envelopes with checks for amounts big and small arrived in the mail at the 100 Club. Bob Parsons, founder of GoDaddy, the Internet domain registrar, gave $120,000 through his foundation. Phoenix's Camelback District of the Boy Scouts Club of America gave $1,900, raised through a daylong car wash. The days passed. The pot of money grew. It paid debts and it paid for counseling. It paid for rent and food. It paid for medical coverage. It also paid for nineteen caskets, bought at a discount.

Butch and Cathy Hampton, husband-and-wife proprietors of the Hampton Funeral Home, needed help. They ran a small business, accustomed to handling a few burials at once, if that. They called up funeral directors they knew and didn't know, colleagues all across the state. It was Tuesday, July 2, two days after the Hotshots' deaths. Fire officials had asked Butch and Cathy to bring the guys home from the Medical Examiner's Office in Phoenix in white hearses. The couple had a single white hearse in their small fleet of hearses. They needed eighteen more.

Autopsies had revealed no surprises: smoke and burns had killed the men.

Someone from the International Association of FireFighters, a labor organization, kindly suggested hiring a national company to take care of the transport and funeral services.

Butch turned it down—"We take care of our own."

Butch and Cathy commissioned white hearses from other funeral directors. They helped identify a piece of land at the Pioneers' Home Cemetery, state-owned, and reserved it for the Hotshots. Nine of them would eventually be buried there, but all nineteen would have headstones, arranged close together, as they'd died.

On Wednesday, Fraijo, the Prescott fire chief, told Prescott's mayor, Marlin Kuykendall, that the place best suited to host the big memorial service was not in town, but in an enclosed, air-conditioned concert arena in neighboring Prescott Valley. It was too hot for an outdoor event. The mayor protested. Fraijo reminded him that Vice President Joe Biden would attend and said, "You can't put the vice president under the blazing sun." Chief Fraijo also admonished the mayor, who'd participated in most news conferences at the Prescott High School gym, but hadn't yet sat down and spoken with the Hotshots' families.

On Thursday, Prescott's Fourth of July fireworks display went on as planned at Pioneer Park, the pyrotechnics bathing the city in color and light. Firefighters stood on the sidelines at the ready, guarding the safety of the public, vigilant lest a spark ignite the brush nearby. After the show, a young man took to the microphone and announced in a booming, reverential tone, "God bless America and the nineteen Granite Mountain Hotshot firefighters!"

That night, the Yarnell Hill Fire was mostly contained. Four hundred firefighters had beaten it back. And with some rain, the odds of its growing and spreading diminished.

On Saturday, Hotshots' parents, children, and wives rode downtown atop a fire truck, opening the Frontier Days parade. The audience cheered along the street as the truck passed by. Behind it, rodeo clowns played tricks and a country-music band strummed a Don Gibson classic, "Oh Lonesome Me."

On Sunday, July 7, 2013, the white hearses lined up outside the Medical Examiner's Office in Phoenix at ten in the morning. Passenger's and driver's side doors had stickers attached— the emblem of the Granite Mountain Hotshots. On a rear side window of each hearse was taped the name of the Hotshot riding inside.

The hearses pulled out in succession. Bagpipes and drums played somberly. The crowd read the names.

The hearses strung out and turned west onto Washington Street, toward the capitol. Hundreds of people stood silently and watched them pass, despite the heat—temperatures reached 107 degrees that afternoon. Many saluted. Some dabbed at tears. Children stared from under plastic red hats handed out by Phoenix firefighters.

The procession veered north on Interstate 17, and after twenty-three miles, pulled west onto the Carefree Highway and its magnificent fields of spiky ocotillo and towering saguaro. It rolled on through Wickenburg, where $30 million of gold has been dug from the ground, and meandered along the winding back roads toward Yarnell. Stephanie Raetz, widow of Daryl Raetz, the police officer killed back in May, stood at an intersection along the way, honoring the fallen firemen—exactly what her husband would have done, she said.

From the foot of Yarnell Hill, Tim LeMieux and his wife watched, their dog sitting by them. They were living in Yarnell when the fire swept through town. "These were the men that were trying to protect my home," LeMieux said as the hearses passed.

The hearses slowed. They kept a set distance apart winding up the slope, negotiating the hairpin twists of the road up Yarnell Hill. At the top, Yarnell stood, a quilt of burned and unburned patches, disorderly stitched together. Purple ribbons fluttered from surviving trees. Banners hung from windows that hadn't shattered. Workers from APS, the state's largest electric utility, were making repairs. They took a break. They'd orchestrated their homage: they'd parked nineteen of their trucks side by side along Highway 89, flags of Arizona and the United States waving from the truck's raised booms.

The procession continued—past Peeples Valley and Skull Valley, through a corner of the Prescott National Forest, and past those guardrails the Doce Fire had melted by the edge of Prescott. It passed before Station 7. Citizens had lined the fence around it with objects and words of remembrance—"19 Forever" and "We ♥ Our Hotshots."

The Granite Mountain Hotshots were always accompanied. In each white hearse were meaningful company—alumni of the crew, blood relatives. At the funeral home, honor guards from communities near and far stood watch, day and night— firefighters, police officers, border and customs agents, Marine Corpsmen.

On Tuesday, thousands convened for the public memorial service in Prescott Valley. Vice President Joe Biden flew in from Washington accompanied by Arizona's junior senator, Jeff Flake. Sally Jewell, the US secretary of the interior, sat next to the secretary of homeland security, Janet Napolitano, a former Arizona governor. Senator John McCain was also there.

Three buses of US Forest Service employees drove up from Phoenix, among them representative members of the agency's eighty Hotshot crews. Firefighters came from Long Beach, California, from Indianapolis, from Lewisville, Texas, and from Ogden, Utah. Wildland firefighters were present in dark-green cargo pants and sun-chapped skin, along with urban firefighters in crisp dress uniforms and walrus mustaches. One of them was Sean Johnson, part of a large contingent in from New York City. They'd helped organize the ceremony, carrying out their end of a pact made after 9/11, when many Arizonan firefighters had come to Ground Zero and done whatever needed doing.

"All these years later, we're coming here to help them out," Johnson said.

Sharon Knutson-Felix was one of those Arizonans who'd spent weeks toiling amid the rubble of the World Trade Center towers, helping police officers process the guilt they felt about their survival and bearing the heavy load of helping the families left behind. Standing at the Arizona memorial that morning, Sharon recollected the grieving she'd witnessed in New York City, the mothers, wives, and children who'd welcomed her consoling presence, and accepted the burden of still more.

Darrell Willis, a wounded man, did the same. "Each and every one of them," he intoned, about the Granite Mountain Hotshots, "was an adoptive son." He spoke from a stage at the Prescott Valley arena, wearing the same dusty boots he'd worn while fighting in the Yarnell Hill Fire, where he'd taken charge of protecting structures in the town of Peeples Valley and heard that the Hotshots were gone.

Willis said, "I thank God for their bravery, courage, loyalty, professionalism, humility. I thank God for their fitness, their work ethic, their cohesion, their teamwork." The crew's leadership, he said, was made up of "the right men," men who led with confidence and mindfulness. "Take comfort in the fact that I would have followed them blindfolded into the place that they were at," he said—the place where they'd died.

In 2011, Willis had accompanied the Hotshots on a run to Colorado—he used to fill in when they were down a man. On their way out of a fire, already driving to the next fire, they'd stopped by Storm King Mountain, where fourteen firefighters had died in 1994, trapped by a wave of flame. The men had hiked a trail that followed the fallen firefighters' path. They'd talked along the way, distilling the challenges and studying the conditions contributing to the deaths.

Willis shared the story at the memorial service, his gaze on the grieving families before him, as if he were speaking to them alone: "They were truly committed to returning to you after every assignment. But there was another plan."

The mournful routine rolled on, minute by minute—a bell rang, a name was read, a family stood up and received a folded American flag and a Pulaski from the hands of a firefighter.

Vice President Biden spoke of the men he'd never met, but admired—"nineteen ordinary men who did extraordinary things."

At home that night, Juliann Ashcraft gathered her four children and told them, not for the first time, that Daddy was in heaven and wasn't coming back.

• • •

Butch and Cathy Hampton, the funeral directors, had kept careful notes on a whiteboard, highlighting the schedule of every private memorial service and burial, so none would coincide. The men had many friends in common, and those friends might want to say several goodbyes.

The day after the big public memorial saw six private ceremonies, at churches, by gravesides. One, by Granite Basin Lake, a reservoir in the Prescott National Forest, honored Eric Marsh. The lake carried special significance for Amanda: she and Eric had spent hours riding its trails on horseback on June 17, the day before Eric had returned to active duty as division supervisor on the Doce Fire, and also her thirty-eighth birthday. Outside the funeral home, firefighters from Milwaukee carried his flag-draped casket to a fire truck. The firefighters wore full dress uniforms of thick polyester, suitable for Missouri's colder weather. It was still early, not even seven in the morning, but the heat and humidity brought by the monsoon season had settled in. The firefighters sweated stoically, carrying on with requisite dignity.

The Heights Church hosted two services that day, for Travis Turbyfill and for Clayton Whitted. Willis spoke of Travis's intention to leave the Granite Mountain Hotshots at the end of the 2013 season and focus on his family. He and Willis had agreed on a plan that would keep Travis nearby, employed by the Wildland Division and working with the crew. He was a Mr. Fix-It, and the Hotshots had felt grateful that he could repair their banged-up buggies, tune up their saws, sharpen their tools. Willis had had to get the position approved by City Hall—a challenge he'd deemed worth fighting for.

Whitted left behind a long and detailed list of planned home repairs—a renovated bathroom, a spruced-up backyard. He'd calculated that the work would occupy his spare time through October 2015.

At Andrew Ashcraft's remembrance, John Mellencamp's "Small Town" played and a slide show rolled on a big screen, displaying the small-town life he cherished. Juliann had hoped to move to the Florida coast, but Andrew felt content right where he was, in Prescott.

At Wade Parker's funeral, Todd League, pastor at Word of Life Assembly of God, made people laugh and cry, recalling Wade's giddiness during a session of premarriage counseling—a frank talk about sex. Wade couldn't wipe the grin from his face. His fiancée, Alicia, had kept her eyes on the floor.

Two hundred miles south, in Marana, Arizona, marines clicked their heels and raised their white-gloved hands in salute after lowering Billy Warneke into his grave. Roxanne stared ahead, rubbing her pregnant belly.

On the other side of the country, from the Senate floor in the Capitol, Senator McCain defined Billy and Wade and Andrew and Clayton and Travis and Eric, and the thirteen others who had died with them, as "men to emulate if you have the courage and character to live as decently and honorably as they lived."

In Yarnell, Highway 89 reopened, evacuees returned. By July 11, 2013, the deadly fire was fully contained, at last.

AN END, AND
NEW BEGINNINGS

JULIANN ASHCRAFT STOOD IN FRONT OF THE YAVAPAI County Courthouse. Its granite façade, quarried from the mountains around Prescott, glistened in the bright sunlight. Seven years earlier, Andrew had proposed to her in the courthouse plaza, in the cool shade of tall American elms. Four weeks earlier, she'd buried Andrew up the street.

That morning, Juliann had a lawyer by her side and reporters recording her every word. She offered thanks "for all that this community has done, for all that the citizens of the world have done." The families of the Granite Mountain Hotshots had received tens of thousands of dollars in donations, and Andrew's four children had been inundated with cards and gifts. People had shipped them so many stuffed animals in the mail that she'd run out of storage space.

Juliann thanked her newfound family of firefighters, and the firemen who'd accompanied her oldest son, Ryder, to his first day of kindergarten.

Then, she took off the gloves:

"There were nineteen men who perished in that fire." Juliann's voice trembled. "For whatever reason, there are people who feel that some of them don't deserve to be treated in the way that the others are."

After deaths, funerals, and memorials; after the confusion and disbelief of those first days with no husband, no father for her children, Juliann had thought about the future. The prospects worried her and infuriated her, too. There had been so much talk about the Granite Mountain Hotshots' esprit de corps, the unity they'd embodied even as they'd died. But then the bureaucratic reality of their unequal standing surfaced. Six of the Hotshots were full-time employees of the City of Prescott. Thirteen were not. That split them into two benefit categories. The survivors of the full-timers would get monthly pension payments, life-insurance payouts, health-insurance coverage. The others were to receive none of that.

Juliann weighed her financial predicament. She was a stay-at-home mother with four kids to clothe, feed, keep healthy, send to school and college. The unfairness of the benefit categories angered her. Those nineteen men had done the same hard work, faced the same dangers, and toiled the same number of hours, on- and off-season, protecting the same now-grateful citizenry. Why should they be treated differently after all had died together?

She had called on Mayor Marlin Kuykendall to make things right. He'd refused to meet with her. To a newspaper reporter, he had said, "She's a neat little lady. . . . But money took hold in this situation real fast." On online message boards, Juliann became a target of criticism, a portrait of greed. On the streets, some people glared at her. Others criticized her openly, as her kids listened.

Juliann decided the time had come to move out of Prescott. She craved anonymity for her kids' sake. She found a home 140 miles away, near three of her siblings and a playground, but far from everything that was familiar. The new home became her way station, a safe place where she could figure out what would come next.

She began a fight for benefits. The City of Prescott's lawyers asserted that the number of hours that Andrew had worked and his leadership position didn't determine his benefit status. It was solely his job classification on payroll records, that ambiguous title: full-time seasonal.

Juliann filed a claim against the city. The city questioned if wildland firefighters were a category of "municipal firefighter," an unquestioned label for those who rode on red trucks and put out structure fires—the guys on "the floor," as they put it. Remarkably, a lawyer for the city argued that the Hotshots were more like parks workers or perhaps janitors, whose jobs entailed only limited exposure to risk. A local board for the state's Public Safety Retirement System heard the two sides and voted 4 to 1 in Juliann's favor, agreeing that her family should get the same benefits as those paid out to the families of the full-time Hotshots, the same benefits given to families of every structural firefighter on the city's payroll. There was no denying, board members said, that Andrew had earned them, and no denying that the Hotshots were also firefighters, even though the board's decision only applied to him.

Mayor Kuykendall cast the only dissenting vote.

On the first anniversary of the tragedy, Juliann joined eighteen other families at the Pioneers' Home Cemetery for an intimate memorial. Bells at the courthouse tolled nineteen times at 4:42 p.m., considered the official time of death for the Hotshots. A moment of silence ensued. The Prescott Veterans Memorial Pipers played "Amazing Grace."

On the following day, July 1, 2014, a majority of the City Council voted to appeal the board's decision favoring Juliann. Mayor Kuykendall recused himself from the vote.

The case landed on the docket of Judge David Mackey of Yavapai County Superior Court. Juliann brought her children to the hearing. Halfway through it, Ryder lay down on her lap and fell asleep.

Andrew's mother, Deborah Pfingston, sat on the bench behind them, surrounded by alumni of the Granite Mountain Hotshots. They were Andrew's brothers-in-arms. Deborah had prepared herself for the prospect of losing a child, but she'd never imagined losing Andrew. Her older son, T.J., had worried her. He was a sargeant in the US Army and had twice spent a year on duty overseas, in Iraq and Afghanistan. T.J. lived by the principle of selfless service, one of the Seven Core Army Values, a soldier's moral guide, learned during basic combat training— "the commitment to go a little further, endure a little longer, and look a little closer to see how he or she can add to the effort"; a commitment "larger than just one person."

In court, Deborah looked at the young men around her, their bodies toughened by the elements, their hands callused by the hardships of a Hotshot's trade. She realized how selfless they'd been, and remained—soldiers of their own accord. These men were grieving, too, she thought.

Outside their tight circles, few seemed to notice.

Judge Mackey gave the sides ninety minutes to state their

cases. Juliann was represented by Patrick J. McGroder III, a son of Buffalo, New York, known for his elegant dress suits—he has a soft spot for Armani—and persuasive arguments. He'd forced Ford Motor Company to fix Crown Victoria police cars so they wouldn't explode on impact. He'd spared a Catholic bishop from serving time in prison despite the bishop's role in a fatal hit-and-run. That day, McGroder summarized for the judge Andrew's schedule with the Granite Mountain Hotshots: He'd labored for ten straight months in 2012 and every month in 2013, averaging fifty-five hours on the clock each week. Officially, Andrew may not have been a full-time firefighter. But, McGroder said, he was undoubtedly a firefighter who worked full-time.

From the bench, Judge Mackey ruled that Prescott had the "responsibility" to pay the benefits Juliann had asked for.

Months later, two other widows, Roxanne Warneke and Amanda Misner, waged their own fights against the city. Their husbands were rookies in 2013; Roxanne and Amanda based their claims on the number of hours Billy and Sean would have worked, during and after fire season, had they not died in Yarnell. McGroder, who also represented them, maintained that Billy and Sean would have toiled enough hours to qualify for the state's public safety retirement system and its generous package of death benefits. McGroder presented his argument before the same local board that had sided with Juliann. Again, the board agreed with him. This time, Mayor Kuykendall voted in favor of the families. The City of Prescott did not appeal.

None of the other families who could have brought a case against the city chose to do so. None of them wanted to poke an open wound, pick a fight. After deaths, funerals, and memorials, one bigger and farther than the next—in Colorado Springs; Boise, Idaho; and Annapolis, Maryland—honoring the Hotshots and all other firefighters killed in the line of duty in 2013, they were ready to grieve in private and to move on, however they could.

• • •

Death hadn't scared Billy Warneke. In the few conversations when he'd opened up to Roxanne about his time as a sniper in Iraq, Billy had spoken about death as an inevitability—"You live, you die, that's the way it goes," he'd said. He'd returned from war in one piece, though he always seemed to sleep with one eye open—always alert, always mindful of the people around him, always assessing his surroundings. Billy had been cautious and deliberate about his actions, and that's why Roxanne had never worried about him. He knew risk.

They used to hike the federal lands behind the trailer home they shared in Avra Valley, sometimes hunting, sometimes wandering. Billy had taught Roxanne to shoot and bought her a Remington 700 tactical rifle with a custom-made scope. She'd used the rifle to bag deer. Together, they'd spray-painted the rifle with khaki-and-green camouflage. She'd loved their adventures and envied his fearlessness. Billy went parasailing, skydiving, deep-sea diving, and bull riding—one thing he'd said he'd never do again. He was terrified of being gored by a bull, he'd told her. But he didn't mind sharks. Billy wanted to swim with them someday, and to hunt lions in Africa, and alligators in Louisiana.

After Yarnell, Roxanne got so angry at him for leaving her she swung a sledgehammer and tore a hole through a wall in their trailer, pregnant belly and all. "Why did I have to be supportive of him?" she'd lamented. Billy had asked what she thought of his fighting wildfires, and she'd told him to go for it. She'd trusted his judgment. She regretted that.

She talked herself into keeping it together after he was gone, for the sake of her daughter. His daughter. She read books on bereavement, which all discussed destructive things that grieving people do—out-of-control drinking, drugs. Those weren't options for her. She was straitlaced and had a child growing inside her.

The baby, Billie Grace Warneke, was born on December 19, 2013, almost six months after her father's death. By the first anniversary, she and Roxanne had moved into a new home. Through one of its ministries, a church in Tucson called Victory Worship Center had collected donations, bought materials, and coordinated teams of firefighters who'd built the house. Dan Klement, a fire captain in the Golder Ranch Fire District, nearby, ran a tiling business on the side and installed the floors at Roxanne's home free of charge. He'd first met Roxanne on that fateful night in 2013, when he'd knocked on her door and told her that Billy was dead.

Roxanne donated the trailer to the church in Tucson—her way of saying thanks. Church members parked it elsewhere and finished the renovation work that Billy had started, repurposing the trailer as a refuge home for women fleeing abusive relationships.

Roxanne's new house occupies the lot where the trailer had stood. Out front, nineteen purple granite bars are mounted on a waist-high circular wall, a memorial to Billy and his crew. Inside the house, on a console table, is a photo of Billy, and the flag that had draped his casket, folded and encased in a triangle of wood and glass. Billie Grace, fresh out of diapers, stops in front of the table, points at Billy's picture, and says, "Dada."

She loves blueberries, as her father had. And she loves to sway to Lee Greenwood's rendition of "God Bless the USA," Billy's favorite song.

After Billy died, Roxanne vowed to finish his bucket list. She has to muster the courage to face lions and alligators in places unknown and wants to wait until her daughter is old enough to join her. But she will hunt where Billy wanted to hunt, and she will swim with sharks.

Until then, Roxanne will keep busy shooting the rattlesnakes that seek the shade of her front porch in the Arizona heat. She fires at them with a .22 revolver that Billy had given her. It had belonged to his grandfather.

She refuses to let grief paralyze her.

Amanda Misner has tried to gain control of her grief, too, but has found it tough. Two years after the Hotshots' deaths, she longs for Sean with the same intensity; time has only reaffirmed how much she misses her man. She has kept him alive on her Facebook page, posting pictures of them together, sharing long-ago memories as if they'd just happened, writing love notes to him in the past tense.

> You were more than just a lover, a husband, a father, you were my soul mate, my other half, my best friend, and I miss you so much Sean Michael Misner. You were my rock, the person who picked me up when I was down. The person who wouldn't give up on me, even when I wanted to give up on myself. I need you! I don't just want you, I literally need you. The fact is that I don't know how to live, only survive is because I don't know how to live without you.

She moved back to California—closer to her mother, and to Sean's mother, and back to the life she'd left behind after she and Sean met. But something inside her had irretrievably changed.

One spring day in 2015, she wrote:

The thing is, I'm not trying to find the old me. She is gone, she left on 6/30/13. For a long time I was trying to find that person I used to be. I can't, because a big part of that person was Sean. I am now trying to figure out who it is I want to be. It truly is a day-to-day struggle.

She got green highlights on her auburn hair, played in an occasional softball game, and took up running. She got puckering lips tattooed on her left shoulder, where Sean liked to kiss her, and his full name inked on her left forearm. She pledged to dedicate her life to their son. She named him Sean Jaxon Herbert Misner, in honor of his father and paternal grandfather, both firefighters, both gone before he came into this world.

Amanda Misner spent days cooped up at home, in pajamas, potty-training Jaxon and living with the ups and downs of depression. One day, she woke up and felt like dressing up. It might have been the phone calls and private messages of encouragement she'd received from Roxanne, or the tactful advice from her mother, or her own realization that she had to pick herself up. It might have been an up before another down—she didn't dwell on it much. Whatever it was, she seized it. She put on high heels and laughed at herself because she could barely walk in heels; she's more of a sweatpants-and-sneakers kind of girl. Then, she got in her car and went to Walmart.

Tiffany Rose closed off the world after Anthony was gone. They weren't married, and that put Tiffany in the "other" category—someone other than a wife or a mother, a woman without legal or blood ties to any of the fallen Hotshots, yet still very much part of their story. She'd adopted Anthony's last name after he was gone so that it would match that of their girl, born on October 10, 2013, the day Anthony would have turned twenty-four. Tiffany named her Willow Mae.

Days before he'd died, Anthony had bumped into a Granite Mountain alumnus, Shane Arollado, at a gym in Prescott. They'd joined the crew together, in 2012, Shane's only season. Anthony had approached Shane in the weight room and showed him a sonogram picture of Anthony's baby that he had stored in his cracked iPhone. Shane told Anthony that Tiffany could call anytime if she needed help while Anthony was away.

After Anthony died, Tiffany did just that.

Shane rode in the white hearse that brought Anthony from the medical examiner's office in Phoenix to the funeral home in Prescott. He handed Tiffany a Pulaski at the big public memorial in Prescott Valley. He accompanied her to a private ceremony in Beach Park, Illinois, Anthony's hometown.

The two grew close, closer than close friends are.

Tiffany, Shane, and Willow moved into a rental home together in Prescott Valley. Willow calls Shane Dada. She calls the other man she sees in the pictures on her bedroom wall Dada, too. Tiffany tells her, "That's your other dada," but leaves it at that. Willow is still too young to comprehend. But she will. "I'm going to tell her all about Anthony," Tiffany said. "But Shane is the dad who's raising her. He is the dad she knows."

Tiffany and Shane married on September 12, 2015. She added his surname to Anthony's surname, wrapping past and present into her name, Tiffany Rose-Arollado.

Stephanie Turbyfill's older girl, Brooklyn, started asking Stephanie for another dad around the second anniversary of Travis's death. Stephanie smiled, not only because Brooklyn's question made the future easier for her—she did hope to let another good man into their life someday—but also because it meant that Brooklyn was emerging unbroken from the depths of her own grief. Stephanie had never imagined a little girl could suffer as much as Brooklyn had, that her expressions of sorrow could be so raw. Brooklyn and Travis had shared a deep connection—she was Daddy's girl, the first baby he'd held in those big, rough hands of his, the first girl he'd rocked to sleep. For months after he was gone, Brooklyn dashed inside her room, slammed the door, and wailed, "My daddy wants me! My daddy wants me!" Each time, Stephanie felt as if she'd lost a piece of herself. She had her own grief to contend with, but had pushed it aside, shelved it somewhere deep inside her, to focus on Brooklyn, and on Brynley, who was only a baby when Travis had died.

It took Brooklyn a long time to warm to other men in the family. She refused her uncles. She refused Stephanie's father, the grandpa she had adored. It was as if something inside Brooklyn had become wary after her father was gone, Stephanie said. Telling her that Travis had died—that her young, handsome, strong superhero of a dad had died—had been hard. Brooklyn was old enough to understand absence, but not dying, other than that it meant her daddy would never come back to her.

With Brynley, the process was different. She was eighteen months old when Travis died, and Stephanie knew no way to explain death to a baby. When Travis had been out on fires, Brynley sometimes fixed her gaze at the door, as if waiting for him to return. Eventually, he had.

She seemed okay with not having Travis at home, perhaps because she felt he'd walk through that door at some point, as he'd always done. She still turned her eyes to it, waiting.

One day, after her second birthday, Brynley pointed to a

family picture that hung in the living room and said, "My daddy. I like him. Coming home."

"No, honey, Daddy isn't coming home. Daddy is in heaven now," Stephanie told her.

Heaven. Somehow, it had become a synonym of dying, and also of hope, for those who believed in it. Stephanie was sure that in heaven the ones who were gone and the ones who'd been left behind would meet again.

That night, she tucked in her girls, planted kisses on their foreheads, and retreated to her room.

The next morning, Brynley walked in there and asked, "My daddy died?"

Stephanie looked at her, equal parts stunned and relieved. Her baby had made it simpler than she'd anticipated. "Yes," Stephanie told Brynley. "Daddy is dead."

Taking care of her girls—"my husband's children" is how she describes them—is what has kept her going.

Amanda Marsh removed the ring she'd given Eric from her finger, and then the ring he'd given her. She'd met a man who knew to laugh at the same silly things Eric Marsh used to laugh at, and who brought children—his own—into her life.

Juliann Ashcraft had to get away to start the next phase of her life. She paid $27,500 for a 1983 Greyhound bus, equipped with eight beds, a kitchen, and a small bathroom. She took her oldest children out of school and headed north—into New Mexico, then Texas, Tennessee, Missouri, and Oklahoma, where they stopped by the Oklahoma City bombing memorial and helped families gather what was left of their belongings after a tornado tore up their homes.

In each state, they visited a person or group of people who had donated to the Hotshots' families—a woman who'd painted the men's names on ceramic tiles, a man who'd sketched their portraits, a Hotshot crew who'd sent the kids T-shirts celebrating their dad and the job he had.

People had called Juliann greedy so many times she'd started to believe them. Then, a boy died of cancer in her neighborhood, and she joined a group who'd volunteered to organize the funeral. Her task was ironing thirty white tablecloths; she ironed late into the night, and that got her thinking about how much money and time strangers had given to help her family and the families of the eighteen other men.

"I needed to give them a hug," she'd said.

She also wanted to teach her children a lesson in gratitude. After each visit, they wrote thank-you cards together to the donors, and she spoke to her kids about the importance of caring for others. She feared they'd grow up feeling entitled because of all they'd received without much sense of where it had come from. They could no longer watch Andrew pull on his ash-smudged pants, lace up his dust-caked boots, and leave home for work. They no longer had their father as an example. But she would teach them the value of hard work, somehow.

Desiree Steed had a child, a daughter, on June 17, 2015. The girl's father, Eric Montejano, coached Desiree's two other children, Jesse's children, in gymnastics.

Desiree and Eric named their girl Cora—a homage to a dear great-aunt of Desiree's, and because the name matches those of her half siblings, Caden and Cambria, which also start with the letter C.

Cora's middle name is Grace and has a connection to her parents' story.

Eric had known Jesse and Desiree's kids before he'd got to know Desiree beyond hurried greetings at pickup and drop-off.

Eric was married and Desiree a widow when they had their first meaningful conversation, toward the end of 2013. His marriage was ending by then. That summer, after just a few months together, his wife had filed for divorce. He and Desiree faced rumors and criticism when they started dating, but she paid them no heed. "When you know it's right, you know it right away," Desiree said. She'd felt it when she'd met Jesse, and she felt it when she met Eric. She also knew not to cling to any illusion of endless tomorrows. She'd learned that everything can change in a moment, or with a lightning strike on a parched mountainside.

The middle name Grace, Desiree said, "is our wish that the people around us will extend a little grace our way."

She felt that in her union to Eric, she regained a sense of being in control of her own story. "There's a certain number of people who are in love with this romantic idea of me and the other wives being sad, and alone, and in this widow status forever," she said. "I refuse to do it."

She hasn't abandoned her past, though. A poster-size portrait of Jesse greets visitors in her new family's new home. Cambria talks to her portrait often, telling her father about her day, and the excitement of preschool graduation and her first day of kindergarten. Caden usually starts his stories with "Remember that day when Daddy . . ." He reminds Desiree of Jesse.

Cora's room has lavender walls with white butterflies etched above her crib. Her full name is Cora Grace Montejano.

Desiree and Eric had held a commitment ceremony in their backyard, but had never married. Marriage, she said, would nullify some of the benefits Jesse's children had been receiving since his death.

"My last name," she said, "is still Steed."

•••

Deborah Pfingston has kept detailed notes on yellow pads and in electronic files. She has scrutinized the documents released since her son's death in the Yarnell Hill Fire, dissected investigative reports, examined the theories and suspicions ardently discussed in online boards. She spoke with anyone who asked and had questions for everyone. She hiked the Weaver Mountains again and again, following the footsteps of the Granite Mountain Hotshots, looking for answers. Who'd abandoned those boys—and her boy—in the blazing wild? Why had Andrew died?

She misses his calls, his voice, his teasing. She misses their morning coffees at Wildflower Bread Company, halfway between her house and his, off the main road into Prescott. She misses his small gestures—his surprise visits, the autumn leaves he'd brought for her from New York's Central Park, the random keys he'd added to their collection. She misses watching him whiz by her on his skateboard, happy and carefree.

She's doing okay, but is still sad. "There will be no filling the hole. There's no moving on."

Deborah and her husband, Jerry, had been together for seventeen years when Andrew died; Jerry has been there whenever she needed someone with whom to hike those hills in Yarnell, to interpret the latest rumor she'd heard, and to weave together the leads she'd gathered, trying to build a coherent sequence of events that preceded the Hotshots' deaths. Yet two years after the fire, Deborah still longed for "truth, transparency, and accountability," she said. She could still not understand why the incident command team running the Yarnell Hill Fire on June 30, 2013, had not been fully staffed, or how the people running the fire—all of them experienced, all of them old friends—could have missed the signs that they had lost control of the blaze.

On a cool midspring morning, with clouds like cotton balls dotting the sky, Deborah and Jerry drove to the high school in Chino Valley where Danny and Michelle Parker were hosting the third annual Wade S. Parker Memorial Baseball Game. The event memorializes one of Andrew's fire brothers and raises scholarship money for graduating seniors interested in firefighting careers. It's one way Danny and Michelle found of honoring Wade's passions, of keeping his joy alive.

Deborah and Michelle had never met until their sons left them. They have forged a tight bond over their shared grief, rooted in tragedy but proceeding in friendship.

•••

Darrell Willis had ruminated on and prayed about the loss. He'd felt the deaths of the Granite Mountain Hotshots weigh on him, cloud his mind, haunt him in his sleep. He'd held up well for a while—in public, at least. He'd gracefully and patiently shared his memories of the nineteen men, as individuals and as the unit they'd become under those leaders of distinct yet complementary styles, Eric Marsh and Jesse Steed. Willis had consoled parents and widows, standing up against the city to help them— not because he'd been blinded by their sadness, or his, but because he'd thought it right. He'd tactfully handled questions and criticism from city officials for years and tamed Marsh when he'd lost his cool—for Marsh's sake, and the sake of the crew.

Twenty-nine years at the Prescott Fire Department had made Willis a savvy navigator of the perils and opportunities brought by wave after wave of political leaders, an expert at when and how to pick fights. He'd harnessed broad support for the creation of the Wildland Division, raising the threat of wildfire to the level it deserved. He'd steered the division into creating the first and only municipal Hotshot crew in the country, arming the city against the threat.

But the time had come to part ways. He had his reasons—unforgiving reasons this time.

In his office at Station 7 on March 9, 2015, he slid on his reading glasses, set his fingers to the keyboard of his desktop computer, and typed a letter to the chief of the fire department, Dennis Light:

> I write to inform you that I am resigning from my position as Division Chief.

Since the deaths in Yarnell, residents of Prescott had wondered what would become of the Granite Mountain Hotshots—could this be the end? Willis had been assured that the city would at least maintain its Wildland Division and also its commitment to prepare against fires in the forests surrounding it. The signs pointed toward another outcome, though, and Willis could read them well. In closed-door meetings of city officials, discussions revolved around questions of money, not necessity. Everyone seemed focused on the costs and liabilities the city would face if the crew became active again, and if deaths in the line of duty happened again. Deaths in the line of duty had happened before that dark day in Yarnell, and they have happened since:

On August 16, 2013, Jesse Trader died when the water truck he'd been driving tumbled down a rural road's embankment outside the Big Windy Complex, in southwest Oregon. He was nineteen.

On August 30, 2013, Token Adams, engine captain for a fire

crew in New Mexico's Jemez Ranger District, died after crashing his all-terrain vehicle while checking on a lightning-sparked fire. He was forty-one.

On September 27, 2013, Mark Urban, a veteran smoke jumper with the Bureau of Land Management in Boise, died after his parachute malfunctioned during a training exercise. He was forty.

In Prescott, someone raised the possibility of contracting with private crews to do the cleanup work the Hotshots used to do in the winter and leave the task of fighting fires to the feds. The idea gained traction.

Willis wrote:

> It seems the handwriting is on the wall, and that the City now wants to take greater risk than any year previous by doing away with the Division that mitigates this great risk of a Catastrophic Wildfire.

He quoted from the Gettysburg Address:

> It is rather for us to be here dedicated to the great task remaining before us—that from these honored dead we take increased devotion to that cause for which they here gave the last full measure of devotion—that we here highly resolve that these dead shall not have died in vain.

He signed, using the motto that Eric Marsh had chosen for his Granite Mountain Hotshots:

> *Esse quam videri.*

To be, rather than to seem.

AUTHOR'S NOTE

T HIS IS A WORK OF NONFICTION, AND A LABOR OF
love. The stories in this book are real, the events are real,
and all of the people presented in these pages are real. When I
wrote that a person felt, thought, wondered, or recalled something, the feeling, idea, question, or memory was either described
to me directly by the person to whom it is attributed or pulled
from transcripts of interviews they gave to investigators who
examined the Yarnell Hill Fire and its nineteen fatalities. I
extracted some direct quotes and dialogue from these interviews,
and from radio communications I reviewed and transcribed.
Other direct quotes and dialogues came from my interviews with
parents, wives, and friends of the Granite Mountain Hotshots;
firefighters; and residents of Yarnell and Peeples Valley, the central Arizona communities affected by the conflagration.

I agreed to change one name: of an inmate on the first team

to respond to the Yarnell Hill Fire, a crew out of the Arizona State Prison Complex–Lewis.

This book tells the stories of nineteen men I couldn't meet. To learn about them, I interviewed members of all nineteen families, and also the men's coworkers, supervisors, roommates, and best friends. I traveled to five states to meet them, logged more than a hundred hours of recorded interviews with them, and filled seventeen notebooks with information and observations from these and other interactions. I was graciously received and sometimes slept in the homes where these men had grown up. I played with the children they'd fathered, and hugged the women, parents, and stepparents they'd left behind. I'm grateful beyond words for the time, patience, and trust these families have bestowed upon me so I can tell this story fully and candidly. No one was paid. No one who talked to me asked for anything in return. None of the families had an advance look at the manuscript.

Notes detail sources. All errors are mine.

I listened to the Granite Mountain Hotshots' favorite bands and musicians on my many, many drives between Phoenix, where I lived while writing this book, and Prescott, the crew's home base—Ted Nugent, Third Day, Paul Simon, Daft Punk, Waylon Jennings, Lee Greenwood, the Kinks. I had access to a diary that one of the firefighters kept and personal writings by three others. I read some of the books they had read, and I particularly enjoyed the ones that Chris MacKenzie and Garret Zuppiger favored—Shel Silverstein's *Where the Sidewalk Ends* and Edward Abbey's *Desert Solitaire*, respectively. Chris, Zupp, you have great taste.

At the Arizona Wildfire and Incident Management Academy in Prescott, I successfully completed basic training in 2014 and returned the following year for another course, on the intrinsic and tricky connection between fire and weather. The Granite Mountain Hotshots' superintendent, Eric Marsh, had helped found the academy, and many of the crew's members had studied or taught there. In the classes I took, I walked baby steps in their shoes, gripping and wielding the tools of their trade, and cutting fire line in the wild, wearing the sort of flame-resistant shirts and pants they wore, similar leather gloves, similar insulated boots. I did that while carrying a loaded backpack and a four-pound fire shelter that I practiced deploying, as they had.

I had first learned about the Granite Mountain Hotshots on June 30, 2013. Next-door neighbors were over for some pizza and wine when my husband read on Twitter about the fire crew's entrapment and shared the news with me. I did what I had to do: packed a bag, jumped in my car, and drove toward the town where the fire that had killed them still burned. It was my duty as Phoenix Bureau chief for *The New York Times*. I led the newspaper's coverage of the story, and the story stayed with me. I knew, from early on, that to explain the great loss would lead far beyond assigning blame for the fatalities. In firefighting, decisions are based on probabilities, on the best information at hand, and they're made quickly, very quickly.

The Granite Mountain Hotshots were justly confident in their abilities and leadership, ambitious in their goals, and focused on going home safe after every run. They had chosen to live on a razor's edge, helped one another elect and survive constructive risk, and rewarded one another with well-founded guardianship and devotion. They have sustained my respect because of the straightforwardness of their lives, the beauty of their work, and the depth of their characters. They believed in the value of working together, in the power of cohesion, and in the endurance of brotherhood, concepts whose meaning I understand better through them. They embraced a culture of loyalty that Eric Marsh had built through a careful selection, hiring a team of people he felt could work together as one.

The Granite Mountain Hotshots loved one another, loved what they did, and chose to stay together until the very end.

ACKNOWLEDGMENTS

My deepest gratitude goes to the families of the nineteen Granite Mountain Hotshots: Juliann Ashcraft, Deborah and Jerry Pfingston, T. J. Ashcraft, Linda and David Caldwell, Claire Caldwell, Leah Fine, Mike and Janice MacKenzie, Suzanne Wagner, Bruce and Judy Lindquist, Emilee Ashby, Karen Norris, Joanna Norris, Ryan DeFord, Stephen DeFord, Tripp Carter, Connie Andersen, Autumn Andersen, Stephanie Turbyfill, John and Mary Percin, Bobby Percin, Matt Percin, Amanda Marsh, John and Jane Marsh, Danny and Michelle Parker, D. J. Parker, Joe and Anna Woyjeck, Maddie Woyjeck, Bobby Woyjeck, Amanda Misner, Tammy and Ron Misner, Tim McElwee, Tiffany Rose-Arollado, Desiree Steed, Taunya Steed, Cassidy Steed, Kristi Whitted, Carl Whitted, Gayemarie Ekker, Marsena Thurston Stevens and Roxanne Warneke. You have a very special place in my heart.

ACKNOWLEDGMENTS

Tony Sciacca, Don Howard, Mike Pickett, P. J. Lingley, Dan Pearson, and Josh Miller welcomed me at the Arizona Wildfire and Incident Management Academy and made sure I worked hard, learned much, and had a good time while at it. Frank "Pancho" Auza, Darby Starr, and Brad Pitassi satisfied my many curiosities about the job. Darrell Willis, Duane Steinbrink, Marty Cole, Tim McElwee, Doug Harwood, Phil "Mondo" Maldonado, Dan "Boon" McCarty, Brandon Bunch, Justin Kaoni, Ted Ralston, Todd Rhines, Bettina Rodriguez, Matt Demenna, and Conrad Jackson taught me what it means to be a Granite Mountain Hotshot.

Greg Smith, Mike Jones, Kirk Warren, Evan Whetten, Andrew Williams, and the other member of the Lewis Crew who worked in Yarnell. Thank you for making sure I had the full story.

Mark Kramer, my mentor and dear friend, held my hand, sharpened my focus, and used his brilliant skills as a narrative writing coach to improve each of the chapters I wrote. Rebekah Zemansky, my assistant, transcribed my interviews, researched and checked historical facts, and asked a lot of smart questions as this book evolved. Mike Saucier, my husband, never wavered in his support for me and his trust in me. You're my rock, Mike.

Christopher Callahan and Kristin Gilger, dean and associate dean of the Walter Cronkite School of Journalism and Mass Communication at Arizona State University, gave me a home from which to write this book. Thank you, and thanks also to Len Downie Jr., who took time to read my manuscript; Peter Bhatia, who always answered my questions and listened to my stories; and Leslie-Jean Thornton, whose collation of tweets about the Yarnell Hill Fire on June 30, 2013, was crucial to my understanding of how—and how quickly—news of the fatalities spread on social media.

Stephen J. Pyne, one of this country's foremost fire historians and a prolific author, shared his immense knowledge with me and painstakingly reviewed my writings to make sure I got it right. Tom Swetnam, director of the Laboratory of Tree-Ring Research at the University of Arizona, patiently explained the centuries-old cycles of fire in the wild. Richard Wrangham, the Ruth B. Moore Professor of Biological Anthropology at Harvard, welcomed me at his home in Cambridge, Massachusetts—on a cold, snowy morning two days before Christmas—for an engaging discussion about fire and its role in human evolution.

Michelle Ye Hee Lee took time to ensure I had the right chronology for her tweets from the fire. John F. McCullagh graciously allowed me to use one of his poems in this book. John Dougherty made sure I never missed any newly released public document.

I learned about fire and weather from Valerie Meyers, manager of the fire weather program at the National Weather Service in Phoenix, and Brian Klimowski, meteorologist-in-charge at the National Weather Service station in Bellemont, Arizona. I learned how fire crews and resources are managed from some great people at the National Interagency Fire Center in Boise, and my special thanks go to John Glenn, Fire and Aviation Operations division chief for the Bureau of Land Management, and Aitor Bidaburu, fire program specialist for the US Fire Administration, members of the National Multi-Agency Coordination Group; Ed Delgado, national program manager for Predictive Services; Herb Arnold, leader of the fire center's Remote Sensing/Fire Weather Support unit; and Mike Tuominen, chief of its Incident Communications Operations. Also, thanks to Andy Delmas, fire management officer at the Boise Fire District, who explained to me the challenges of fighting wildfires so close to homes.

ACKNOWLEDGMENTS

Chuck and Leah Tidey put me up at their home in Yarnell and, along with Kathy Montgomery, introduced me to many people there and in Peeples Valley, helping bring an important aspect of this story to life. Joy Collura and Sonny Gilligan guided me on several hikes along the path traveled by the Granite Mountain Hotshots and shared recollections of their encounter with the men on the day they died. Katie Cornelius, a volunteer curator for the Prescott Fire Department, generously shared notes and documentation she had collected for an exhibit commemorating the first anniversary of the fatalities.

I'm thankful to my employer, *The New York Times*—and, in particular, to Janet Elder, Alison Mitchell, Sam Sifton, and Ethan Bronner—for believing in me, believing in this book, and giving me the time I needed to write it. I thank Susan Edgerley and Brent Staples for their kind guidance and wise advice, and my friends Jack Healy, Ian Lovett, Ray Rivera, and Dan Frosch for expertly and compassionately helping me cover the Yarnell Hill Fire when it happened, and for cheering me on as I wrote this book.

In my agent, Eric Lupfer, of William Morris Entertainment, I found a perfect champion for this book. At Flatiron Books, I found a perfect home for it. Bob Miller and Colin Dickerman shared my vision for this project and were nothing short of devoted to making it shine. I thank Colin and James Melia for their surgical editing and careful choices. I thank Flatiron's publicist, Marlena Bittner, and its associate publisher, Liz Keenan, who crafted a stellar promotion and marketing campaign for this book.

Finally, I thank my parents, Daniel and Vera, for raising me right.

CHRONOLOGY

June 28, 2013

4:30 p.m.—Granite Mountain Hotshots report for duty at the West Spruce Fire in the Prescott National Forest.

5:40 p.m.—First calls reporting lightning strikes, fire on Yarnell Hill.

10:07 p.m.—Forecast for Saturday, June 29, at the fire area calls for a hot (102–104 degrees) and dry (10–11 percent relative humidity) day, with likelihood of thunderstorms and gusty winds.

11 p.m.—Granite Mountain Hotshots wrap up a day's work at the West Spruce Fire.

June 29, 2013

6 a.m.—Granite Mountain Hotshots report for duty for the Mount Josh Fire in the Prescott National Forest.

10:11 a.m.—Aerial crew says Yarnell Hill Fire has "few smokes," or limited flame activity.

10:48 a.m.—BLM helicopter drops off seven firefighters, among them four state prisoners, at the burning ridge, the first crew to reach the Yarnell Hill Fire.

12:22 p.m.—Aerial crew estimates size of the fire at 2 acres.

4:15 p.m.—Incident commander Russ Shumate tells dispatchers he is "still having problems catching" the fire, estimates its size at "possibly 3–4 acres."

5:18 p.m.—Fire jumps over its containment line on the east side and grows to about 6 acres.

8:10 p.m.—Fire has grown to 100 acres, burning through brush one-and-a-half miles from closest structure.

9:01 p.m.—State dispatcher logs e-mail order sent to Eric Marsh, assigning Granite Mountain Hotshots to Yarnell Hill Fire on Sunday, June 30.

9:38 p.m.—Flame lengths at 20–30 feet. Yarnell Hill Fire moving north. Firefighters on fire line "ineffective" because chain saws ran out of gas.

June 30, 2013

6:29 a.m.—Size of the fire estimated at 600 acres.

approximately 7 a.m.—Granite Mountain Hotshots attend briefing at Yarnell fire station. Boulder Springs Ranch identified as "bomb-proof" safety zone.

9:45 a.m.—Forecast calls for isolated thunderstorms in the evening, with lightning, strong winds, and no rain over fire area.

10:21 a.m.—Russ Shumate officially transfers command of the fire to Roy Hall, who is certified to manage more complex fires.

10:45 a.m.—Aerial crew reports fire at 800–1,000 acres, flame lengths at 15–20 feet, moving one-eighth of a mile per hour to the northeast.

11:45 a.m.—Granite Mountain Hotshots carve out an anchor point on the burning mountain.

12:27 p.m.—Flame lengths at 15–20 feet. Fire moving N-NE at half-mile per hour, one hour from nearest structures in Peeples Valley. Fire grew by 700 acres in previous two hours.

12:37 p.m.—Brendan McDonough dropped off at lookout spot about a mile northeast of the rest of the Granite Mountain Hotshots.

1:24 p.m.—Wade Parker texts his mother, "We're on a 500-acre fire in Yarnell. Temps supposed to get up to 116. I gotta pretty good headache. Pray for me."

1:56 p.m.—Pre-evacuation orders issued for Yarnell. Residents given four hours to leave.

2:02 p.m.—National Weather Service issues the day's first weather alert, forecasting thunderstorm activity on fire's east side.

3:19 p.m.—Andrew Ashcraft texts his wife, Juliann: "We could really use a little rain down here."

3:26 p.m.—National Weather Service issues second alert for thunderstorm-driven winds approaching fire from NE, blowing at 40–50 miles per hour.

3:30–3:45 p.m.—Wind direction shifts by 180 degrees, to W-NW. Heavy ash starts falling on crews near Shrine of St. Joseph in Yarnell. Two-mile wall of flames marches southeast.

3:42 p.m.—Paul Musser, of incident command team, asks Granite Mountain Hotshots Superintendent Eric Marsh if he can bring his men down to Yarnell to help protect its homes.

3:50 p.m.—Brendan McDonough hikes down from lookout spot and catches a ride out of the wild.

3:50 p.m.—Marsh tells Todd Abel, a member of the incident command team, that "winds are getting squirrely up here." Abel asks if crew is "in a good spot." Marsh answers: "Yes, we're in the black."

3:55 p.m.—Marsh says on radio that Granite Mountain Hotshots were "picking our way through the black" and "going out toward the ranch." Incident commander who hears it presumes it is the bomb-proof safety zone that had been identified at morning briefing.

4:03 p.m.—Fire officials say thunderstorm is pushing fire in multiple directions, 600 buildings threatened.

4:04 p.m.—Wade Parker texts his mother, "This thing is running for Yarnell, just starting to evac. you can see fire on the left town on right."

4:04 p.m.—Juliann texts Andrew, "Are you sleeping down there?"

4:08 p.m.—Mandatory evacuation ordered for Yarnell.

4:24 p.m.—Image on Doppler radar shows fire plume at 31,500 feet.

4:30 p.m.—Thunderstorm-driven winds reach northern edge of the fire, pushes it south. Flames double their size and triple their speed.

4:33 p.m.—A Granite Mountain Hotshot screams over the radio, "Breaking in on Arizona 16, Granite Mountain Hotshots, we are in front of the flaming front."

4:35 p.m.—Marsh says on the radio, "Yeah, I'm here with Granite Mountain Hotshots. Our escape route has been cut off. We are preparing a deployment site and we are burning out around ourselves in the brush and I'll give you a call when we are under the sh—the shelters."

4:47 p.m.—Aerial crew announces over the radio an unknown number of shelter deployments, at an unknown location.

6:25 p.m.—Eric Tarr, police officer-paramedic with the Arizona Department of Public Safety, confirms nineteen fatalities.

NOTES

Prologue

4 *"I've got eyes on you":* Yarnell Hill Fire Serious Accident Investigation *Report,* 23, http://www.iawfonline.org/Yarnell_Hill_Fire_report.pdf.

5 *Eric Tarr, a police officer:* Information on *Ranger 58's* assignment and its role in searching for the Hotshots from interview with Charles Main and Eric Tarr and transcripts of the interviews given by them and the helicopter's pilot, Clifford Bursting, to investigators.

6 *The shelters are not supposed to hug:* Information on fire-shelter requirements and components from "The New Generation Fire Shelter," a publication of the National Wildfire Coordinating Group. Information on how to deploy a fire shelter from the author's basic training at the Arizona Wildfire and Incident Management Academy.

7 *At the crest of the rise, he halted:* Descriptions of the scene, gear he carried, and his discovery of the Hotshots from interview with Eric Tarr.

7 *Billy Warneke lay between Marsh:* Yarnell Hill Fire Serious Accident *Investigation Report,* 88.

The Guys

11 *"I'm Darrell Willis":* Descriptions and quotes from first day of the 2013 season for the Granite Mountain Hotshots from interviews and notes

taken in advance of that day by Darrell Willis, as well as interviews with Ted Ralston, a code-enforcement officer in the Prescott Fire Department Wildland Division who was present.

12   *Seven of them were veterans:* From personnel files and crew manifest, obtained through public records requests.

12   *he'd fulfilled a childhood dream:* Based on interviews with Kevin Woyjeck's parents, Joe and Anna.

12   *"Objective: To be part of":* From Kevin Woyjeck's personnel file, obtained from the City of Prescott through a public records request.

12   *Woyjeck wanted to work for the Los Angeles County Fire Department:* This and other professional information on Kevin Woyjeck from his personnel file with the Prescott Fire Department, obtained through public records requests, and interviews with Joe and Anna Woyjeck.

13   *Woyjeck joined the Granite Mountain Hotshots:* Interviews with Joe Woyjeck.

13   *Fire Order No. 2:* See US Forest Service's "Standard Firefighting Orders and 18 Watchout Situations," http://www.fs.fed.us/fire/safety/10_18/10 _18.html.

14   *His father had taped a card:* Interviews with Joe Woyjeck.

14   *kept a similar card in his wallet:* Interview with Grant McKee's fiancée, Leah Fine, and his aunt, Linda Caldwell.

14   *one of six official full-time positions:* According to personnel files, obtained under public records requests.

14   *On eighties nights at Coyote Joe's:* Interview with Robert Caldwell's wife, Claire.

14   *On his first job:* Interview with Robert Caldwell's mother, Linda.

15   *"I see you when I see you":* Interview with Caldwell's wife, Claire.

15   *rather die in his boots:* Interviews with Linda and Claire Caldwell.

15   *one of 107 Hotshot crews:* National Interagency Coordination Center Hotshot Crew status report for June 28, 2013.

15   *only one of two to operate:* The other was the Ironwood Interagency Hotshot Crew, formed by the Northwest Fire District in Tucson, Arizona. That crew was officially disbanded on October 3, 2014.

16   *In 2011, the crew traveled 16,150 miles:* From Granite Mountain Interagency Hotshot Crew end-of-season reports for 2011 and 2012, courtesy of Katie Cornelius, curator, Prescott Fire Department.

16   *On hikes along Trail #33:* Interviews with Granite Mountain alumni Doug Harwood, Brandon Bunch, Justin Kaoni, and Matt Demenna.

17   *"Every decision you make from now on":* Interview with Marsh's wife, Amanda.

17   *entirely different from the dispassionate:* Author registered on usajobs
      .gov and filled out forms and applied for a job on a wildland crew.

18   *Their names are organized on lists:* Interviews with officials at the
      National Interagency Fire Center.

18   *an average of ninety applications:* Interviews with Darrell Willis and
      Todd Rhines, a longtime friend of Marsh's and the supervisor of the
      Wildland Division's fuels crew.

18   *"When was the last time you lied?":* Several of the wives of the fallen
      Granite Mountain Hotshots recalled that question. Willis recalled the
      conversation with Marsh and Steed's mastery of the job interviews.

19   *Billy Warneke, twenty-five, had written:* Descriptions of Warneke's
      practicing for the Granite Mountain Hotshots' interview, his attire on
      the day of the interview, and his answer to the question of when he'd
      told his last lie from the author's interviews with his wife, Roxanne.

20   *car break-in at a Walmart:* "Prescott Police Arrest Two Men in Walmart
      Vehicle Burglary," *Prescott Daily Courier,* December 29, 2010, http://
      dcourier.com/main.asp?SectionID=1&SubSectionID=1086
      &ArticleID=89007&TM=435.701.

20   *He'd felt remorseful and ashamed:* "Brendan McDonough, Sole Survivor
      of Firefighting Crew, Was 'Remorseful' After 2010 Conviction for Stolen
      Property," *Phoenix New Times,* July 3, 2013, http://www.phoenixnewtimes
      .com/news/brendan-mcdonough-sole-survivor-of-firefighting-crew
      -was-remorseful-after-2010-conviction-for-stolen-property-6626985.

20   *He told the Overhead that:* McDonough's job interview from Todd
      Rhines, who was present.

21   *his command called him Papa:* Interviews with Amanda Marsh, Darrell
      Willis, and crew alumni. Universally, that was their nickname for Eric
      Marsh.

21   *he'd shouldered a tree as it fell:* Interview with Granite Mountain
      alumni Philip Maldonado, who witnessed the event.

21   *getting back in shape:* Interviews with Jesse Steed's wife, Desiree, and
      the official finish-line picture of Steed on the P. F. Chang's Rock 'n'
      Roll Marathon.

22   *If he pulled out an eight:* Description of deck-of-cards workout from in-
      terviews with Darrell Willis and several crew alumni.

22   *"Having fun yet?":* Justin Kaoni, a Granite Mountain alumnus, and
      other alumni recalled Steed's asking this or a similar question during
      the deck-of-cards workout.

22   *he could hold a tiny brush:* Travis Turbyfill's eulogy, written by his wife,
      Stephanie, and posted on a temporary public memorial erected weeks
      after the fire in Yarnell.

22   *list of items the men needed:* "Items to bring for your first day" handout provided by Darrell Willis, which also included instructions on appearance, hair regulations, and boot purchasing.

23   *made $12.09 an hour:* Starting salaries and benefits information on Warneke, Misner, and Woyjeck from their personnel files, obtained through a public records request. Information on the City of Prescott's dismissal of seasonal employees and its exemption on covering their benefits from administrative hearing over posthumous benefits for Warneke, Misner, and Andrew Ashcraft, who was among the fourteen seasonal employees of the crew. Calculations on the ratio of seasonal firefighters on Hotshot crews based on requirement of "a minimum of seven permanent/career positions" in a crew of twenty, as stipulated in the "Standards for Interagency Hotshot Crew Operations," published by the National Interagency Fire Center, http://www.fs.fed.us/fire/people/hotshots/ihc_stds.pdf.

24   *Some of the guys didn't know much:* Interviews with crew alumni and others connected to the crew, such as Ted Ralston and Todd Rhines. The seasonal alumni I spoke with told me they had no idea they could make a case for benefits.

24   *In high school, one was:* Author's analysis of eulogies and obituaries for the nineteen Granite Mountain Hotshots.

24   *He got his GED in 2012:* Anthony Rose's personnel file, obtained through public records requests, and interviews with his fiancée, Tiffany.

25   *At ten, he'd caught his first:* Interview with Wade Parker's father, Danny.

25   *He painted the cabinets:* Interview with Clayton Whitted's wife, Kristi.

25   *He'd written the names:* Ibid.; and Clayton Whitted's pastor, Bob Hoyt, and Darrell Willis.

25   *He and his father followed each other:* Interview with Joe and Anna Woyjeck.

26   *Woyjeck phoned his mother:* Interviews with Anna Woyjeck.

26   *He was wary of spending:* Interviews with Bobby, Joe, and Anna Woyjeck.

26   *Andrew Ashcraft had got in trouble:* Interviews with his mother, Deborah Pfingston.

27   *Travis Carter, thirty-one, went:* Interview with Travis Carter's father, Tripp, and his aunt Connie Anderson.

27   *Scott Norris, twenty-eight, and Dustin DeFord, twenty-four:* Personnel files, obtained through public records requests.

27   *He had moved to work:* Interviews with Scott Norris's mother, Karen, and sister, Joanna.

27   *DeFord, a minister's son:* Interviews with Dustin DeFord's brother Ryan and their father, Steve DeFord.

28   *His uncle A. C. Ekker was:* Interview with Joe Thurston's mother, Gayemarie Ekker, and A. C. Ekker's obituary in *The Times Independent,* reproduced on the Web site findagrave.com, http://www.findagrave.com/cgi-bin/fg.cgi?page=gr&GRid=33437687.

28   *Thurston didn't grow up the:* Interview with Joe Thurston's mother, Gayemarie Ekker, and questions answered by e-mail by Thurston's wife, Marsena. For more on A. C. Ekker's life and his appearance on the cover of *National Geographic.*

28   *a bit of a Don Juan:* Interview with Chris's father, Mike MacKenzie.

29   *"If it's thin and white, it's safe":* Interviews with Sean Misner's mother, Tammy, and his uncle Tim McElwee.

29   *They'd had a modest ceremony:* Interviews with Amanda Misner and wedding pictures she shared with the author.

29–30   *Amanda bought two pregnancy tests:* Interviews with Amanda Misner.

30   *made about a dollar less:* Pay for Hotshots employed by federal agencies from descriptions on Bureau of Land Management's Web site, http://www.blm.gov/nv/st/en/fo/carson_city_field/blm_programs/fire_management/silver_state_hotshots/hours_pay_benefits.html. All federal land-management agencies follow the same formula.

30   *But the Granite Mountain Hotshots had:* Interview with Tim McElwee and Amanda Misner.

30   *Whitted had deployed his goofy:* Interviews with Pastor Bob Hoyt at Heights Church, where Whitted worked as a youth minister.

30   *He'd planned on making it his last:* Interviews with Garret Zuppiger's mother, Suzanne Wagner, his grandfather Bruce Lindquist, and his girlfriend, Emilee Ashby.

30   *Robert Caldwell's wife had introduced:* Interview with Claire Caldwell and John Percin's parents, John and Mary.

31   *He was a recovering methamphetamine addict:* Interviews with Percin's roommate Kirk Warren and Mike Jones, a manager at Chapter 5, the recovery program from which Percin had successfully graduated.

31   *Prescott has long been a place of healing:* I learned about Prescott's history as a recovery hub primarily from several articles, including "Noted Scientist Urges High Altitudes of Arizona for Summer Time," *Yavapai Magazine,* August 1914, 14; "Advantage of Accruing from Life a Mile High in the Arid Southwest," *Yavapai Magazine,* October 1914, 14; "Promise of Prescott: Climate and Tuberculosis," *Yavapai Magazine,*

April 1921, 13; and " 'Recovery City': Sober-Living Homes Prep Clients for Real Life," *Prescott Daily Courier,* June 7, 2011.

32 *There's no exact count:* According to a spokeswoman for the Arizona Department of Health Services, sober-living homes are not licensed, and for this reason the State of Arizona does not keep track of how many there are.

32 *$70-million-a-year industry:* According to Bob Morse, longtime owner of one of the largest drug rehabilitation programs in Prescott, Chapter 5, which John Percin Jr. attended.

32 *Percin had worked hard* and *hurt his knee:* Interviews with Ted Ralston, Kirk Warren, and Mike Jones.

32 *Percin had bared his heart:* Interviews with Todd Rhines and Ted Ralston, whose office was next to Marsh's and with whom Percin worked while on light duty, recovering from his injury.

32 *Marsh told him just that:* Several people relayed the same conversation to me, among them Todd Rhines and Ted Ralston, who worked from the office next to Marsh's at Station 7, and Percin's roommate, Kirk Warren. Current and former members of the crew all knew that Marsh was determined to keep Percin on track.

33 *He'd become sober on September 7, 2000:* Interviews with Marsh's wife, Amanda, and his ex-wife, Kori Kirkpatrick.

33 *Marsh grew up an only child:* Interview with Marsh's parents, John and Jane.

33 *Marsh told the Hotshots to:* Every crew member I interviewed talked about Marsh's insistence that they behave as gentlemen and go out of their way to help others. The examples listed in this passage—opening doors, helping someone cross the street, changing tires—all came from these conversations.

34 *On the walls, posters reminded them:* Author's visit to the ready room at Station 7.

34 *The men were all clean shaven:* Descriptions of the men's appearances and clothing from interviews with Darrell Willis.

34 *So he stayed awake late:* Interviews with Joe Woyjeck and Darrell Willis.

Saving a Tree

36 *In Prescott, they'd found themselves:* Based on crew's schedule for May 2013, obtained through public records request.

37 *Travis Turbyfill kept calculating the hours:* Interview with Travis Turbyfill's wife, Stephanie.

37 *It was their first significant run:* June 2013 work timeline for Granite Mountain Hotshots, obtained through a public records request.

37   *"It's a Long Way":* Interview with Eric Marsh's wife, Amanda.

37   *The Hotshots again rushed out:* InciWeb Incident Information System page on Doce Fire, http://inciweb.nwcg.gov/incident/3437/.

37–38   *"I'm no spring chicken":* From Marsh's "employee self-evaluation," April 2009, obtained through public records request.

38   *he'd fallen and broken his collarbone:* Interviews with Darrell Willis and Amanda Marsh.

38   *The sun blazed up above:* I relied on stories and photo galleries published by the *Prescott Daily Courier* for descriptions of the fire's behavior, the terrain in which it burned, and the homes it threatened, including "Photo Gallery—Doce Fire—Reader and Staff Photos," first posted online on June 18, 2013; "Fast-Moving Wildfire Churns over Granite Mountain, Threatens Williamson Valley Homes near Prescott," published in print on June 19, 2013; and "Firefighters 'Holding Their Own' on Doce," posted online on June 19, 2013. I also interviewed Tony Sciacca, incident commander of the Type 1 team that managed the Doce Fire, for insights on strategies, personnel, and specific duties of the Granite Mountain Hotshots.

38   *One man placed his Sony NEX-7:* The video was posted on Vimeo by Clark Pettit, https://vimeo.com/68893379.

38   *leaving them more vulnerable:* See "Forest Health—Bark Beetle" on the Prescott National Forest's Web site, http://www.fs.usda.gov/detail /prescott/alerts-notices/?cid=fswdev3_009832.

39   *more than 3 million residences:* CoreLogic's 2013 Wildfire Hazard Risk Report, http://www.corelogic.com/research/wildfire-risk-report/2013 -wildfire-hazard-risk-report.pdf.

39   *an average of thirteen thousand homes:* See "Northern California, Homes, and Cost of Wildfires," Headwaters Economics, 2011, http:// headwaterseconomics.org/wildfire/homes-risk/northern-california -homes-and-cost-of-wildfires.

39   *each consisting of twelve thousand:* This is the formula of the most common type of fire retardant used in the West, called Phos-Chek. http:// phoschek.com/industry/wildland/.

39   *Still, by nightfall, 460 families:* See "Hundreds Displaced by Doce Fire near Prescott," Associated Press, June 19, 2013, http://ktar.com/22 /1643276/Hundreds-displaced-by-Doce-Fire-near-Prescott.

40   *They each had a right-hand man:* Roles and descriptions from interviews with Granite Mountain alumni; crew's personnel files, obtained through public records request; and information displayed on exhibit attended by author at Hotel St. Michael in Prescott, Arizona, marking the one-year anniversary of their deaths. Travis Turbyfill's reading

of *Goodnight Moon* to his daughters from interview with his wife, Stephanie.

40 *First came the ones whose job was:* Description of the work of sawyers and swampers from interviews with Granite Mountain alumni Doug Harwood and Brandon Bunch, former saw bosses on the crew.

41 *Not Carter. He loved running a saw:* Ibid.

41 *one of three Hotshots certified:* Personnel files, obtained through public records request.

41 *Ashcraft had hoped to master:* Interviews with Darrell Willis, Doug Harwood, and Juliann Ashcraft.

42 *he'd lasted six months:* Interview with Juliann Ashcraft.

42 *But while others tired and complained:* Interviews with Phil Maldonado and Dan "Boon" McCarty, alumni of the crew.

42 *He ignored the pain and swelling:* Interview with Ashcraft's mother, Deborah Pfingston.

42 *Marsh had pushed city officials:* Interviews with Darrell Willis, Juliann Ashcraft, and Amanda Marsh.

42 *he played rock, paper, scissors:* From passage relayed by Brandon Bunch to Prescott Fire Department curator and included in exhibit on first-year anniversary of the Hotshots' deaths.

43 *Warneke thought he'd prepared:* Interviews with Warneke's wife, Roxanne.

43 *Granite Mountain's diggers carried:* Description of use and order of tools from Granite Mountain alumni interviewed by the author.

44 *district ranger credited with their invention:* See US Forest Service's Northern Region Web page on Edward Pulaski, http://www.fs.usda.gov/detail/r1/learning/history-culture/?cid=stelprdb5122876.

44 *series of fires christened the Big Burn:* For additional information on the Big Burn, see the Forest History Society Web page on the 1910 fires, http://www.foresthistory.org/ASPNET/Policy/Fire/FamousFires/1910Fires.aspx.

45 *The ten o'clock policy ruled:* Interviews with Stephen J. Pyne. Also, see Pyne's *Fire in America: A Cultural History of Wildland and Rural Fire* (Princeton, N.J.: Princeton University Press, 1982).

45 *between 2000 and 2010, they consumed an average:* National Interagency Fire Center's "Total Wildland Fires and Acres," http://www.nifc.gov/fireInfo/fireInfo_stats_totalFires.html.

45 *40 percent by fiscal year 2012:* James Hubbard, deputy chief of state and private forestry for the US Forest Service, statement before the Committee on Natural Resources, Subcommittee on Public Lands and

Environmental Regulation, US House of Representatives, July 11, 2013, http://democrats.naturalresources.house.gov/sites/democrats .naturalresources.house.gov/files/2013-07-11_PLER_hubbardtestimony .pdf.

45 *In 2014, the Forest Service estimated:* "USDA Fiscal Year 2014 Budget Overview," http://www.fs.fed.us/aboutus/budget/2014/FY2014Forest ServiceBudgetOverview041613.pdf.

46 *Forest Service predicts a net loss:* Susan Stein, Mary Carr, Ronald E. McRoberts, and Lisa G. Mahal, "Forests on the Edge: The Influence of Increased Housing Density on Forest Systems and Services," http:// www.fs.fed.us/openspace/pubs/Stein%20et%20al%20URI-%20 Ch%204.pdf.

46 *Within twenty-four hours, 672:* "Doce Fire Outside of Prescott Grows to 7,000 Acres," *Arizona Republic,* June 20, 2013, http://www.azcentral .com/news/arizona/articles/20130618prescott-wildfire-abrk.html.

46 *Fire hadn't threatened Prescott since:* "Fire Grips City," *Prescott Daily Courier,* May 16, 2002. Handout provided by Darrell Willis.

47 *The five types of hand crews:* "About Hand Crews," US Forest Service Fire & Aviation Management, http://www.fs.fed.us/fire/people /handcrews/about_handcrews.html.

47 *giving him an ultimatum:* Eric Marsh's City of Prescott Performance Appraisal, October 10, 2005, obtained through public records request.

48 *burned as many as six thousand calories:* "University Researches Firefighter Nutrition," Associated Press, August 18, 2001, http:// billingsgazette.com/news/local/university-researches-firefighter -nutrition/article_6acf2ee1-83cc-51b0-a75f-414fe4f826f8.html.

48 *Marsh enjoyed sharing his battle stories:* Interviews with Granite Mountain alumni.

48 *even if his crew still drove:* Interview with Marty Cole, part of the first leadership team of Crew 7, Granite Mountain's predecessor.

48 *Marsh nailed down the Hotshots':* "Hotshot Crew History in America, Granite Mountain Interagency Hotshot Crew," produced by the National Interagency Hotshot Crew Steering Committee, November 2013, http://gacc.nifc.gov/swcc/dc/nmsdc/documents/Crews/NMSDC _Hotshot_Crew_History_2013.pdf.

48 *He got the surplus-sale vans:* Interview with Duane Steinbrink, former chief of the Prescott Fire Department Wildland Division.

49 *Up on the fire line, Marsh announced:* Interviews with Duane Steinbrink and Bettina Rodriguez, the female member of the Granite Mountain Hotshots at the time.

49   *Yet until the Doce Fire came along* and *"dust bunnies"*: Interviews with Darrell Willis, Todd Rhines, Amanda Marsh, and former Prescott City manager Steve Norwood, among others.

49   *In a memo to Craig McConnell:* Dan Fraijo to Craig McConnell, March 28, 2013.

49   *Willis had offered his own list:* Darrell Willis, "Wildland Division White Paper 2013."

50   *The city got reimbursed $39.50:* Per Darrell Willis, chief of the Prescott Fire Department Wildland Division.

50   *Marsh typed up his own:* The text has no title, but it's widely referred to by its first line, "Who are the Granite Mountain Hotshots?" According to Darrell Willis, it was written by Eric Marsh. It is signed and undated.

50   *He named the file:* Interview with Ted Ralston.

50   *so named because the bones:* See Federal Writers Project, "How Skull Valley Got Its Name?," circa 1935, http://www.sharlot.org/library -archives/days-past/how-skull-valley-got-its-name/.

51   *While mowing his lawn, he'd spotted:* Interviews with Darrell Willis and Tony Sciacca.

51   *With students on summer break:* See "Prescott High School Trans- forms into Doce Fire Command Post," *Daily Courier,* June 23, 2013, http://dcourier.com/main.asp?SectionID=1&subsectionID=1086 &articleID=120495.

51   *The direction of the wind:* Interviews with Tony Sciacca.

52   *Steed directed the crew to dig:* All details and descriptions from the Granite Mountain Hotshots' work on the Doce Fire from Tony Sciacca.

52   *Granite Mountain Hotshots became local heroes:* Several of the Hot- shots' wives told me of their husbands sharing with them stories of recognition and thanks by people in Prescott after the Doce Fire. Travis Turbyfill specifically told Stephanie that the Doce Fire had made the Hotshots cool.

52   *The men spent their nights:* Interviews with some of the wives who vis- ited the crew during the Doce Fire, including Stephanie Turbyfill, Amanda Misner, and Juliann Ashcraft.

54   *Juliann Ashcraft baked cookies:* Interview with Juliann Ashcraft.

54   *"Family comes first":* Interview with Brandon Bunch. Bunch had two children and a pregnant wife at home when he was out in New Mexico, fighting the Thompson Ridge Fire with the Granite Mountain Hotshots. His wife called; she was having a hard time with the pregnancy and the kids. Bunch decided he should go home to his family, so he quit the crew after the New Mexico fire. Steed told him, "Family comes first," when Bunch announced the reason for his departure.

54 *He was on his third marriage:* Interview with Amanda Marsh.

55 *Then, he kept going east:* Interviews with Amanda Marsh and Kirk Warren, John Percin's roommate.

55 *"full-time temporary employees":* Interviews with Willis and Dan Fraijo, chief of the Prescott Fire Department at the time, and transcripts of administrative hearing over full-time benefits for Andrew Ashcraft.

55 *"equivalent employment authority": Standards for Interagency Hotshot Crew Operations,* chap. 2, "Standards and Qualifications—Minimum Leadership Staffing."

55 *Ashcraft had worked sixteen months:* Testimony at administrative hearing over posthumous benefits.

56 *The circumference of the alligator juniper:* See "Fire Has Brought Change to Granite Mountain Wilderness," *Prescott Daily Courier,* June 26, 2013; and "Spring 2014 National Register of Big Trees," *American Forests,* 20, http://www.americanforests.org/wp-content/uploads /2014/06/Spring-2014-Register-PDF-web.pdf.

57 *"Granite Mountain Hotshots saved this":* Several of the families received a copy of the signed piece of paper the crew had left inside the geocache. Anthony Rose's fiancée, Tiffany, showed her copy to me and I photographed it. She and others relayed to me the story that is described in this chapter.

57 *Chris MacKenzie pulled out his cell phone:* The picture was one of several found inside Chris MacKenzie's cell phone, which survived the Yarnell Hill Fire. Chris's father, Mike MacKenzie, copied them onto a CD and gave them to me. ·

A Bolt of Lightning

58 *five times hotter than the surface:* "Is Lightning Hotter Than the Sun?," *Discovery News,* May 13, 2010, http://news.discovery.com/earth/is -lightning-hotter-than-the-sun.htm.

59 *An unforgiving heat wave:* "Deadly Heat Wave in the West Brings Fires and Travel Delays," *The New York Times,* June 30, 2013.

59 *638 year-round residents:* American FactFinder, 2013. http://factfinder .census.gov/faces/nav/jsf/pages/community_facts.xhtml?src=bkmk.

59 *twenty-four minutes from residents:* Recording of calls obtained through public records request.

60 *calls followed the fire's unsteady cadence:* Ibid.

60 *Brendan McDonough had called in sick:* Time sheets obtained through public records request and interviews with Darrell Willis.

61 *Alarmed, she called 911:* From interview with Barbara and Kim Kelso

61 *He swept his binoculars across:* Interviews with Bob Brandon.

61   *In Yarnell, two firefighters were on duty:* From Yarnell Fire dispatch records, obtained through public records request.

61   *She reached out to the:* Yarnell Fire dispatch records and interview with Sally Foster.

62   *Wildfires are classified by complexity:* "Fire Complexity Analysis," Southwest Coordination Center, http://gacc.nifc.gov/swcc/management _admin/Agency_Administrator/AA_Guidelines/pdf_files/ch5.pdf.

62   *Thirty-seven fires burned in Arizona:* National Interagency Fire Center, Incident Management Situation Report, Friday, June 28, 2013, 2, http://www.predictiveservices.nifc.gov/IMSR/2013/20130628IMSR .pdf.

62   *The largest of these, the Silver Fire:* Ibid.

62   *rising to thirty-nine thousand feet:* "Silver Fire Containment Increases to 35%," Gila National Forest news release, June 29, 2013, http://www .fs.usda.gov/detail/gila/news-events/?cid=STELPRDB5426240.

62   *Shumate had worked for forty-three days:* Shumate's time sheets for May, June, and parts of July 2013, obtained through public records request, Shumate's last full day off before he was called to respond to the Yarnell Hill Fire had been May 18, 2013. On some days, such as June 16, he did not work on a fire, but answered phone calls. (He billed the state for a half hour that day.) On other days, such as June 19 and June 21, he billed the state for sixteen hours.

62   *He pulled a single-engine air tanker:* Russ Shumate interview with investigative teams from Arizona State Forestry Division and Arizona Division of Occupational Safety and Health, obtained through public records request.

63   *The Doce Fire was 92 percent:* "Yavapai County Emergency Management Regional Alert, Doce (aka Dosie) Fire," http://www.regionalinfo -alert.org/?ycalertgroups=doce-fire.

63   *He told Shumate the difficulties:* Yarnell Hill Fire IA (Initial Attack) Action Log, compiled from handwritten notes and recollection by Russ Shumate, July 19, 2013. Obtained through public records request.

63   *Shumate wondered if such a small blaze:* Unofficial transcript of Russ Shumate interview with OSHA compliance officers, August 8, 2013, 9.

63   *Shumate huddled with a range technician:* Unofficial transcript of Russ Shumate interview with OSHA compliance officers, August 15, 2013, 7. Obtained through public records requests.

63   *He consulted with Bob Brandon:* Interviews with Bob Brandon.

64   *A team of BLM firefighters extinguished:* Shumate interview with OSHA officers, August 15, 2013, 9: "Yes, the fire we did take action on was the Oso Fire."

64 *The peaks, canyons, and valleys:* Yarnell Hill Fire Serious Accident Investigation Report, 14.

64 *Temperatures in the region:* US Environmental Protection Agency, "Climate Change Indicators in the United States," http://www.epa.gov /climatechange/science/indicators/snow-ice/snowpack.html.

65 *His wife, Judy, the town's:* Interview with Peter and Judy Andersen.

65 *The work had fallen to a crew:* According to the Andersens and interviews with Ryan DeFord, who was crew boss at Lewis at the time. Ryan was also a brother of Dustin DeFord, one of the fallen nineteen.

65 *one dollar an hour for each:* Information provided by the Arizona Department of Corrections. See also "Battling Flames in Forest, with Prison as the Firehouse," *The New York Times,* November 26, 2013, http://www.nytimes.com/2013/11/27/us/as-costs-are-cut-inmates-fill -gap-in-fighting-wildfires.html.

65 *The last measurable rain had:* "From Tragedy to Recovery: The Yarnell Hill Wildfire of 2013," Yarnell-Peeples Valley Chamber of Commerce, June 2014, pt. II, chap. 8—June 28, 2013, 42.

65 *Daily relative humidity had averaged:* Statistics from Weather Underground.

66 *"No," Shumate had replied:* Interviews with Bob Brandon.

66 *At 9:00 p.m., the Yarnell Hill Fire flared up:* Shumate interview with OSHA officers, August 15, 2013, 11.

67 *spot weather forecast for Yarnell Hill:* Spot forecast completed at 10:12 p.m. on June 28, 2013, for latitude 34.2283 N and longitude 112.7915 W, in Congress, Arizona.

68 *Shumate left Yarnell at 10 p.m.:* Yarnell Hill Fire IA Action Log, 2: "I started back to quarters at approximately 2200."

Calculating Risk

69 *engaged, corralled, and tamed by 11 p.m.:* Time sheet submitted by the crew to the Prescott Fire Department Wildland Division, showing that the Granite Mountain Hotshots were demobilized from the fire at 11:00 p.m. Time sheet provided by Darrell Willis.

69 *By chance, the forest's home crew:* "Hotshots Vital in Many Ways, Experts Say; Crew Helped Prescott Become the Leader in National Firewise Efforts," *Prescott Daily Courier,* September 1, 2013.

70 *The men sat by seniority and experience:* The author visited both of the crew's buggies on more than one occasion, taking note of seat assignments—the name of each Hotshot was taped by his seat's window so that families would know where they were when they rode to fires. Each buggy had a list of assignments the squads had prepared—taking

out trash, cleaning windows, etc. The lists were affixed to the door on the back.

70 *a DVD player taped to a board:* Noticed by author when she visited Bravo's truck.

70 *popped in the R-rated stoner comedy:* Recalled by Rose's mother, Athena Rose.

71 *One was Tone Loc:* Crew alumni, including Doug Harwood and Brandon Bunch.

71 *"Give us a tough one":* Several crew alumni recalled hearing Marsh say these words to incident commanders while on fires.

72 *direct attack:* Account of the crew's declined assignment on the Wesley Fire from Marsh's handwritten unit log on the fire, his official description of the events. Courtesy of Darrell Willis.

72 *Marsh was furious:* In his unit log, dated September 22, 2012, Marsh wrote, "Points: 1. Resources need the ability to refuse unsafe assignments without fear of reprisal. 2. Crew's side of the story needs told. This is not about me vs. DIV A [a supervisor on the fire], but rather about a crew being punished with a bad eval for trying to go home safe."

73 *they'd have to come back by 6:00 a.m.:* The crew's time sheet for the month of June lists its starting time on the Mount Josh fire as 6:00 a.m.

73 *His shyness could be charming:* from interviews with Carter's father, Tripp, and his aunt Connie Anderson.

73 *Carter had already arranged some of his clothes in hangers and drawers:* From interview with Carter's father, Tripp Carter, at the ranch. Mr. Carter showed his son's clothes hanging in a closet in a bedroom upstairs.

74 *"I'm tired. It's a lot":* Recalled by Misner's wife, Amanda.

74 *It was his favorite biblical verse:* Interviews with Misner's mother, Tammy, and wife, Amanda.

74 *five feet nine inches, and:* Ibid.

A Sleeping Fire Awakens

75 *Lewis Crew were up at 5:00 a.m.:* This and additional details on the movements of the Lewis Crew on June 29, 2013, are based on the author's interviews with two inmates who were part of the crew at the time and subsequently confirmed by the crew's boss.

75 *The buildings were dull gray:* Description of buildings and location of Lewis prison from author's observations.

76 *They're placed in specific units:* This and other descriptions of inmate assignments at Lewis prison from spokesmen of the Arizona Department of Corrections Andrew Wilder and Bill Lamoreaux.

76 *One of them is Sandra Bachman:* I learned about the Dude Fire and its fatalities, including Sandra Bachman, from articles and the investigative report on the fire, but none struck me as more comprehensive than a piece headlined "Burn," by Jaime Joyce, published by the Big Roundtable on June 23, 2013, http://www.thebigroundtable.com/stories/burn/.

76 *Another is Paul Rast:* Arizona Department of Corrections, "ADC Staff Killed in the Line of Duty," https://corrections.az.gov/adc-staff-killed -line-duty-4.

76 *416 cells equipped with sliding doors:* Arizona Department of Corrections news release, "Corrections Prepares Newest Facility," November 7, 2014, https://corrections.az.gov/article/corrections-prepares -newest-facility.

77 *forty-three hundred men and women:* CAL Fire Conservation Camp Program, http://www.fire.ca.gov/fire_protection/fire_protection_coop _efforts_consrvcamp.php.

77 *Prisoners dig line in orange jumpsuits:* For distinctions in attire worn by inmate firefighters in California and Arizona, see "Battling Flames in Forests," *The New York Times.*

77 *"A gated community":* Ibid.

77 *They'd had to qualify for their places:* Requirements for inmates who joined prison fire crews in Arizona provided by Arizona Department of Corrections spokesmen Andrew Wilder and Bill Lamoreaux.

78 *Leo Vasquez and another corrections officer:* Lewis Crew manifest, provided by the Arizona State Forestry Division.

78 *It's a feat of engineering:* Details on the construction and enlargement of the Yarnell Hill portion of State Route 89 from "It Took Time to Tame Scary Yarnell Hill," *Arizona Republic,* November 26, 1972.

78 *Still, school buses heading downhill:* Yarnell old-timers all recalled the close calls and lost side-view mirrors on school buses taking them back and forth to Wickenburg. The first to tell me this story was John Paulic, who was brought up in Yarnell in the 1960s and still lived there when we met in 2013.

79 *From the fire station, Williams looked:* Andrew Williams and the inmate I'm calling Steve Parker shared their observations with me and answered my questions about their work on the fire in several interviews by phone, in person, and through text messages.

79 *He'd worked for the state forestry division:* Unofficial transcript of Russ Shumate's interview with OSHA compliance officers, August 15, 2013, 1–3.

79 *Using his authority to mobilize:* Yarnell Hill Fire IA Action Log, 2: "I coordinated with BLM for our next day's actions. It was thought that

multiple smokes would show in the morning in this area. I ordered AZ State Forestry Division (ASFD) crews (Lewis and Yuma), and ASFD engine 151 to report to Peeples Valley store at 0800 to stage. I ordered Air Attack to show up as soon as they came on duty Saturday morning. SEATS were in SE AZ at the time, and I talked with dispatch about timeframes for getting them in play Saturday morning."

80 *Two weeks earlier, the readings:* "Granite Mountain IHC Entrapment and Burnover Investigation," 18, prepared by Wildland Fire Associates for the Arizona Division of Occupational Safety and Health.

80 *On Friday night, the National Weather Service:* The spot forecast for the Yarnell Hill Fire completed at 10:12 p.m. on Friday, June 28, 2013, for the next day, Saturday, June 29: "Sky/weather. Partly cloudy. A slight chance of showers and thunderstorms in the late afternoon. Max temperature . . . 102 to 104. Min humidity . . . 9 to 11 percent."

80 *At 9:00 a.m., the crews gathered:* Yarnell Hill Fire IA Action Log, 3, under June 29, 2013: "0900 Briefed on scene resources with weather, and plan for the day."

80 *An hour later, he came back:* Ibid.: "Lewis CRWB [crew boss] reports that none of the roads are drivable and that a hike would not be achievable with the crew."

81 *four corrections officers, one sergeant:* Manifests of Yuma and Lewis Crews, obtained through public records requests.

81 *He'd spotted an opening:* Shumate interview with OSHA officers, August 15, 2013, 23

81 *In aviation, that creates:* Shumate's concern about high-altitude density from his interview with OSHA officers, August 15, 2013, 23. Description of density altitude from Federal Aviation Administration's "Density Altitude" pamphlet, 2008, https://www.faasafety.gov/files/gslac/library/documents/2011/Aug/56396/FAA%20P-8740-02%20DensityAltitude[hi-res]%20branded.pdf.

81 *Guadiana, Leo Vasquez, and four prisoners:* Unofficial transcript of OSHA compliance officers interview of Justin Smith, an incident commander Type 4 trainee assigned to the fire, on October 16, 2013, 24.

81 *Nate Peck, a firefighter assigned:* Unofficial transcript of Russ Shumate follow-up interview with OSHA compliance officers, October 18, 2013, 10. Shumate recalled his first name as Wayne. See also notes from Nate Peck's interview with investigators dated July 13, 2013, archived by *Arizona Republic,* http://archive.azcentral.com/ic/pdf/1213-yarnell-interview-notes.pdf.

81 *shot an eight-second video:* Guadiana's cell phone video obtained through public records request.

81 *State dispatchers prepared for a long haul:* Arizona Dispatch logs, June 28, 2013, at 21:05:48 ("need Prescott Armory open for both crews tomorrow and need Justin and Jake here @ 0800 // copy and will you need Water and Gatorade at all we have ENG 151 coming in early // copy yeah lets go ahead and load up the eng with what ever is possible and we will buy ice from the station"); and Saturday, June 29, 2013, at 09:46:27 ("I'M GUNNA NEED AN S NUMBER FOR THE GOLDEN CORRAL FOR 48 PEOPLE FOR DINNER").

82 *Seen through binoculars:* Interview with Lewis Crew inmate Steve Parker.

82 *Shumate had ordered it open:* Yarnell Hill Fire IA Action Log, 3: "At 0700 ordered 2 SEATS and for Wickenburg SEAT base to be opened." Entry in Arizona Dispatch logs for June 29, 2013, at 11:54:50 reads, "ADVISED PRESCOTT THAT WICKENBURG IS NOT OPEN YET SO T-413 & T-830 WILL BE HOLD AT PRESCOTT SEAT BASE."

82 *The National Weather Service warned:* Arizona Dispatch logs, June 29, 2013, at 13:48:06, a message from dispatch to Russ Shumate reads: "LOOKS LIKE THERE ARE STORMS BUILDING UP NORTH EAST OF KINGMAN NEXT TO THE 40 MOVING SOUTH// NOT TWO WORRIED ABOUT WHATS GOING TO HAPPEN NEAR SALIGMAN MAYBE A COUPLE SINGLE TREES// JUST WANTED TO GIVE YOU A HEADS UP."

Dialogue and description of Shumate's conversation with a state dispatcher over the storm near Kingman from Russ Shumate IA Action Log, July 19, 2013, P. 4. Obtained through public records requests.

83 *He released the air tankers at 2:42 p.m.:* Dialogue between dispatch and Shumate in Arizona Dispatch logs at 14:42:48: "any need for AA (Air Attack) or can we release them back to PIFC (Prescott Interagency Fire Center) // how long is the flight time from DVT to wickenburg about 20–30 mins // copy we can release them back to PIFC // copy will do."

83 *Justin Smith, a trainee under Shumate:* Unofficial transcript of Smith's interview with OSHA compliance officers on October 15, 2013, 3, obtained through public records request.

83 *twelve bladder bags* and *five gallons:* Shumate interview with OSHA officers, August 15, 2013, 25.

84 *They drained the bladder bags quickly:* Smith interview with OSHA officers, October 15, 2013, 16.

84 *Smith arrived around 4:30 p.m.:* Ibid., 5: "Q: 'And—and what time did you get there?' A: 'I don't recall the exact time.' Q: 'Give me an approximate.' A: 'Um, 5:00 ish, 4:30, 5:00.'"

84 *Smith didn't like what he saw:* Ibid., 14

84 *In Phoenix, the thermometer reached 119:* "Deadly Heat Wave in the West," *The New York Times.*

84 *On the ridge, flying embers:* Shumate interview with OSHA officers, August 15, 2013, 24.

85 *Lewis Crew ran out of gas:* Interview by state investigators with Nate Peck, July 13, 2013.

86 *a strong high-pressure system:* National Interagency Coordination Center Incident Management Situation Report for Saturday, June 29, 2013.

86 *They tallied the number of new:* Ibid. New large fires are specified in the reports for each geographic area. Older fires of significance determined by subtracting new large fires from the number of significant fires listed under each geographic area.

86 *at 3, halfway up a scale:* Ibid.

86 *Shumate could tell he was losing:* Arizona Dispatch logs, June 29, 2013, 16:15:45, on communication from IC, acronym for "incident commander" (Shumate) to one of the dispatchers: "Still having problems catching it."

87 *Shumate heard they'd been grounded:* Ibid., 17:42:09: "T-06 decline mission due to weather as well as HT out of PDC // ok ill [*sic*] advise incident" [*T-06* stands for "tanker 06," *HT* for "helitanker," and *PDC* for "Prescott Dispatch Center"]. Shumate was notified at 17:43:51.

87 *Shumate decided that wasn't:* Ibid., June 29, 2013, 17:50:39, on communication from Shumate: "No need for VLAD [*sic*] // copy."

87 *dispatchers had kept track of:* Activities handled by Southwest Coordination Center from its dispatch logs for June 29, 2013: Silver Fire at 0948, Mount Washington Fire at 1038, Willow Creek Fire at 1611, and Fort Apache Hotshots at 1710.

89 *By 7:38 p.m., the fire had:* Arizona State Forestry Division's Initial Synopsis of Yarnell Hill Fire Resources Deployed, June 28–July 1, 2013, 2: "The fire was estimated at 100 acres at 7:38 p.m." and "The fire was estimated to be one mile from the closest structures in Peeples Valley."

89 *Shumate told state dispatchers:* Arizona Dispatch logs, June 29, 2013, 18:10:40: "Called Golden Corral—Laura mgr—advised need to cancel for the evening. Called Sgt David Stidham and left msg on vm to close armory not needed tonite."

89 *keep everyone safe while monitoring:* Interview with Justin Smith by OSHA compliance officers, October 16, 2013, 12–14.

89 *Shumate prepared to move the command:* Arizona Dispatch logs, June 29, 2013, 18:51:32: "Board members and everyone has agreed. The Peeples Valley School."

90   *drafting an ambitious wish list:* Yarnell Hill Fire IA Action Log, July 19, 2013, 6. Obtained through public records requests.

90   *The coordination center agreed to:* Southwest Coordination Center dispatch logs, June 29, 2013, entries at 2025 ("Granite Mountain IHC will be released off West Spruce fire to home. Granite Mountain is the only Type 1 crew available for Arizona tomorrow") and 2044 ("Arroyo Grande IHC will be released off Creek Fire tomorrow morning").

90   *Granite Mountain got its orders anyway:* Ibid., 2115: "AZ-ADC [acronym for Arizona Dispatch Center] will assign Granite Mountain IHC internally to Yarnell Fire."

90   *149 hours on the clock:* "June 2013 Work Timeline for Granite MTN IHC," courtesy of Darrell Willis.

91   *"I really need some help"* and *"they really needed me":* Darrell Willis interview with OSHA compliance officers, August 19, 2013, 2.

92   *got to Peeples Valley around midnight:* Ibid.: "And so at that point I figured they really needed me and so I headed down about 10:30." The Arizona Dispatch logs note that at 22:42:19, Willis told Shumate, "I'll head down in about an hour."

Promises and Goodbyes

93   *well-ordered and often-used telephone tree:* Universally relayed to me as the way through which the crew received its orders.

93   Respond fast, solve the problem: Prescott Fire Department, "Prescott Fire Way, Our Mission."

94   *rated in annual performance reviews:* Hotshots' "City of Prescott Performance Appraisal," under "City Core Values."

94   *"Kill 'em with kindness":* Ted Ralston and Philip Maldonado, alumni of the crew.

94   *Caldwell's phone blared like a fire alarm:* Interview with Caldwell's wife, Claire.

94   *They'd tussled from sunup:* "Crew Times Report, Granite Mountain Hotshots" on the Mount Josh Fire, June 29, 2013. On at 6:00 a.m., off at noon. Then on at 12:30 p.m., off at 10:30 p.m.

94   *Just before his phone rang:* Rose's fiancée, Tiffany.

95   *A little after eight o'clock:* Steed's wife, Desiree.

96   *Woyjeck had planned to go:* Woyjeck's father, Joe.

96   *fishing rods were among the few:* McKee's fiancée, Leah Fine.

96   *singing Daft Punk's "Get Lucky":* Ibid. Fine was there.

97   *Zuppiger had rushed out of:* Zuppiger's girlfriend, Emilee Ashby.

98   *Dustin DeFord texted his brother:* Ryan DeFord.

99　*Warneke had last driven out* through *"You just need to rest":* Warneke's wife, Roxanne.

99　*At Andrew Ashcraft's house, the call:* Ashcraft's wife, Juliann.

100　*Juliann had given Andrew a blank journal:* Juliann Ashcraft kindly loaned me the diary so I could read and use it freely as I wrote this book.

101　*"I'm exhausted":* Juliann Ashcraft.

101　*Marital counseling had helped:* Juliann Ashcraft and Andrew's mother, Deborah Pfingston.

101　*"Team Ashcraft Contract":* Dated and signed by Andrew Ashcraft on May 2, 2013. Juliann Ashcraft kindly provided a copy to me.

102　*Andrew's handiwork surrounded her:* Juliann Ashcraft described the pieces that Andrew had made for their house during one of my visits.

102　*Choice is the baby:* Juliann Ashcraft and Andrew's mother, Deborah Pfingston.

103　*Travis and Stephanie Turbyfill were schooled:* Stephanie Turbyfill.

103　*4,003 by the end of:* Defense Department, based on an account by the Associated Press, whose death toll as of March 31, 2008, totaled 4,011, but included 8 civilian military contractors, http://usatoday30.usatoday.com/news/world/iraq/casualties/2008-03-01-march-toll_N.htm.

103　*During a training exercise:* Stephanie Turbyfill.

104–105　From *Stephanie grilled him a ham-and-cheese* to *"I could never replace you":* Ibid.

105　*Thurston picked up Rose:* Rose's fiancée, Tiffany.

106　*Steed planted a kiss on Desiree's lips:* Desiree Steed.

106　*Ashcraft approached the couch:* Juliann Ashcraft.

107　*He picked up the phone:* Darrell Willis's interview with OSHA compliance officers, August 19, 2013, 2.

107　*"Off to Yarnell Arizona":* Roxanne Warneke.

107　*At 6:09 a.m., Rose texted Tiffany:* Tiffany Rose.

A Treacherous Combination

111–112　*Ancient traders plying the Indian Ocean:* Ojha Sayantani, C. Gnanaseelan, and J. S. Chowdary, "The Role of Arabian Sea in the Evolution of Indian Ocean Dipole," Royal Meteorological Society, August 2013.

112　*interacts with the Mogollon Rim* and other descriptions of monsoon season in Arizona: Valerie Meyers, fire weather program manager, and Ken Waters, warning coordinator meteorologist, at the National Weather Service office in Phoenix, and Brian Klimowski, meteorologist in charge of the National Weather Service office in Flagstaff.

115　*the years since 1950 had been warmer:* "Assessment of Climate Change in the Southwest United States," prepared for the National Climate Assessment in 2013, http://swccar.org/sites/all/themes/files/SW-NCA -color-FINALweb.pdf.

113 *rainfall patterns had ranged from:* National Centers for Environmental Information, "Drought, June 2013," http://www.ncdc.noaa.gov/sotc /drought/201306.

113 *Austrian mathematician Christian Doppler:* Christian Doppler's page, biography.com, http://www.biography.com/people/christian-doppler -9277346.

114 *Klimowski and his team near Flagstaff:* Interviews with Brian Klimowski during two visits to the National Weather Service office in Flagstaff.

114 *eighty-five of these meteorologists:* "Incident Meteorologists Are on Front Lines of Wildfires," Climate Central, July 3, 2013.

114 *They interpret upper-air soundings:* Description of work of IMETs from interviews with Valerie Meyers and Stewart Turner, fire-behavior analyst assigned to Yarnell Hill Fire on July 1, 2013.

115 *Byron Kimball, a veteran of the:* Byron Kimball's interview with OSHA compliance officers, August 15, 2013, 1–4.

116 *Kimball checked in at the:* Ibid., 12.

116 *Shumate's replacement, Roy Hall:* Ibid.

116 *The fire covered about three hundred acres:* Roy Hall's interview with OSHA compliance officers, August 16, 2013, 16.

117 *The scene reminded him of:* Kimball interview with OSHA officers, August 15, 2013, 12–13.

117 *Shumate got one Friday night:* The National Weather Service fulfilled requests for spot forecasts on June 28, 2013 at 2155 MST, then on June 29, 2013, at 730 MST, 1652 MST and 2033 MST.

Trouble in the Sky

119 *The fresh team of incident commanders trickled in:* Hall interview with OSHA officers, August 16, 2013, 5–6.

119 *Shumate's replacement, Roy Hall, had:* Ibid., 5: "I could see the fire from there."

119 *adult furniture hadn't yet arrived:* Interviews with Barbara Kelso.

119–120 *Shumate had assigned* and *He sought help:* Willis interview with OSHA officers, August 19, 2013, 8–10.

120 *In the Yarnell neighborhood of:* Gary Cordes interview with OSHA compliance officers, September 11, 2013, 8–9.

120 *"we'll lose it":* Cordes interview with Osha officers, August 16, 2013, 5.

121 *Cordes described it as a "bombproof":* Ibid., 10.

121 *"Of course, you still have the black"*: Ibid.

121 *Abel pulled Marsh aside* and subsequent descriptions of fire and veg-etation: Todd Abel's interview with OSHA compliance officers, August 22, 2013, 9.

122 *Building an anchor would become:* Ibid., 16.

122 *The fire in Yarnell was now:* Southwest Coordination Center dispatch logs, June 30, 2013, 0859: "Yarnell is first priority."

122 *ahead of seven other troublesome:* National Interagency Coordina-tion Center Incident Management Situation Report, July 1, 2013, 0530 MT.

122 *The Dean Peak Fire, at:* Southwest Coordination Center dispatch logs, June 30, 2013, 0901: "Established first priority fire as Yarnell, then Dean Peak."

122 *On his way to the school, Shumate:* Shumate interview with OSHA of-ficers August 15, 2013, 47. Size of fire from Arizona Dispatch Center, Saturday, June 29, 2013, 12:22:35, "Sizeup: The only smoke was the Yarnell Hill, AA is calling it two acres on the top of the ridge. . . ."

122 *the fire had consumed five hundred acres:* Southwest Coordination Center dispatch logs, June 30, 2013, 0900: "Darrell Willis is on scene and says 300–500 acres."

122 *At 9:18 a.m., a hiker snapped:* Time stamp of picture provided by the hiker, Joy Collura.

123 *as he climbed to fifty-six hundred:* Joy Collura and her hiking compan-ion, Sonny Gilligan, guided me on two hikes along most of the path followed by the Granite Mountain Hotshots on June 30, 2013. The al-titude was measured by Ms. Collura when we reached the spot where she crossed paths with Eric Marsh that day.

123 *Conrad Jackson and Mark Matthews:* Interviews with Conrad Jackson and Mark Matthews.

123 *It rose twenty feet high:* Arizona State Forestry Division Initial Synopsis of Yarnell Hill Fire Resources Deployed, June 28–July 1, 2013, 3.

123 *undeterred by twenty-four thousand:* In Willis's interview with OSHA officers, August 19, 2013, 17, he says that a DC-10 had dropped "a couple of loads" of fire retardant on the flames. DC-10s can carry twelve thou-sand gallons of fire retardant per load.

123 *light up the brush west:* Ibid., 18.

124 *tapped into the ranch's ninety:* Interviews with Conrad Jackson.

124 *the Haines index:* According to the US Forest Service's Wildland Fire Assessment System, the Haines index "is used to indicate the potential for wildfire growth by measuring the stability and dryness of the air

over a fire." For additional information, see http://www.wfas.net/index
.php/haines-index-fire-potential—danger-34.

124 *a thousand acres of land:* Arizona Dispatch logs, June 30, 2013, 10:54:20,
Air Attack to dispatch: "Fire is 800 to 1000 acres moving quickly to the
northeast."

125 *Bar Double A Ranch, to evacuate:* Ibid., 11:02:32: "AA Bar Ranch is
being evacuated."

125 *twenty-eight cats, several dogs:* Interview with Gerry McCullough.

125 *Now, with Hall officially in:* Arizona Dispatch logs, June 30, 2013,
11:02:32: "1000 Type 2 Team Hall taking over fire." Also, Shumate's interview with OSHA officers, August 15, 2013, 47: "So I left the fire
scene, um, and went home and went to bed."

125 *Hall was a veteran of thirty-nine:* Hall interview with OSHA officers,
August 16, 2013, 1–2.

125 *repeat himself again and again:* Ibid., 6

126 *full complement of twenty-seven members:* Ibid., 16.

126 *His mandate was simply to:* Ibid.: "There was—there was no discussion
on objectives except for, go take the fire and suppress the fire."

126 *He asked . . . for three additional Hotshot:* Arizona Dispatch logs,
June 30, 2013, 11:29:21: "Placed orders for 3 IHC crews."

126 *In Yarnell, Cordes picked three:* Cordes interview with OSHA officers,
September 11, 2013, 19.

127 *At 11:36 a.m., a single-engine:* Granite Mountain IHC Entrapment and
Burnover Investigation, 11: "ATGS [Air Tactical Group Supervisor]
directed two SEAT drops at 1136 and 1145 directly onto the burnout
operations."

127 *With McDonough and a few:* Ibid., 12: "a short squad of the GMIHC
moved to the west side of the ridge and tied into the burned area and
steep rocky terrain. DIVS A considered this connection a good anchor
point." McDonough's participation in the job of carving the anchor
point detailed in "No Exit," *GQ*, December 2013: "Donut breaks off
with Marsh and the short squad, following the charred perimeter of the
fire until they reach cold black, where nothing is smoldering and the
heat has dissipated. They scrape a line two feet wide down to mineral
earth, cut away any fuel another foot from either side, dig a cup trench
on the downslope side to catch anything that might roll into the chaparral below, and they keep doing that until they've tied in with the cold
black. It's a good anchor, solid and secure."

127 *Frisby complained of the poor briefing:* Redacted statements by Frisby
and Brown. They were not identified in such statements, but two officials involved in the investigation confirmed the authorship of each of

the statements to me—Frisby's written on July 3, 2013, and Brown's on July 1, 2013.

128 *real estate agency's road map:* At least one engine crew, with firefighters from Sun City West and other suburban Phoenix communities, received a local real estate agency's map as its guide.

128 *Blue Ridge had been assigned no:* Granite Mountain IHC Entrapment and Burnover Investigation, 37.

128 *A Blue Ridge squad leader:* In their interviews with investigators, Blue Ridge crew members said the bulldozer operator didn't know his assignment, didn't have a supervisor, and didn't have a working radio.

128 *Marsh and Frisby decided that:* Notes written by Brian Frisby and three other members of the crew, obtained, with redactions, through public records requests.

129 *Marsh assigned the post to:* McDonough's interview with OSHA compliance officers, August 20, 2013, 25: "Tie back into Eric and that's when he decided I was gonna be the lookout."

129 *radioed Marsh to tell him:* Granite Mountain IHC Entrapment and Burnover Investigation, 12.

129 *BLM employee with twenty-five years:* Rance Marquez interview with OSHA compliance officers, September 23, 2013, 2.

129 *Marquez had been appointed* and *none were available:* Ibid., 6, 9.

129 *Still, Abel instructed Marquez to:* Abel interview with OSHA investigators, August 22, 2013, 15.

129 *They argued:* In Marquez's interview with OSHA officers on September 23, 2013, 18, he says the conversation "wasn't exactly cheery and rosy, it was—it was direct."

129 *Marsh told Marquez to move:* Ibid., 22: "He just suggested that I drive around, um, to that far end to where that—where that field kind of opens up and try to find another way in."

130 *At noon, at the school:* Hall interview with OSHA officers, August 16, 2013, 22.

130 *all twenty-one were committed:* Interagency Hotshot Crew report for June 30, 2013, provided by the National Interagency Fire Center.

130 *Dispatchers at the Southwest Coordination Center:* Arizona Dispatch logs, June 30, 2013, 12:10:18: "Per SWC [Southwest Coordination Center], they need to go out of GACC [geographic area] for IHC orders, possibly Northern California."

130 *At 12:27 p.m., Hall gave David Geyer:* Geyer's assessment detailed in Arizona Dispatch logs, June 30, 2013, 12:27:55.

130 *covering nearly two thousand acres:* Geyer's assessment of the fire says

it "increased 700 acres in the last 2 hours," and the previous acreage of the fire put it at a thousand acres.

130 *Hall paused and considered the precarious:* Hall interview with OSHA officers, August 16, 2013, 24.

131 *The fire hissed, whooshed, and roared:* Barbara Kelso and Lewis Crew inmate Steve Parker.

131 *They made their way back:* Granite Mountain IHC Entrapment and Burnover Investigation, 13: "After lunch, the crew worked their way back, reinforcing their line as they went, ensuring they had a good anchor point."

131 *justify calling a Type 1 team:* Hall interview with OSHA officers, August 16, 2013, 16.

132 *several states in the West:* The fire behavior analyst, for example, came from Illinois.

133 *Linda Ma stood by the side:* Interview with Linda Ma.

133 *Bob Brandon ran one of:* Interviews with Bob Brandon and Darby Starr.

134–135 *Joki had realized that orders:* Glenn Joki interview with OSHA compliance officers, August 15, 2013, 7–13.

135 *"Well, look it," Hall replied:* Tony Sciacca interview with OSHA compliance officers, August 20, 2013, 10: "Came in and tied in with Roy. And I said, you know, asked him what he had and he said, 'Well look it, I got a mess.'"

135 *Sciacca used Willis's radio to "clone":* Ibid.

135 *"We got a hell of a rainstorm":* Ibid., 11.

136 *"Everybody out!" he commanded:* Willis interview with OSHA officers, August 19, 2013: "And I told them, 'Everybody out.' I just had a—just had everybody get out of here."

137 *"We're going to lose Peeples Valley":* Interviews with Conrad Jackson.

Change in the Winds

138 *The winds might be fierce and erratic:* Granite Mountain Entrapment and Burnover Investigation, 13.

139 *"Do you have eyes on both of them?"* and subsequent dialogue between Todd Abel and Eric Marsh from Abel's interview with OSHA investigators, August 22, 2013, pp. 39–40.

139 *Bob Brandon, working west of:* Interviews with Bob Brandon. See also "A Narrow Escape: Peeples Valley Firefighters Recount That Frightening Day," *Prescott Daily Courier,* June 30, 2014.

139 *Darby Starr heard something about:* Interviews with Darby Starr.

139 *At 3:33 p.m., the Yavapai County:* According to a timeline of the evacuations of Peeples Valley and Yarnell posted on AZCentral.com on

November 16, 2013, the county issued a CodeRED alert with a mandatory evacuation notice for Peeples Valley: "All residents west of Highway 89 and north of Yarnell please report to Yavapai College" (in Prescott, where a shelter had been set up for evacuees), http://www.azcentral.com /news/arizona/articles/20131116yarnell-hill-fire-evacuation-timeline .html.

139 *"Puff," Willis thought. "No problem":* Willis interview with OSHA officers, August 19, 2013, 20: "I mean, we were having trouble holding it and then all of sudden it was, like, puff, no problem. Wind stopped and we had a good—good dirt road there."

140 *Jackson and Matthews high-fived each:* Interviews with Conrad Jackson.

140 *"pray for rain"* Text message exchange between Wade Parker and his mother, Michelle, provided by Michelle Parker.

140 *On the radio, Marsh and Abel:* Abel interview with OSHA officers, August 22, 2013, 39–40.

140 *The winds are getting squirrely:* Ibid., 40.

141 *"Are you guys in a safe place?":* Ibid.: "I said are you guys in a safe place? He said affirmative, we're in the black. I said copy that, just—once again everybody's in a good spot? Yes we're all in a good spot, we're in the black. I said copy that."

141 *"I'm trying to work my way off the top"* This radio communication between Marsh and Abel was unearthed by the author John N. Maclean and Holly Neill, a former wildland firefighter who has been investigating the Yarnell Hill Fire with Maclean. It was one of several background conversations they found in the audio and video recordings used by investigators who prepared two separate reports on the fire and released to the media. Maclean and Neill wrote about their findings on the Web site *Wildfire Today,* http://wildfiretoday.com/2014/01/19/discoveries-in -yarnell-hill-fire-recordings-provide-new-information-about-location-of -eric-marsh/.

141 *They acknowledged the fire's proximity:* Granite Mountain IHC Entrapment and Burnover Investigation, 14. McDonough also described the events of June 30, 2013, in a video interview with *The Prescott Daily Courier,* posted on its Web site on July 26, 2015, http://dcourier .com/main.asp?SectionID=257&SubSectionID=1117&NewsVideoID =247.

142 *"I've got eyes on you":* "No Exit," *GQ,* December 2013, http://www.gq .com/long-form/no-exit.

142 *"This fire is running at Yarnell!!!!":* Scott Norris's mother, Karen.

143 *From his cockpit, a pilot:* Yarnell Hill Fire Serious Accident Investigation, 22

143 *On his way out, he gave:* Granite Mountain IHC Entrapment and Burn-over Investigation, 15.

143 *Musser, one of the fire's:* Arizona Division of Occupational Safety and Health's Inspection Narrative for the Arizona State Forestry Division, 18.

No Answer

144 *Marsh called Frisby on the radio:* Notes from Blue Ridge Hotshots' unit logs transcribed in the Arizona Division of Occupational Safety and Health's Inspection Narrative for the Arizona State Forestry Division, 19.

144 *deduced that Marsh and his men:* Cordes interview with OSHA officers, September 11, 2013, 33.

145 *He thought they would have:* Ibid., 34.

145 *Its crew told dispatchers that:* Arizona Dispatch logs, 16:03:37, from Bravo 33: "Will place additional 6 HEAVYs (heavy air tankers) due to wind shift, 600 structures threatened, have structures on both flanks of the fire and Yarnell is still threaten [*sic*] to the SE."

145 *Flying toward Yarnell:* "Deaths of Granite Mountain Hotshots Expose Fight over Airtankers," ABC News, September 30, 2013: "And, as first reported by ABC News, the investigation team found that the lone plane flying toward Yarnell as the hotshots called for help—Tanker 43, a P2V retired sub hunter owned by Neptune Aviation—suddenly 'suffered a left reciprocal piston engine mechanical failure that forced them to jettison their retardant load and return to the base of departure.'"

145 *At 4:04 p.m., she picked:* Text message provided by Juliann Ashcraft.

146 *McDonough turned the key, started:* Truck radios turned themselves off automatically after the truck was shut off for some time, but came back on as soon as a key was turned in the ignition.

146 *By radio, Marsh and Steed:* Fragments of this conversation were captured on the background of a video recorded by one of the Hotshots, Christopher MacKenzie, at 4:01 p.m., https://www.youtube.com/watch?v=omfw_Unt_VQ.

147 *but through dense, unburned brush:* Based on author's observations from three visits to the edge of the saddle through which the Granite Mountain Hotshots descended, photographs of the area taken by hikers Joy Collura and Sonny Gilligan prior to the fire, and observations made on two visits to the Hotshots' shelter-deployment site, at the bottom of the canyon.

149 *waving her arms, "Get out now!":* From Tragedy to Recovery: The Yarnell Hill Wildfire of 2013, a narrative of the fire by residents of Yarnell

and Peeples Valley (Yarnell-Peeples Valley Chamber of Commerce, June 2014), 167, "Embers Raining Down."

150 *"Do we need to call a time-out?":* Yarnell Hill Fire Serious Accident Investigation, 27: "At approximately 1600, ASM2 [aerial supervisory module 2, a role fulfilled by Burfiend's Bravo 33] overhears a comment on the radio referencing a crew and a safety zone. ASM2 calls OPS1 [Operations 1, Todd Abel] and clarifies, 'I heard a crew in a safety zone, do we need to call a time-out?' OPS1 replies, 'No, they're in a good place. They're safe and it's Granite Mountain.'"

150 *Burfiend then asked Marsh, "Is everything":* Ibid.: "Following this conversation, ASM2 hears DIVS A (Eric Marsh) announce on the radio, 'We're going down our escape route to our safety zone.' ASM2 asks, 'Is everything okay?' to which DIVS A replies, 'Yes, we're just moving.'"

150 *He directed the firefighters:* Cordes interview with OSHA officers, September 11, 2013, 29: "Right, and Of—Musser showed up and met with me where I was parked on the road, asked me what I thought and I basically said this thing's gonna move, it's moving pretty aggressively towards town. Um, during . . . that time, within that time frame, as you drop to the next line, the trigger point for crew rem—uh, removing the crew was met so I, I got on the, uh, told the guys to start picking up and, and getting ready to get out of the area."

151 *They ordered their men to:* Interview with Bob Brandon.

151 *"Start driving very slow":* Interview with Brandon; and also "A Narrow Escape," *Prescott Daily Courier.*

151 *He had thought he wouldn't make it:* "A Narrow Escape," *Prescott Daily Courier.*

151 *He stood like a chaperone to the path ahead:* Interviews with Darby Starr.

152 *When the single raindrop struck him:* Ibid. See also "Dude Fire Still Smokin'," *Wildfire Magazine,* June 1996, http://www.fireleadership .gov/toolbox/staffride/downloads/lsr11/lsr11_still_smoking.pdf.

152 *"Shit," he said, "that was close":* Interview with Starr.

153 *He peeked in his rearview mirror:* Interview with Marty Cole.

153 *sixteen miles per hour, fourteen:* Granite Mountain IHC Entrapment and Burnover Investigation, 15: "At 1618, the outflow boundary neared the northern end of fire area moving at 16 miles per hour" (16 miles per hour=84,480 feet per hour / 60=1,408 feet per minute).

153 *the smoke plume had soared:* Ibid.: "At 1624, Dopplar radar showed a fire plume at a height of approximately 31,500 that grew to 38,700 feet by 1633."

153 *Cordes understood that he had underestimated the fire's potential:*

On pp. 18–19 of the transcript of his interview with state investigators, dated September 11, 2013, Cordes described his "trigger points" or landmarks he'd selected that would prompt certain actions, including the evacuation of crews working his end of the fire, once flames hit these landmarks. On p. 49, he acknowledges that he had miscalculated his trigger points: "I miscalculated my trigger points that, that got ate up in 15 minutes that I figured I had over an hour."

153 *"There goes Yarnell," she thought:* Interview with Barbara Kelso.

154 *They could see the fire to:* Author's observations during hikes along the route taken by the Granite Mountain Hotshots throughout the day on June 30, 2013.

154 *On the radio, a desperate cry:* Radio communication transcribed from audio captured in a video of the last three minutes of radio transmissions from the Granite Mountain Hotshots before they were entrapped by fire and killed, https://www.youtube.com/watch?v=BbrlWTng2JU &feature=youtu.be (link from *Wildfire Today*'s YouTube channel, posted on December 13, 2013).

Gone

158 *Abel phoned Willis and asked:* Willis interview with OSHA officers, August 19, 2013, 22. Also, Abel interview with OSHA officers, August 22, 2013, 50.

159 *"Keep mopping, keep watching this":* Willis interview with OSHA officers, August 19, 2013, 22.

159 *A pair of horses dashed:* Ibid., 23: "Ah, as I was driving into Yarnell along this highway right about here there's, ah, two horses running down the middle of the road."

159 *"What's going on?":* Ibid.

159 *Dispatchers were calling every hospital:* Interviews with *Ranger 58* police officer–paramedics Eric Tarr and Charles Main.

159 *"You gotta pray for these guys":* Willis interview with OSHA officers, August 19, 2013, 24.

160 *"The worst-case scenario is":* Ibid.

160 *"Bullshit," Cordes fired back:* Cordes interview with OSHA officers, September 11, 2013, 39: "It was Engine 59 that told me that they had transmitted over the radio, over air to ground that they had deployed and I, and I, it was Charlie Reyes who's the, who's the engine boss down there and I told him BS, that uh, they didn't need to deploy 'cause the safety's, they were in their safety zone and it was bomb proof and he said no, they never got—made it there, they got cut off. And that's when I knew obviously something bad had most likely occurred."

162 *They were the last people Cordes rescued:* Ibid., 37–38; and "Mystery Man Rescued Residents During Yarnell Hill Fire," *Arizona Republic,* March 31, 2014.

163 *"Any word?":* Hall interview with OSHA officers, August 16, 2013, 35.

163 *He called the state forester:* Ibid., 37.

164 *they all barged through fire:* Narrative of actions by Frisby and Brown to reach the Granite Mountain Hotshots constructed from redacted statements by four members of the Blue Ridge Hotshots, including Frisby and Brown; interviews by Roy Hall and Gary Cordes with OSHA investigators, and helmet-camera videos recorded that afternoon and released by the Arizona State Forestry Division.

165 *At 6:08 p.m., one of them* and subsequent tweets: Compilation by Leslie-Jean Thornton, an associate professor at the Walter J. Cronkite School of Journalism and Mass Communication at Arizona State University, of tweets about the fire posted in the afternoon and evening of June 30, 2013. Lee kindly searched through her feed and confirmed the times of her tweets posted in this chapter.

166 *John Percin's name had been left off:* Hall interview with OSHA officers, August 16, 2013, 37.

166 *In its 128-year history:* Interviews with Wade Ward, Darrell Willis, and Dan Fraijo.

168 *Stephanie Turbyfill had gone to her* and details of her evening: Interviews with Stephanie.

169 *"It's them. They're gone":* Interview with Kristi Whitted.

169 *A disturbing alert from the Fox:* Interview with Tiffany Rose.

169 *The alert, relayed at 7:30 p.m.:* Fox 10 Phoenix, https://twitter.com /fox10phoenix/status/351528088544354304 (time listed on the link is CST).

169 *Back from a shopping trip:* Interviews with Desiree Steed.

169 *Juliann ran to her bedroom:* Interviews with Juliann Ashcraft.

170 *She touched her stomach:* Interviews with Amanda Misner.

170 *In Seal Beach, California, Joe:* Interviews with Joe and Anna Woyjeck.

170 *In the buggy, McDonough heard the beeps, rings, and buzzes:* "19: The True Story of the Yarnell Hill Fire," *Outside* magazine, September 2013.

170 *Amanda Marsh arrived with her neighbor:* Interview with Amanda Marsh.

171 *where Andrew Ashcraft, class of 2003:* Interviews with Ashcraft's mother, Deborah Pfingston.

172 *The fireman held Tripp's hands:* Interviews with Matt Demenna.

172 *For Roxanne Warneke, who lived:* Interviews with Roxanne Warneke.

Two Thousand Degrees

174 *A fire shelter's skin is:* Yarnell Hill Fire Serious Accident Investigation *Report*, Appendix C: "Personal Protective Equipment Analysis," 82.

174 *If the sack heats to 500:* Ibid., 87, table.

174–175 *more than three hundred lives:* "New Generation Fire Shelter Developed for Wildland Firefighters," US Forest Service, May 2003, http://www.fs.fed.us/t-d/pubs/htmlpubs/htm03512313/.

175 *Firefighters must hold the sides:* Positioning inside a deployed fire shelter from author's basic training at Arizona Wildfire and Incident Management Academy, March 9–13, 2014.

176 *Donning chaps of nylon and Kevlar:* Chaps, worn by sawyers, listed among clothing they were wearing when they died.

176 *twenty-four feet by thirty feet:* Yarnell Hill Fire Serious Accident Investigation Report, 88, diagram.

176 *Ten of the nineteen men had gone in* and other positioning, as well as description of clothing in the shelters: Ibid., appendix C, 89–94.

177 *Sometime during the winter:* Interviews with Juliann Ashcraft. Also, "Firefighter's Widow Finds Peace, Comfort in 'Be Better' Bracelet," *Salt Lake City Deseret News,* July 8, 2013.

"We Take Care of Our Own"

189 *Sharon had lost a son* and accompanying information on the death of her first husband: Sharon Knutson-Felix, with Allen R. Kates, *Gifts My Father Gave Me: Finding Joy After Tragedy* (Cortaro, Ariz.: Holbook Street Press, 2006).

190 *On Sunday, Sharon had heard* and other descriptions of Knutson-Felix's activities on June 30, 2013, and beyond: Interview with Sharon Knutson-Felix.

190 *In one day:* See "Firefighter, Police Officer Lose Lives on Same Day in Tragic First for Phoenix," *Arizona Republic,* May 22, 2013.

191 *the club's connection to the site:* Interview with Sharon Knutson-Felix.

191 *helped set up an incident command:* Interviews with Dan Fraijo.

192 *Thirty-five thousand visitors were:* Estimates from Prescott tourism officials in "Tributes to Firefighters Added to Prescott Rodeo, July 4th," *Arizona Republic,* July 2, 2013, http://archive.azcentral.com/travel/articles/20130702tributes-firefighters-prescott-rodeo-july-fourth-yarnell-hill-fire.html.

192 *handmade signs had appeared:* Observations by the author during her stays in Prescott following the deaths.

192 *Eighteen fire crews:* From updates on the fire by the Type 1 incident

management team, posted on the Web site *Wildfire Today,* July 1, 2013, http://wildfiretoday.com/2013/06/30/arizona-yarnell-fire/.

193 *$120,000 through his foundation:* "Yarnell Charitable Donations Mostly Distributed," *Arizona Republic,* June 28, 2014, http://www.azcentral .com/story/news/arizona/2014/06/28/yarnell-donations-distributed /11657993/.

193 *$1,900, raised through a daylong:* "Over $13 Mil Raised After Yarnell Tragedy," *Arizona Republic,* December 24, 2013, http://archive .azcentral.com/business/news/articles/20131207yarnell-tragedy -millions-raised.html.

193 *They needed eighteen more:* "Honoring Heroes: How a Small-Town Funeral Home in Arizona Handled the Services for 19 Fallen Hotshots," *International Cemetery, Cremation and Funeral Association Magazine,* November 2013.

194 *"We take care of our own":* Interview with Butch Hampton.

194 *Chief Fraijo also admonished the mayor:* Interview with Dan Fraijo.

195 *rodeo clowns played tricks:* "Prescott Frontier Days Parade Honors All Heroes, Fallen Hotshots," *Prescott Daily Courier,* July 7, 2013, http:// dcourier.com/main.asp?SectionID=1&SubsectionID=1&ArticleID =121030.

195 *Stephanie Raetz, widow of Daryl:* "Yarnell Hill Fire: Fallen Firefighters Brought Home in Stirring Procession," *Arizona Republic,* July 8, 2013, http://www.azcentral.com/news/articles/20130707yarnell-fire -firefighters-procession-prescott-brk.html.

195–196 *"These were the men that were trying to protect my home":* Ibid.

197 *"All these years later, we're coming":* "Thousands Gather to Honor 19 Arizona Firefighters," *The New York Times,* July 9, 2013, http://www .nytimes.com/2013/07/10/us/arizona-firefighters-remembered-at -memorial-service.html.

197 *"I thank God for their bravery":* C-SPAN video of memorial service, http://www.c-span.org/video/?313826-1/vp-biden-speaks-service -arizona-firefighters.

198 *"nineteen ordinary men who did extraordinary":* Ibid.

199 *The lake carried special significance:* Interview with Amanda Marsh.

200 *"men to emulate if you have":* "Statement by Senator John McCain Honoring the Granite Mountain Hotshots," July 9, 2013, http://www .mccain.senate.gov/public/index.cfm/press-releases?ID=c4a6ecbd -0a2d-5fbe-1dcd-50972c470094.

200 *By July 11, 2013, the deadly:* According to InciWeb, the Yarnell Hill Fire was 100 percent contained on July 10, 2013, http://inciweb.nwcg .gov/incident/article/3461/19114/.

An End, and New Beginnings

202 *He'd refused to meet with her:* Interviews with Juliann Ashcraft and Dan Fraijo, former chief of the Prescott Fire Department.

202 *"She's a neat little lady":* "City Won't Budge on Ashcraft Status: Widow Takes Her Plea to the Courthouse Plaza," *Prescott Daily Courier,* August 8, 2013, http://dcourier.com/m/Articles.aspx?ArticleID=122048.

203 *It was solely his job classification:* The author attended one day of hearings on the case and read the transcript of the proceedings, provided by Juliann Ashcraft's lawyer, Patrick J. McGroder III.

203 *voted 4 to 1 in Juliann's:* "Prescott Public Safety Retirement Board OKs Ashcraft Benefits," *Prescott Daily Courier,* May 23, 2014, http://dcourier.com/main.asp?SectionID=1&SubSectionID=1&ArticleID=132023.

204 *On the following day, July 1:* "Board That Ruled for Ashcraft Disputes Claims in City Appeal," *Prescott Daily Courier,* July 3, 2014. Specifically: "The filing came after the Prescott City Council's vote on Tuesday"—July 1, 2014—"to appeal the decision."

204 *Deborah had prepared herself for:* Interviews with Deborah Pfingston.

205 *He'd labored for ten straight:* Evidence introduced by McGroder during the legal proceedings on Andrew Ashcraft's benefits.

205 *Judge Mackey ruled that Prescott:* "Judge: City Had 'Responsibility' to Treat Ashcraft Like Other Full-Time Hotshots," *Prescott Daily Courier,* January 22, 2015, http://dcourier.com/main.asp?SectionID=1&subsectionID=1086&articleID=140885.

205 *Again, the board agreed with him:* "Board Oks Benefits to the Hotshot Families of Misner, Warneke," *Prescott Daily Courier,* January 30, 2015, http://dcourier.com/main.asp?SectionID=1&SubSectionID=1&ArticleID=141238.

206 *"You live, you die":* Interview with Roxanne Warneke.

207 *The baby, Billie Grace Warneke:* "Nearly 6 Months After Yarnell Fire, a Final Hotshot Legacy Begins," *Arizona Republic,* December 20, 2013, http://www.azcentral.com/news/arizona/articles/20131204arizona-yarnell-granite-mountain-hotshot-baby-warneke.html.

207 *Billie Grace, fresh out of diapers:* Witnessed by author during a visit to Roxanne Warneke's home.

210 *Shane told Anthony that Tiffany could call:* Interviews with Tiffany Rose.

212 *Amanda Marsh removed the ring:* Interview with Amanda Marsh.

212 *She paid $27,500 for a:* Interviews with Juliann Ashcraft.

213 *Desiree Steed had a child:* "Birth: Cora Grace Montejano," *Prescott Daily Courier,* July 8, 2015.

INDEX

Abel, Todd, 120, 158–59
  Marquez and, 129
  Marsh, E., and, 121–22, 138–41, 150
Adams, Token, 217–18
air tankers
  in Doce Fire, 39
  Ranger 58, 5
  Southwest Coordination Center on,
    130, 145
  in Yarnell Hill Fire, 79–82, 86–87,
    127, 130, 145
alligator junipers, 56–57
American Ranch community, 38–39
Andersen, Judy, 65
Andersen, Peter, 64–65
Arizona Department of Public Safety,
    164, 189–90
Arollado, Shane, 210
Arroyo Grande Hotshots, 90, 122
Ashby, Emilee, 98, 105–6
Ashcraft, Andrew, 21, 30, 41–42, 73,
    99–103, 106, 177
  background on, 26–27, 42
  in Doce Fire, 42

employment status of, 55
funeral for, 199–200
remains of, 1, *1,* 176–78
in Yarnell Hill Fire, 133
Ashcraft, Juliann, 54, 99–103, 106, 133,
    145, 169–70
  background on, 26–27, 41–42
  Kuykendall on, 202
  after loss, 177, 198, 200, 212–13
  news coverage on, 201–2
  on pensions, 202–5
Ashcraft, T. J., 204
autopsies, 193

Bachman, Sandra, 76
Bambi, 44
Bates, Dan, 171
Bear Mountain Hand Crew, 13
Bellemont's National Weather Service
    office, 117
Biden, Joe, 194, 196, 198
Big Burn, 44
BLM. *See* Bureau of Land
    Management

Blue Ridge Hotshots
  Frisby and, 127–29
  in Yarnell Hill Fire, 88, 127–28, 143,
    153
Boulder Springs Ranch, 144–45, 151,
    184–85
Boy Scouts Club of America, 193
Brandon, Bob, 61, 63, 68
  on Yarnell Hill Fire, 66, 82, 83,
    133–34, 137, 139, 150–52
Bravo 33, 143, 145, 150, 158
  Division Alpha and, 155–57
Brown, Rogers Trueheart, 128, 150–51
  in search party, 163, 164, 165
budget cuts, 49, 115–16
buggies, 16, 48, 69–70
Bunch, Brandon, 182
Bureau of Land Management (BLM),
    63, 67, 81
Burfiend, John, 150
Bursting, Clifford, 6, 164, 165, 166

Cal Fire. *See* Department of Forestry
    and Fire Protection
Caldwell, Claire, 15, 30–31, 177
Caldwell, Robert, 30–31, 69, 93
  background on, 14–15, 36
  in Doce Fire, 40
  remains of, 1, *1*, 178
  Turbyfill, T., and, 40
Carter, Travis, 57, 73–74, 93
  background on, 27
  in Doce Fire, 41
  remains of, 1, *1*, 177
Carter, Tripp, 172
Central Yavapai Fire District, 91, 120
City of Prescott Oath of Office, 34
city officials, 15, 49–50, 55
climate, 45
Cole, Marty, 135, 153
combis, 43
Cordes, Gary
  in Glen Ilah, 120, 126–27, 134,
    150
  Marsh, E., and, 121
  rescues by, 160–62
  Yarnell Hill Fire and, 91, 120–21,
    126, 133–34, 144–45, 150, 153

Coyote Joe's, 14
Crockett, Joe, 106

DC-10, 87
Dean Peak Fire, 85, 90, 122, 131
DeFord, Dustin, 49, 54, 57, 70, 97–98
  background on, 27
  remains of, 1, *1*
DeFord, Ryan, 97–98
Delgado, Ed, 86
Demenna, Matt, 182–88
Department of Forestry and Fire
    Protection, 77
Department of Public Safety, 164,
    189–90
diggers, 42–43
Disney, 44
Division Alpha, 121, 129
  Bravo 33 and, 155–57
Division Zulu, 129
Doce Fire, 62–63
  air tankers in, 39
  Ashcraft, A., in, 42
  Caldwell, R., in, 40
  Carter, Travis, in, 41
  evacuations, 39–40
  fire line in, 40–41, 52
  Granite Mountain Hotshots in,
    37–43, 46–47, 49, 50–57
  incident commanders in, 39, 40, 51,
    134
  Marsh, E., in, 38–39, 40, 51–52
  McKee in, 53
  Parker, W., in, 54
  under Sciacca, 51, 134
  Steed, J., in, 40, 52, 53–54, 56–57
  Turbyfill, T., in, 53
  Warneke, W., in, 43
  water drop at, 39
  Whitted, C., in, 40
  Willis, D., in, 38
donations, 191, 193, 201
Doppler, Christian, 113
doppler radars, 113–14
Double Bar A Ranch, 119–20, 123–24,
    136–37, 139, 158
Downey, Jim, 125–26, 131–32
drip torches, 52

drug rehabilitation, 31–32
Dude Fire, 76

Eighteen Watchout Situations, 13–14
Ekker, A. C., 28
Ekker,Gayemarie, 28
equipment and gear, 15, 22
    combis, 43
    for diggers, 42–43
    drip torches, 52
    medical kit, 6
    monkey paws, 43
    MRE, 70
    psychrometer, 4
    Pulaskis, 43–44
    rhinos, 43
    sprinklers, 123–24
    in Yarnell Hill Fire, 87
escape route, 144–45, 153–57
evacuations
    Doce Fire, 39–40
    rescues after, 160–62
    Yarnell Hill Fire, 124–25, 132–33,
        136–37, 139, 150

families
    financial assistance for, 190–92, 193,
        201
    get-togethers, 53–54
    after loss of Granite Mountain
        Hotshots, 167–73
    telephone tree, 167–71
Felix, David, 190
financial assistance, 190–92, 193,
    201
    pensions, 202–5
Fine, Leah, 53
fire ecology, 44–45
fire line
    in Doce Fire, 40–41, 52
    in Yarnell Hill Fire, 3, 83
fire shelters
    description of, 5–6, 174–75
    lives saved by, 174–75
fire-behavior analyst, 115
Flake, Jeff, 196
Flora Mae Park, 163
forensic investigators, 185–86

Forest Service, US
    establishment of, 44
    guidelines by, 13–14
    wildfire policy by, 44–46
forestation cycles, 44–45
Fort Apache Hotshots, 88
Fort Whipple, 31–32
Foster, Sally, 61, 65–66
Fraijo, Dan, 49–50, 160, 191–92, 194
French, Tom, 150
Frisby, Brian
    Blue Ridge Hotshots and, 127–29
    Marsh, E., and, 127–29
    McDonough and, 129, 142, 145–46
    in search party, 163–65
Frontier Days parade, 192
funeral service
    for Granite Mountain Hotshots,
        193–94, 198–200
    by Hampton Funeral Home, 191,
        193–94, 198–99

gear. See equipment and gear
Geronimo Hotshots, 88
Geyer, David, 130
Glen Ilah, 4
    Cordes in, 120, 126–27, 134, 150
Granite Mountain Hotshots. See also
        specific crew members
    announcing death of, 170–72
    autopsies of, 193
    buggies, 16, 48, 69–70
    carrying home, after Yarnell Hill
        Fire, 179–88
    city officials on, 49–50
    in Doce Fire, 37–43, 46–47, 49,
        50–57
    employer of, 15, 23
    entrapment of, 2–5, 153–57, 175–78
    families, after loss of, 167–73
    founding of, 48–49
    full-time permanent positions, 42,
        55, 202
    full-time temporary positions, 23–24,
        55, 202–3
    funeral service for, 193–94, 198–200
    future for, 217, 218
    guidelines for, 13–14

Granite Mountain Hotshots (*continued*)
  hierarchy in, 13, 69–70
  hiring process, 17–20
  inauguration of, 11–14, 34–35
  incident commanders and, 128,
    146–47
  job requirements of, 16–17, 22–23
  last contact with, 153–57
  life as, 16
  loss of, 153–57, 175–78
  memorial service for, 191–92, 194–98
  mobilization of, in Yarnell Hill Fire,
    90–94
  on morning of Yarnell Hill Fire, 105–8
  news coverage on loss of, 164–65,
    166–67, 169
  pay and salary of, 23–24, 50
  in Payette National Forest Fire, 72
  profits of, 48–49
  remains of, 1, *1*, 176–77, 186–88
  search party for, 5–7, 163–66
  spending by, 48–49
  *Standards for Interagency Hotshot
    Crew Operations*, 55
  under Steed, J., 16–17
  in Thompson Ridge Fire, 37, 70
  training, 16–17, 23
  in Wesley Fire, 72
  in West Spruce Fire, 69–73
  in Yarnell Hill Fire, 1–7, 90–94,
    105–8, 120–22, 126–32, 137–57
Granite Mountain Wilderness, 38
Ground Zero, 197
Guadiana, Jake, 79, 80, 81

Haines index, 124
Hall, Roy
  background on, 125–26
  as incident commander, 116, 125
  in search party, 163
  Shumate and, 116, 119–20, 122, 125
  in Yarnell Hill Fire, 116, 119–22,
    125–28, 130–32, 135–36, 162–63
Hampton, Butch, 193, 194, 198
Hampton, Cathy, 193, 194, 198
Hampton Funeral Home, 191, 193–94,
    198–99
Harper, Brad, 190

Hart, Bob, 161–62
Hart, Ruth, 161–62
heat wave, 59, 64, 65
high wildfire risk areas, 39, 46
Highland Pines, 60
hiring process, 17–20
homebuilding, in high wildfire risk
    areas, 39, 46
honesty, 18–19
Hotshot crews, 15–16, 47–48, 88, 90,
    130, 197
Hunt, Scott, 46, 116, 131–32, 163

IMETs. *See* incident meteorologists
incident commanders, 72
  in Doce Fire, 39, 40, 51, 134
  Granite Mountain Hotshots and, 128,
    146–47
  in Yarnell Hill Fire, 116, 125–28,
    134–35, 146–47
incident meteorologists (IMETs), 115–16
Indian Fire, 46–47

Jackson, Conrad, 123, 124, 136–37,
    140, 186
Jaroso Fire, 98
Jewell, Sally, 196
Johnson, Sean, 197
Joki, Glenn, 134–35

Keehner, Matt, 151–52
Kelso, Barbara, 60–61, 66, 119, 131,
    132–33, 153
Kelso, Kim, 60–61, 66, 131, 132–33
Kimball, Byron, 115–17, 124, 132, 138
Klement, Dan, 207
Klimowski, Brian, 114, 118–19
Knutson, Doug, 189–90
Knutson, Ricky, 189
Knutson-Felix, Sharon, 189–91, 193,
    197
Koile, Jim, 61
Kuykendall, Marlin, 49, 194
  on Ashcraft, J., 202
  on pensions, 202–4, 205

lawsuits, 202–5
Lee, Michelle Ye Hee, 164–65

LeMieux, Tim, 195–96
Lewis inmates, 65
  in Yarnell Hill Fire, 67, 75–79, 81,
    83–85, 87, 136
Lewis state prison, 65, 76
Light, Dennis, 217
Lindquist, Bruce, 97–98
lookout, 4–5, 129, 141–42

Ma, Linda, 58–59, 133, 149–50
MacKenzie, Christopher, 40, 57, 98
  background on, 28
  employment status of, 55
  remains of, 1, *1*, 178
  Whitted, C., and, 40
MacKenzie, Mike, 28, 178
Mackey, David, 204–5
Mann Gulch Fire, 34
Manzanita Drive, 161
Marquez, Rance, 129–30
Marsh, Amanda, 54, 92, 105, 167–68,
    170–72
  after loss, 178, 199, 212
Marsh, Eric, 7, 37, 47, 60, 105
  Abel and, 121–22, 138–41, 150
  background on, 32–34, 48, 54–55, 94
  Cordes and, 121
  Division Alpha and, 121
  in Doce Fire, 38–39, 40, 51–52
  Frisby and, 127–29
  funeral for, 199
  hiring process by, 17, 18–20
  Marquez and, 129–30
  memo, to city officials, 50
  remains of, 1, *1*, 178
  Steed, J., and, 20–21, 71
  on weather awareness, 115
  on Wesley Fire, 72
  Willis, D., and, 33–34
  Yarnell Hill Fire and, 6, 90–91,
    121–22, 127, 138–41, 143–53,
    155–56
Matthews, Mark, 123, 124, 136–37,
    140, 186
Matt's Saloon, 26
McCain, John, 196, 200
McConnell, Craig, 49–50
McCullough, Gerry, 125

McCullough, Kate, 125
McDonough, Brendan, 2, 54, 60, 98,
    153, 160
  background on, 20
  Frisby and, 129, 142, 145–46
  as lookout, 4–5, 129, 141–42
McElwee, Herbert, 29
McElwee, Tim, 29, 170
McGroder, Patrick J., III, 205
McKee, Grant, 14, 23, 57, 96–97
  in Doce Fire, 53
  remains of, 1, *1*
meals ready to eat (MRE), 70
medical kit, 6
memorial service, for Granite Mountain
    Hotshots, 191–92, 194–98
Mile High Middle School, 169, 179
Misner, Amanda, 29–30, 74, 169–70
  background on, 53
  after loss, 208–9
  on pensions, 205
Misner, Sean Jaxon Herbert, 209
Misner, Sean, 70
  background on, 28–30, 36, 74
  remains of, 1, *1*
Misner, Tammy, 74
Model Creek School, 116, 119, 130–31,
    136
Model Creek subdivision, 124–25
monkey paws, 43
monsoons, 111–13
Montejano, Cora Grace, 213–14
Montejano, Eric, 213–14
Moore, Pearl, 162
Moser, Cory, 186, 187
Mount Josh Fire, 73, 90, 92, 94
Mount Washington Fire, 88
MRE. *See* meals ready to eat
Muleshoe Animal Clinic, 125
Musser, Paul, 120, 135, 143, 153,
    155–56, 159
  in search party, 162–63

Napolitano, Janet, 196
National Fuel Moisture Database, 80
National Interagency Fire Center, 85
National Multi-Agency Coordinating
    Group, 85

National Park Service, 45
news coverage
  on Ashcraft, J., 201–2
  on Granite Mountain Hotshots,
    164–65, 166–67, 169
911 calls
  reverse-911 system, 132
  on Yarnell Hill Fire, 59–60, 61, 67,
    68
Norris, Scott, 142
  background on, 27
  remains of, 1, *1*

off-season work, 24–25, 36–37
100 Club of Arizona, 189, 191, 193
oral traditions, 48
Oso Fire, 64
Owens, Alicia, 181, 184

Parker, Danny, 179–82, 185–88, 216
Parker, Michelle, 140, 180, 216
Parker, Steve, 76
  in Yarnell Hill Fire, 77, 79, 84, 136
Parker, Wade, 140
  background on, 25, 180–84
  in Doce Fire, 54
  remains of, 1, *1*
Parsons, Bob, 193
Pattersen, Karen, 59
pay and salary, 23–24, 50
Payette National Forest Fire, 72
Peck, Nate, 81, 83, 87
Peeples Valley, Arizona, 3–4, 91–92,
    119–20, 131, 139
Peeples Valley Fire Department, 61, 63
pensions
  Ashcraft, J., on, 202–5
  court rulings on, 204–5
  description of, 202
  Kuykendall on, 202–4, 205
  lawsuits over, 202–5
  Misner, A., on, 205
  Warneke, R., on, 205
Percin, John, Jr., 60, 70, 73, 166
  background on, 30–31, 32
  remains of, 1, *1*
pets, 125, 162
Pfingston, Deborah, 204, 215–16

pilots, 81, 143, 150. *See also* air tankers
Pioneers' Home Cemetery, 194, 203–4
preparedness levels, 86
Prescott, Arizona
  City of Prescott Oath of Office, 34
  as place of healing, 31–32
  population, 12
Prescott Fire Department, 120, 184
  under Fraijo, 49–50, 160, 191–92
  Wildland Division, 11, 33, 46–47,
    49–50, 217–18
Prescott firefighters, 69
Prescott Hotshots, 69
prisoners. *See* Lewis inmates
psychrometer, 4
Public Safety Retirement System, 203
Pulaski, Edward, 43–44
Pulaskis, 43–44

Raetz, Daryl, 190
Raetz, Stephanie, 195
Ranger 58, 5
Rast, Paul, 76
Redford, Robert, 28
Remmerde, Cheryl, 149–50
rescues, 160–62
reverse-911 system, 132
rhinos, 43
Ridge Way Drive, 162
risk-management, 147
Robbers Roost, 28
Rookie of the Year award, 42, 182
Rose, Anthony, 94–95, 105, 107–8
  background on, 24–25, 36
  remains of, 1, *1*
Rose, Tiffany, 95, 105, 107–8, 169
  after loss, 177–78, 209–10
Rose, Willow Mae, 209–10

safety officers, 134–35
saw bosses, 41
sawyers, 40–41
Sciacca, Tony
  Doce Fire under, 51, 134
  in Yarnell Hill Fire, 134–35, 152–53
search party
  Brown in, 163, 164, 165
  Bursting in, 6, 164, 165, 166

INDEX

Frisby in, 163–65
for Granite Mountain Hotshots, 5–7,
  163–66
Hall in, 163
Musser in, 162–63
Tarr in, 5–7, 164–66
Shayne, Adria, 4
Shumate, Russ, 61
  background on, 79
  Hall and, 116, 119–20, 122, 125
  Kimball and, 116
  on Yarnell Hill Fire, 62–63, 66–68,
    79–91, 115, 119–22, 125, 128
Silver Fire, 62, 88
Skull Valley, 50–51, 108
slop-over, 84
Smith, Bryan, 162
Smith, Justin, 83–84
Smith, Ron, 151
Smokey Bear, 44
snow storm, 94
South Canyon Fire, 34
Southwest Coordination Center, 87–88,
  90, 122
  on air tankers, 130, 145
  in hiring process, 18
spot forecasts, 117, 124
sprinklers, 123–24
*Standards for Interagency Hotshot
Crew Operations,* 55
Starr, Darby, 133–34, 137, 151–53
State Route 89, 78
Station 7, 12, 18
Steed, Desiree, 96, 106, 169, 171
  background on, 21
  after loss, 177, 213–14
Steed, Jesse, 95–96, 106
  background on, 20–22
  after dirt bike accident, 21–22
  in Doce Fire, 40, 52, 53–54, 56–57
  Granite Mountain Hotshots under,
    16–17
  Marsh, E., and, 20–21, 71
  remains of, 1, *1,* 178
  in Yarnell Hill Fire, 4–5, 93, 128–29,
    146–49, 154
Steinbrink, Duane, 33, 170–71
  in Indian Fire, 46–47

Storm King Mountain, 198
Sun City West Fire District, 133
swampers, 40–41
Swiss-cheese model, 147

Tarr, Eric, 5–7, 164–66
teamwork, 15, 16–17
ten o'clock policy, 45
Ten Standard Firefighting Orders, 13–14
Thompson Ridge Fire, 37, 70
Thumb Butte, 16–17, 183
thunderstorms
  monsoons relating to, 112
  Yarnell Hill Fire relating to, 3–4,
    121, 132–34, 138, 152
Thurston, Joe, 105
  background on, 27–28
  remains of, 1, *1*
Thurston, Marsena, 28
Trader, Jesse, 217
training, 16–17, 23
trees, 56–57
trigger points, 126, 141, 145
tuberculosis, 31–32
Turbyfill, Brooklyn, 210–11
Turbyfill, Brynley, 53, 211–12
Turbyfill, Stephanie, 103–5, 106,
  167–69, 171–72
  background on, 22, 37, 53
  after loss, 177, 210–12
Turbyfill, Travis, 37, 57, 103–5, 106
  background on, 22–23
  Caldwell, R., and, 40
  in Doce Fire, 53
  funeral for, 199
  remains of, 1, *1,* 177
Type 1 crew, 88, 131–32
Type 2 crew, 47, 90, 125–26
Type 3 crew, 47

uniforms, 49
Urban, Mark, 218

Vasquez, Leo, 78, 81
Vicente, J. P., 179, 182, 184–86

Ward, Wade, 166–67
Warneke, Billie Grace, 207

Warneke, Roxanne, 19, 36, 99, 107, 172–73
  background on, 206–7
  after loss, 200, 207–8
  on pensions, 205
Warneke, William ("Billy"), 7, 23, 36, 54, 57, 99, 107
  background on, 19, 43, 206
  in Doce Fire, 43
  funeral for, 200
  remains of, 1, *1*
Warren, Kirk, 60
water drop, 192–93. *See also* air tankers
  at Doce Fire, 39
weather
  awareness, 115, 121
  Bellemont's National Weather Service office, 117
  doppler radars, 113–14
  forecasters, 86, 113–15, 117, 118–19, 132
  heat waves, 59, 64, 65
  monsoons, 111–13
  spot forecasts, 117, 124
  thunderstorms, 3–4, 121, 132–34, 138, 152
  wildfires and, 111–15
weather forecast, 3–4, 67–68, 80, 82–83, 113–19, 124
  wind changes, 68, 118–19, 138
Weaver Mountains, 58, 62–63, 64
Wesley Fire, 72
West Spruce Fire, 60, 62
  Granite Mountain Hotshots in, 69–73
Whiskey Row, 14, 26, 98
Whitted, Clayton, 7, 49, 57, 69, 93, 183
  background on, 25–26
  in Doce Fire, 40
  funeral for, 199
  MacKenzie, C., and, 40
  remains of, 1, *1*
  Willis, J., and, 159–60
Whitted, Kristi, 25–26, 169
Wiederaenders, Tim, 167
wildfire policy
  background on, 44–45
  by Forest Service, 44–46
  ten o'clock policy, 45

wildfires
  acres lost to, 45–46
  classification of, 15, 62
  fire-behavior analyst for, 115
  weather and, 111–15
Williams, Andrew, 76
  in Yarnell Hill Fire, 77, 79, 84
Williamson Valley, 50–51
Willis, Darrell, 13, 55, 148
  description of, 11–12
  in Doce Fire, 38
  at Granite Mountain Hotshots' memorial service, 197–98
  in Indian Fire, 46–47
  after loss, 166, 185, 186–87, 216–18
  Marsh, E., and, 33–34
  resignation of, 216–18
  in Yarnell Hill Fire, 91, 119–20, 123–24, 126, 135–37, 139, 158–60
Willis, Judy, 159–60
Willow Creek Fire, 88
wind changes, 68, 118–19, 138
World Trade Centers, 197
World War II, 44
Woyjeck, Anna, 170, 192
Woyjeck, Bobby, 26, 170
Woyjeck, Joe, 12, 13, 170, 172
Woyjeck, Kevin, 23, 25–26, 57, 70, 96–97
  background on, 12–13, 26
  description of, 12
  inauguration of, 12, 13–14, 34–35
  remains of, 1, *1*

Yarnell, Arizona
  demographics, 59
  population, 2
  topography of, 64–65, 78
Yarnell Hill Fire. *See also specific firefighters*
  air tankers in, 79–82, 86–87, 127, 130, 145
  Arroyo Grande Hotshots in, 90, 122
  Ashcraft, A., in, 133
  Blue Ridge Hotshots in, 88, 127–28, 143, 153
  Brandon on, 66, 82, 83, 133–34, 137, 139, 150–52

classification of, 66–67, 120
Cordes and, 91, 120–21, 126,
    133–34, 144–45, 150, 153
damage assessment, 184
equipment and gear in, 87
escape route, 144–45, 153–57
evacuations, 124–25, 132–33,
    136–37, 139, 150
fighting, after loss of Granite
    Mountain Hotshots, 185, 192–93,
    194, 200
fire line in, 3, 83
Granite Mountain Hotshots in, 1–7,
    90–94, 105–8, 120–22, 126–32,
    137–57
Guadiana in, 79, 80, 81
Hall in, 116, 119–22, 125–28,
    130–32, 135–36, 162–63
incident commanders in, 116,
    125–28, 134–35, 146–47
Kimball on, 115–17
Lewis inmates in, 67, 75–79, 81,
    83–85, 87, 136
Marsh, E., and, 6, 90–91, 121–22,
    127, 138–41, 143–53, 155–56
mobilizing ground and air teams for,
    79–87
911 calls on, 59–60, 61, 67, 68
origin of, 3, 58–59
Parker, S., in, 77, 79, 84, 136
Peck and, 81, 83, 87

Sciacca in, 134–35, 152–53
Serious Accident Investigation
    Report, 1
Shumate on, 62–63, 66–68, 79–91,
    115, 119–22, 125, 128
size of, 81, 88, 120, 122, 130
Smith, J., in, 83–84
Starr and, 133–34, 137, 151–53
Steed, J., in, 4–5, 93, 128–29,
    146–49, 154
Sun City West Fire District in, 133
Swiss-cheese model relating to,
    147
thunderstorm relating to, 3–4, 121,
    132–34, 138, 152
trigger points, 126, 141, 145
Williams, A., in, 77, 79, 84
Willis, D., in, 91, 119–20, 123–24,
    126, 135–37, 139, 158–60
wind changes in, 118–19, 138
Yuma Crew in, 70, 80, 119–20, 123
Yavapai County Sheriff's Office, 59–60,
    67–68, 124–25
Yavapai County Superior Court, 204
The Yellow Sheet, 65
Yuma Crew, 70, 80, 119–20, 123

Zuppiger, Garret, 97–98, 105–6, 182,
    183
background on, 30
remains of, 1, *1*